Unlikely Fame

UNLIKELY FAME
POOR PEOPLE WHO MADE HISTORY

DAVID WAGNER

with Jenna Nunziato

Paradigm Publishers
Boulder • London

All rights reserved. No part of the publication may be transmitted or reproduced in any media or form, including electronic, mechanical, photocopy, recording, or informational storage and retrieval systems, without the express written consent of the publisher.

Copyright © 2014 Paradigm Publishers

Published in the United States by Paradigm Publishers, 5589 Arapahoe Avenue, Boulder, CO 80303 USA.

Paradigm Publishers is the trade name of Birkenkamp & Company, LLC, Dean Birkenkamp, President and Publisher.

Library of Congress Cataloging-in-Publication Data

Wagner, David.
 Unlikely fame : poor people who made history / David Wagner.
    pages cm
 Includes bibliographical references and index.
  ISBN 978-1-61205-714-9 (pbk: alk. paper) — ISBN 978-1-61205-717-0 (consumer ebook)
1. Poor—United States—Social conditions. 2. Poverty—United States—History. 3. Celebrities—United States—Biography. 4. Fame. I. Title.
 HV4044.W34 2014
 362.5092'273—dc23

2014012412

Printed and bound in the United States of America on acid-free paper that meets the standards of the American National Standard for Permanence of Paper for Printed Library Materials.

Designed and Typeset by Straight Creek Bookmakers.

18 17 16 15 14   1 2 3 4 5

CONTENTS

Introduction · vii

1 **Poverty as a Serious Disability** · 1

2 **Childhood Poverty: Abandonment, Loss, Hurt, and Shame** · 15

3 **Hedonism, Pain, and Suffering in Adult Life** · 44

4 **Class Consciousness** · 69

5 **Rebels against Authority** · 93

6 **Fame and Poverty** · 116

7 **Contemporary Fame and Poverty** · 143

Appendix: Bibliographic Essay for Chapter 1 · 172
Bibliography · 179
Index · 189
About the Authors · 194

INTRODUCTION

❧

As a teacher, writer, and sometime organizer, I have worked much of my life on issues about poverty and poor people. Like others who have embraced these issues, I have found a huge chasm in public understanding of people who have suffered poverty. Most readers of academic books or journals—or for that matter many more popular venues—have only a vague idea of what it is like to grow up in poverty. The fact that most academics, journalists, publishers, researchers, and other writers are almost always from the middle class or above furthers this distance. As someone who has tried to engage readers, I have used a variety of more personal descriptions of the poor, whether ethnographic (from participant observation study) or historical (where fragments of the lives of the poor can be found). This book is still another attempt to engage readers who are not from impoverished backgrounds with the lives of the poor.

Writing about the lives of poor people who became famous has the advantage of a certain amount of public interest. Moreover, there is an availability in most cases of far more data about their lives than most poor people of the past or current times will ever leave. In this sense they are a wonderful source of data. Of course, there are some dangers—the individuals presented here are hardly representative of the poor. Overwhelmingly, my study of famous American figures shows that the poor are scarce, and in fact the working class is fairly absent,[1] at least after the Civil War. Some professions, such as scientists, professors, politicians, and bureaucrats, are found almost entirely in the middle class or higher. Only in several fields, particularly in the twentieth and twenty-first centuries, have some poor people succeeded—generally in the entertainment industry and sports. So this book is not meant to support the old Horatio Alger myth about the poor rising in class very easily. Nor am I suggesting the figures I present are in all ways representative of the poor, their genders, race or ethnicity, or anything else. They are by definition special.

Still, the fact that the twenty-seven profiles included here (twenty from the past and seven who are still alive) represent childhoods with much pain and suffering, and that despite their fame, for the most part, they continued to suffer from the effects of a low-income background, is particularly significant. For after all, if these great authors, reformers and leaders, movie stars and music stars suffered so long after they were famous (and at least in some cases, affluent) this tells us a great deal about the effects of poverty.

Because my main focus in the book is in showing ways in which poverty influences life experience I have not included a chronological biography of each figure. For those who are interested, I present this list showing the order, by birth, of the individuals to be discussed:

- the "miracle worker" Anne Sullivan (1866–1936)
- author Theodore Dreiser (1871–1945)
- author, adventurer, and political figure Jack London (1876–1916)
- heavyweight boxing champion Jack Johnson (1878–1946)
- birth control reformer Margaret Sanger (1879–1966)
- comedy figure and actor Charlie Chaplin (1889–1977)[2]
- radical organizer Elizabeth Gurley Flynn (1890–1964)

---

1. In studying the American National Biography Online, I recorded approximate class positions for the entire database of those born after the Civil War. Although in some cases information was too vague to use, in most cases it was clear. Overwhelmingly those who warranted inclusion in the database were middle class or higher by a factor of 2:1 or more. Poor people ranged from 2 to 10 percent. The remainder was split between farm families and working-class families.

2. Charlie Chaplin is the only figure I selected who was not born in the United States. Because the majority of his life was spent in the United States, he seemed a worthy exception.

- poet Edna St. Vincent Millay (1892–1950)
- baseball star Babe Ruth (1895–1948)
- writer Richard Wright (1908–1960)
- playwright William Saroyan (1908–1981)
- artist Jackson Pollock (1912–1956)
- actor John Garfield (1913–1952)
- jazz singer Billie Holiday (1915–1959)
- civil rights organizer Fannie Lou Hamer (1917–1977)
- Black Muslim icon Malcolm X (1925–1965)
- actress Marilyn Monroe (1926–1962)
- actor Steve McQueen (1930–1980)
- singer Johnny Cash (1932–2003)
- comedian and actor Richard Pryor (1940–2005)

Although I have tried to include the most obvious variables of diversity in American history between the Civil War and recent American history including birth dates, geographical location, gender, and race, I do not claim this list of subjects to be scientifically representative. In Chapter 7 I examine the following seven living persons:

- entertainer and singer Dolly Parton (1946–)
- author Stephen King (1947–)
- entertainer Mr. T (1952–)
- talk show host and entrepreneur Oprah Winfrey (1954–)
- basketball player Larry Bird (1956–)
- comedian and actor George Lopez (1961–)
- rapper and entrepreneur Jay-Z (1969–)

ACKNOWLEDGMENTS

I want to thank two superb former students for their help with this book. Penny Collins worked with me on the Bibliographic Essay, and Jenn Gilman assisted me in the beginning of the project. As always my wife and colleague Marcia B. Cohen was my first reader and picked up some glaring errors. I wish to also thank my Homelessness and Poverty class at California State University–Dominguez Hills for their reading of the unpublished manuscript in progress. And another "usual suspect" in my writing, Dean Birkenkamp, and the great staff at Paradigm Publishers deserve praise.

Chapter 1

POVERTY AS A SERIOUS DISABILITY

> Poverty is humiliation, the sense of being dependent on them, and being forced to accept rudeness, insults, and indifference when we seek help.
>
> Poverty is ... pretending that you forgot your lunch, being teased for the way you are dressed, feeling ashamed when [your] dad can't get a job, not getting a hot dog on hot dog day, being afraid to tell your mom that you need gym shoes, not getting to go to birthday parties, not buying books at the book fair. (Carr and Sloan 2003)

This chapter will briefly review the considerable literature—both national and international—on the serious impact of poverty on people's lives, particularly in childhood. Too often, poverty or low income is presented as a simple gradient or at the end of the class spectrum (from rich to poor or upper to lower), which provides no sense of what it is like to be poor. I argue that suffering poverty is more akin to suffering a serious disability, illness, or other serious tragedy. As we shall see, while some people do escape their backgrounds, even then they carry around serious wounds that affect their whole lives.

Although the data about poverty are widely acknowledged, they are not highlighted in either American academic or popular literature. Many Americans are so wedded to the Horatio Alger "pull yourself up by the bootstraps" ideology that they tend to deny the devastation poverty brings. To conservatives, and not a few political moderates, the poor still represent failure and personal blame. On the other hand, when I discussed this book project with some leftist friends, I was cautioned that stories about poor people who became famous might be seen as "incorrect" as it would convey too much free will in the social system. Whereas women, and individuals of different races, ethnicities, or sexual orientations, are now allowed a history with some diversity, apparently poorer people are not. Because of the history of discussions of the "culture of poverty" and "pathologies" of the poor particularly in the 1960s (and continuing), many American scholars on the liberal-left are reluctant to confront the disabling issues of poverty. Despite this silence, the fact is that poor people are likely to die earlier, have poorer physical and mental health than those in higher social classes, and are more in danger of social problems such as crime and substance use.

DEFINING POVERTY

One problem in any discussion of poor people is who do we mean by the "poor"? Poverty is both an *absolute* condition—an individual or family does not have enough to survive in terms of food, transportation, health care, education, or housing—and a *relative condition* in that it exists at a particular time and particular culture in which a certain standard of living is required (see Iceland 2009 for a good discussion of absolute and relative poverty). That is, deprivation exists at a particular time and in a particular culture. A family in 1850 without running water was not necessarily poor or deprived. However, in 2012 in America this would be a sign of both absolute and relative poverty. A family without a telephone in 1920 was hardly deviant, but in 2012 a family without at least a telephone or a computer or a television might have little access to what their society requires to be a citizen. As Adam Smith wrote 250 years ago, poverty destroys one's credibility in society, making one a nonperson (cited in Marmot 2005).

Different societies choose to measure and count the poor in different ways. Since the early 1960s, the United States has used a "poverty line" to measure poverty: the poverty rate calculated based on an extremely old formula, which was in turn based on a US Department of Agriculture study that a minimal modest diet required one-third of a household's income. Although food is no longer as large a part of a typical family's budget, housing, fuel, and other medical costs have soared. According to many critics, the poverty level should be raised as much as twice its current level to accommodate the current costs of living. Further, the US poverty rate admits no distinction by geography, even though it is common knowledge that someone living in rural Mississippi needs less money than a resident of New York City or Los Angeles. A further problem, frequently a criticism of conservatives, is that "in kind" benefits (e.g., food stamps, Medicaid, and other noncash subsidies) are not costed out and counted, so that a family with many benefits does not show an increased standard of living over a family without these benefits.

Despite the weaknesses and many conflicts about the poverty rate, this measure still has value in a comparative way. To say we have 46 million people under the poverty line may be underestimating poverty and simplifying poverty to a rather arbitrary statistical standard, but it can be used in studies and to compare over time the number of people in poverty or the number of poor people in the United States as compared with other nations.

Many other countries favor a comparative approach, which uses median income as a measure. The number of people who fail to meet a percentage of the median income are then considered poor. The conception here is that the median represents some culturally agreed upon standard of living in a nation, and those individuals and families who are dramatically below this are excluded or disenfranchised from the tools they need for successful participation in their societies. The United Nations and other world groups have been moving toward this relative condition of poverty definition, by which count America would have a highly uneven distribution of wealth with many more poor than we currently count.

There are many other disputes and complexities worthy of mention. Statistical measures of all kinds tend to miss the fluidity of social class status as most sociologists or anthropologists would understand it. To be eighteen and on your own as a college student and living on $5,000 a year does not make you poor, nor does being a medical resident at a hospital at age twenty-four and making $15,000. Social class is a status that is both *prospective* and *retrospective*: it is prospective in including your family's assets and your human capital, which determines what you will be; it is retrospective in that coming from poverty is significant in that most individuals even moving above a poverty line will have few assets and few people to assist them. Poverty requires some length of time that one's family and self see their lives as limited. We know the medical resident is likely to become a physician and hence her or his scrimping is temporary; the college student is likely to earn more money after graduation, although much depends on where the student came from in social class. We instinctively realize income does not tell us everything. Even wealthy people have bad years, but they can draw on their assets to overcome a low income or investment year. Poverty means at least low income and little or no assets, but it also brings with it a retrospective and/or prospective poverty. Your parents were poor, you are poor, and you see no way out. Or, for whatever reason, you have dramatically fallen from the middle classes (or more rarely the upper classes) and for lack of appropriate education, for which to dress, travel, and qualify for good work or inheritance, see your future as bleak.

As many sociologists encounter, I had difficulty always separating out the "poor" from those of the working class, which historically has been the most numerous class and which, particularly in hard times such as depressions and recessions, has suffered greatly. In my research I have looked for descriptions of the families of the people I studied that expressed the fact that they were deprived of material goods to such a degree as to be "poor," and that in many cases, although not all, a form of relief whether the poorhouse in the nineteenth century, the orphanage or town and city relief, or a form of welfare in more modern cases was given to the family. Over time, of course, conditions change and some of the individuals studied had families that moved up depending on the historical period.

DISABILITIES ABOUT BEING POOR

The summary below shows some of the severe consequences of being poor in recent years (some of these consequences were far worse years ago). Of course, they do not mean all poor people will suffer from the particular social problems. As I will explain, there are a number of mediating factors in life that help people survive. But before we discuss this, the overall awful fate of poverty should be noted.

Life Expectancy and Physical Health

- A study of Louisville, Kentucky, found an over ten-year difference in life expectancy from the highest to lowest class.

- Taking a subway ride from Washington, DC, to the end of the line in Montgomery County, Maryland, researchers find a twenty-year difference in life expectancy.
- On 5th Avenue in New York City a walk uptown shows a fifteen-year drop in average life expectancy.
- Another study found that relative risk of death is four times higher among low-income people than high-income people.
- In the nineteenth century, poor people died overwhelmingly from tuberculosis; in the twentieth and twenty-first centuries they are far more at risk than higher classes for cardiovascular disease, stroke, lung diseases, chronic respiratory disease, diabetes, diseases of the digestive tract, kidney disease, deaths and injuries in accidents and from violence, suicide, and HIV and AIDS.
- Although both obesity and smoking tobacco are associated with low social class, "bad lifestyle" choices account for only a part of class difference, estimated at a quarter or a third.
- Poor people are shorter than rich people; are more likely to suffer from chronic stress, bad cholesterol, depression, and low birth weight and thinness in infancy; and are more likely to have lower IQs. They are also more likely to be without teeth, suffer from deafness and other hearing problems, have speech and vision problems, and have high blood pressure. Experts say the poor have inferior development of nervous systems. Children in poverty have higher levels of lead, methyl mercury, polychlorobiphenyls, dioxins, and pesticides in their systems.
- Concentrated poverty exacerbates all these findings and is an independent variable. In other words, there is a big difference between being poor in a relatively "average" neighborhood and living in an area that is seen as a "slum" or "ghetto."

Mental Health

- Studies going back fifty years and continuing to today have found mental health disorders are diagnosed more among the poor than the affluent. This link is particularly evident with children's mental health, in which attention, conduct, and other behavioral disorders are three times higher among the poor. Childhood anxiety and depression also correlate with poverty.
- Among adults, schizophrenia and personality disorders are most linked to poverty and low class, as are alcoholism and drug

addiction. Some studies also find a high rate of depression among poor women.
- In earlier periods of American history, poverty and "pauperism" were almost completely associated with insanity, and the mental hospitals were filled with poorer people. The increased popularity of mental illness as an explanatory device for behavior has changed some of this, but the more serious diagnoses still often go to the poor.
- As with physical health, some studies have shown the concentration of poverty ("neighborhood poverty") has a great additive effect on people in poverty in terms of mental health problems and hopelessness and despair. That is, the higher the rate of poverty in a community, the more severe its social psychiatric problems.

Education

- Studies show strong correlations between poor cognitive development and lack of school achievement with poverty; the number of behavior problems, lower test scores, and higher dropout rates correlate with poverty as well as special education placements. IQ tests rise with income.

Social Problems: Alcohol, Drugs, Crime

- Teen pregnancy has historically been associated with low income.
- Crime rates and arrests (except for white-collar crime) are dominated by lower income people. One study showed that boys living in poverty in their first five years of life were more than twice as likely to be arrested as those whose incomes exceeded the poverty line by two times. Interestingly, cross-national studies have also found that the higher rates of inequality there are (for example, in the United States), the more crime there is.
- Classic studies of alcoholism find that while the rate of drinking may not differ by social class, overwhelmingly "problem drinking" among men is associated with lower class status. This includes binge drinking and problems with police, work, and finances as a result of alcohol. Similarly, studies of drug use suggest more associated problems with low-income drug use than in higher classes.
- Lower class standing and poverty are major correlates of cases of child abuse and neglect and domestic violence.

REASONS FOR THE LINKS BETWEEN POVERTY AND SOCIAL AND PHYSICAL PROBLEMS

Much of this book will show how anxiety, stress, pain, suffering, and depression—as well as, at times, aggression—mark the lives of the poor. A complete review of social science and medical literature is beyond the scope of these pages (though I have provided a bibliographic essay in the Appendix). Briefly, I note that there are some genetic and biological explanations, though the vast majority of studies stress environmental causes. There is also a school of thought that ties the very labeling of social problems to what activities and behaviors the poor engage in. Finally, some academics and political activists maintain a marked skepticism about certain statistics because of how data are collected.

Genetics

In a society eager to find (natural) scientific explanations for everything, the relationship between poverty and poor health and problem behavior is sometimes seen as a biological problem. Although in general this view can support a harsh Social Darwinist position, there is no question that certain aspects of health carry some inheritable elements. Increased vulnerability to alcoholism, schizophrenia, cognitive problems, high blood pressure, low birth weight, and poor immune systems, for example, may have genetic elements. The difficulty is that most good studies prove biology is rarely destiny and that a predisposition to a problem is nowhere near such a level to make it likely. The child of a schizophrenic or alcoholic absent an environment conducive to developing these issues will most likely *not* develop them.

Most problems, including issues of life expectancy, carry some genetic elements, some prenatal elements, and a large number of environmental elements from the time the child is born until he or she reaches adulthood.

Environmental Stress

Most social scientists and health researchers identify the dominant cause of problems in life to be the social environment. In this analysis, living in a poor family of origin, particularly over a long period of time, is a public health problem in itself.

No aspect of poverty can be separated from its harmful effects. Poor people often lack good prenatal care and are unable to provide good nutrition, stimulation, and other needs when the child is in utero. Many poor people live in crowded, substandard housing that exposes children to a host of physical problems. Crowded housing along with poor wages (or unemployment) adds to family stress. Large families living in small places can result in conflict among family members including abuse and violence. Families with little access to education do not stimulate their children as much, and cannot provide them a "head start" with school studies. The cost and unavailability of day care sometimes results not only in lack of stimulation but also an absence of any break time for caretaking parents. When children grow up in a neighborhood of intense poverty, they lack places to get nutritious food and are unlikely to have safe playgrounds or other areas in which to play. Concentrated poverty areas often include violence and weak protection against adult drug use, drinking, or crime.

While poverty is not one experience and varies widely, generally the most recent studies have shown that stress and lack of control are the greatest correlates between social class and life expectancy and health. As noted earlier, although habits such as cigarette smoking and poor diet limit good health, these behaviors account for a relatively smaller part of the equation than stress. The film *Unnatural Causes*, which uses several long-term studies to show social class correlates of health and life expectancy, points to how stress can be measured through the presence of cortisone in the blood system. While everyone has stress, long and repeated exposure to stress begins to eat away at one's physical and mental functioning. Michael Marmot, who contributed to the film, in his book *The Status Syndrome* emphasizes the lack of control people at the bottom of society have over their lives as compared with middle- and upper-class people. When your life is unpredictable, dangerous, hostile, without rewards, and without support, your ability to ward off physical illness is lower, and your chances of being mentally ill or using substances are higher.

Labeling and Class

Although some measures are fairly objective, many "social problems" have a more subjective element. Some "problems" are arguably not social problems when they involve nonpoor people, and some acknowledged problems have considerable labeling differences among the classes.

Teen pregnancy is an example of what might be called a "pseudo-problem" or a problem related to finances and class, not to either sex or mothering. It's interesting to note that teen pregnancy was not an issue when it was most frequent, in the pre-1960s era. This appears to be because most young mothers were forced into "shotgun" weddings with the father. What was illicit was unmarried sex and pregnancy, not the age at which people had children. When "social problem" experts declared teen pregnancy a problem in the 1970s they aimed their fire at young unmarried women, many of them low income and nonwhite. Studies have found that teen mothers do not differ substantially from their sisters (who were not young mothers) when looked at over a longer period of time. That is, what is problematic in modern America where women are expected to finish school and prepare for work is the earning potential that may be lost due to time spent caring for a child at an early age. This, however, is not a concern for teen parents with money or single-parent families with money. Nor on further examination does it prove to always be a concern among lower-class mothers.

Another type of issue where labeling comes to the fore is mental health diagnosis. On one hand, there is considerable subjectivity in psychiatric diagnoses, and on the other hand, many DSM (the *Diagnostic Statistical Manual* of the APA) diagnoses themselves arguably include class features (the "anti-social personality," for example, clearly defies middle-class morality), so determining what is "valid" is difficult. A long pattern has existed among clinical personnel to label the poor and people of color with what used to be called "psychotic" diagnoses, while middle-class people often get what were called "neurotic" disorders.

Substance use can also arguably be looked at historically through a class and racial lens. Alcohol use among the rich has rarely been considered a problem, but alcohol use by the poor, blacks, and immigrants surfaced as the subtext of the temperance and prohibition movements in the nineteenth and early twentieth centuries. As historians of drug use have argued, each illegalized substance (opium, cocaine, and marijuana, for example) came about through association with people of color and poor people. Opium was fought as the "Chinese drug" while "cocaine" was said to make African Americans crazy and strong, and marijuana's "reefer madness" was associated with Mexicans.

Many of the above examples represent needed correction to the view of some moralists that the poor practice bad morals or that all we see as "bad" is so. Nevertheless, as I will discuss, it does not make sense to throw out all objective measures of distress either because we suspect some differences in diagnosing and labeling or because we know many "problems" are "socially constructed" in a society divided by social class and race.

Overskepticism of Data

Some leftist social scientists and activists have stretched the skepticism of labeling and counting in such a way that (except for presumably the health statistics) they challenge the accuracy of the association of problems with poverty. This issue, to take two examples, comes up with family violence and with crime.

The denial appears to develop, on the one hand, because various behaviors are so stigmatized—child abuse, spousal abuse, crime, for example—and, on the other hand, because the language of public service announcements and charities has become so universal ("*everyone* is at risk of domestic violence or crime or cancer or whatever") that many nonexperts and some experts are confused.

For example, we know that child abuse and neglect are overly policed on the poorest families. Part of this is the visibility the poor have; poor mothers and children are on streets or plazas of housing projects where neighbors see them, whereas middle-class people are often hidden behind fences and hedges and have bigger homes. More important, because the state welfare departments house the divisions of child protection, they police most those they come in contact with. But the problem here is one of degree and extent: are there middle- or higher income people who harm their kids that go unapprehended? Yes! But by the same token, the overwhelming evidence determined from death certificates or serious injuries shows that the worst abuse (both child and spousal) does occur in poverty-ridden families and is worsened by unemployment, crowded housing, and other conditions in the lower classes. I have actually had people imply the upper class can hide these offenses, but it is kind of a stretch to believe there are bodies buried in the grounds of rich people. People turn a truism into a denial of the special problems that people at the low end of society have more of because of social conditions.

Radical criminology has also at times emphasized corporate, upper-class, and white-collar malfeasance to argue that class determines that the poor get prison, which is of course much less true for the rich. These views also contain an important truth, but when people talk about murder or assault, for example, they do not mean income tax evaders or those who skim from clients' accounts. Perhaps society should change its values, but in the meantime, it goes against all facts to not admit that because of the conditions the poor live in, they are more likely to turn to violence and other crime than the more affluent classes.

MEDIATING AND MITIGATING CIRCUMSTANCES OF POVERTY

As we explore the lives of those born poor who obtained some fame and presumably success, we will become aware of a considerable number of circumstances that may determine the chances of rising out of poverty.

First, it is important to note that every historical period has a different economic context for mobility in the economy, downward or upward. Growing up during an economic depression or a long recession (such as the one that began in 2008) does not bode well for success even for the most ambitious and talented people of any class. As jobs are scarce, education expensive, and new enterprises slow to start, generally the poor will lack the tools to succeed even more than other classes. On the other hand, some periods of American history, such as the years during World Wars I and II as well as the affluent "Pax Americana" (1945–1973), also aided by a war economy, have provided help for workers and poor people by a scarcity of labor and decline in discrimination against groups (racial and gender, for example) because of the desperate need for labor.

Second, as I have noted above, highly concentrated poverty is most conducive to many of the most negative impacts of poverty. For whites in America in recent decades, poverty has been far more scattered than, for example, African American and Native American poverty, both of which were highly concentrated. In the past, poor people of all colors were often further segregated from opportunities in the workplace and education, and many grew up among other poor, particularly in the case of immigrants. The more individuals received some sort of passage out of their neighborhood or ghetto, the more it helped them.

Third, poverty has been shown to be most horrific for young children. Growing up in poverty particularly before the age of five or six is especially difficult because of its constraints on socialization and good health. All other things being equal, a family that grew up working class and fell into poverty when the children were age ten, twelve, or fourteen, for example, may find that its children escaped some of the worst of poverty's effects.

Another variable is the length of time in poverty. It was quite frequent in American history for large percentages of people to experience poverty.

Chapter 1

Even today over a few years' time and even using our low poverty line, many families and individuals pass through poverty. But a year or two of tightening the belt is quite different from spending many years in poverty, which has a more serious effect.

As we will see, a key mediating factor is to what extent individuals are lucky enough to meet people outside of their family who will serve to mentor them and assist them in educational or occupational development. Quite a few of the people considered in this book received help from teachers. To name a few, "miracle worker" Anne Sullivan was helped by several teachers at the Perkins School for the Blind, where she came to love learning and intellect; writer Theodore Dreiser had a favorite teacher who helped him complete one year at college; Edna St. Vincent Millay, living in poverty in a small Maine town, was lucky enough to have her poetry discovered while still a teenager; comedian Richard Pryor spoke highly of a teacher in his otherwise dreary school who encouraged his "clowning around." For others, though, it need not be strangers: birth control pioneer Margaret Sanger's private-school education was funded by older sisters, and country singer Johnny Cash's mother encouraged his singing.

Of course, no one's life can be boiled down to just parenting or mentoring. A complex role of luck and talent enters the mixture as well, and opportunity structures are different in various fields of endeavor. In the nineteenth century and even the early twentieth century, high levels of professional and organizational cloture were not yet in place, and it's then that some of our subjects were able to become writers or intellectuals. For most of the twentieth century and continuing today (see Chapter 7), however, only the entertainment and sports industries have served an important role in the ambitions of poor people and disenfranchised ethnic and racial groups. While the numbers who succeed in these fields are miniscule compared to those who seek openings, it would appear that only these areas are even somewhat open to people without much capital, either economic or human.

BIOGRAPHIES AND THE NATURE OF POVERTY

The remainder of this book will consider twenty-seven famous Americans who were born into poverty. Our sample for the first six chapters spans much of American history since the Civil War. I intentionally left out earlier periods because the nature of American life, and particularly its economy, was so different between the American Revolution and the end of the Civil War as to make comparisons to poverty in recent history irrelevant. For a variety of reasons I initially chose not to consider living Americans. However, interest on the part of many people in the issue of relatively recent Americans who were mobile was quite extensive, and fortunately my work with Jenna Nunziato, a student in the master's program at the University of Southern Maine, led us to collaborate on Chapter 7, which discusses seven living American figures who were born poor.

In Chapter 2 I review the childhood experiences of some of our subjects to provide real-life examples to the generalizations presented in this chapter about growing up in poverty. While each person is different, there were quite a number of negative experiences that these subjects experienced, particularly abandonment by one or more parents, and feelings of shame from both poverty itself and other ill effects that were correlated with poverty.

In Chapter 3 I will utilize how the pain and suffering experienced from poverty from childhood on structured the lives and personalities even of these "successful people" who escaped poverty and became world famous. Some subjects were able to keep the pain mostly to themselves, while others had such pain or aggression that it helped bring them down from fame or led to other problems, or early death.

In Chapters 4 and 5 I examine a commonality in these poor people born between 1866 and 1940 in their class consciousness and antiauthoritarian views. Although these two tendencies can of course be related, they are conceptually different. Some subjects were always aware of and loyal to their roots and expressed in their writings or actions a consciousness of similarity with poor and other people near the bottom of society (e.g., the working class). Other subjects had a more instinctive attitude of "damning authority" but without apparent reference to a political or even social loyalty to the poor or working class. Both aspects of these subjects' lives are of great help in understanding not only them but perhaps also many other poor people.

In Chapter 6 I bring us back to another ingredient of our story: fame and success. Tyler Cowen, who wrote the book *What Price Fame?*, raises the point that "fame-seeking often harms the achiever. The famous live under stress and many die young." Additionally he quotes an old Jewish proverb stating, "If you wish to live long, don't become famous." Although our sample may be too small to be truly representative, nearly every individual story seems to reinforce the many dangers of fame, bringing into question what constitutes success in society. Some of our subjects no doubt grew addicted to fame, and yet they and others also sought relief from the constant pressure of fame.

I will try to sort out the issue of social class (poverty) from what personality and social effects the achieving of fame had on our subjects. This inquiry can help raise another area of inquiry for future research. Another interest of mine in Chapter 6 is to see to what degree poverty obviously impeded success, yet in the more recent world has occasionally been a virtue—particularly in the entertainment industry and sometimes in the political world. An affluent Malcolm X with a large African American following would be hard to picture; Johnny Cash and many other (broadly) country and western singers would have had difficulty springing from riches; and Latino comedian George Lopez would be quite different emanating from the upper middle or upper classes.

In Chapter 7, Jenna Nunziato and I use the biographies of seven contemporary figures to review as far as possible what trends found among the earlier sample of twenty seem to still hold today. It is clear that the pain and problems bred by poverty remain severe, but it is less clear that the responses earlier figures had to their backgrounds remain.

CHAPTER 2

CHILDHOOD POVERTY
ABANDONMENT, LOSS, HURT, AND SHAME

❧

This chapter focuses on the experience of some of our subjects during childhood, in particular with abandonment or loss—death of a parent, separation or disappearance of a parent, placement in a poorhouse or workhouse, orphanage, or juvenile home—and the feeling of shame and hurt that accompanied poverty and other unfortunate events of youth. Like most of the poor they experienced shame, and often the subjects felt they or their families were "deviant" or different from others in the community. Many felt rejection by their own families.

Stephanie Coontz has written eloquently on how the traditional family in America with two parents (one supposedly working, one not) and children was the "way it never was" (2000). She is correct, but poor families have always been among the most visibly different from societal expectations. The lower life expectancy in the poorer classes made for more widows and widowers among the poor. Second, the difficulty financially and legally in obtaining divorce made many partners living in poverty more likely to leave the partnership for reasons ranging from insufficient financial provision by the father to domestic violence or other difficulties in the family (see Gordon 1988; Wagner 2008). The poor or working-class family was often married in name only, at least until one of the pair moved upward and then remarried. Further, those without property have always lived more frequently without the benefit of matrimony, and children who were unwanted or at least felt to be economically unsupportable were often abandoned to institutions or other family arrangements (a sample of the many studies of desertion and abandonment in the American family includes Calhoun 1945; Gordon 1988; Schwartzberg 2004; and Ten Broek 1971).

Lest the stories of our subjects from years ago seem archaic to the reader, I remind them that while poorhouses and workhouses are no more, and we have few orphanages left, in the case of the poor large numbers of institutional and stigmatized arrangements continue to exist. Our prison and jail cells hold millions of poor people, and our homeless shelters, housing projects, foster homes, and group homes, for example, hold many millions more. While we hope there are some differences today, for the most part, the stigma of poverty and abandonment, loss, hurt, and shame may be about the same.

ANNE SULLIVAN: A YOUNG IRISH GIRL GOES TO THE POORHOUSE

Few people had a more traumatic childhood than "the miracle worker" to be, Anne Sullivan (1866–1936). The firstborn child of Irish immigrants Tom and Alice Sullivan, who had arrived in the western Massachusetts town of Agawam in 1863, Sullivan grew up in impoverished circumstances worsened by an alcoholic father who may have abused her. Further, she was born with a disability called trachoma, a granular inflammation of the eye, which though now treatable, in those days limited her vision for most of her life. Sullivan remembered someone saying to her in her early years "she would be so pretty if not for her eyes" (Braddy 1933a, p. 1). Adding to the difficulties of the family were her mother's bout with tuberculosis (TB) and the birth of her brother Jimmie in 1869 with a tubercular hip. Not surprisingly, Sullivan painted herself as "blindly rebellious" and passionate, throwing things around the small room in which the family lived. Yet, of course, we do not know what came first, abuse or rebellion, or if they occurred together.

Life worsened for the family with the depression of 1873 (one of the worst in American history) and the death of Annie's mother that year from TB. Evidently, Tom Sullivan acknowledged his lack of ability to care for Annie and Jimmie (although he did keep a third child with no disability in his home), and the two were sent to an aunt and uncle. In

1876, unbeknownst to the young children, it was decided that Annie and Jimmie would be sent nearly 100 miles east to the State Almshouse at Tewksbury, Massachusetts (near Lowell). On a gloomy February day the two children were accompanied by a state agent for a train ride and picked up by a "black Maria" vehicle that transported them to one of the largest almshouses (or poorhouses) in the nation (Lash 1980, p. 7).

From colonial times on, the Americana poor relief system, copied after the English, used two ways of providing relief—"outdoor" or aid at home, and "indoor" or relief through being placed in a poorhouse or workhouse. Help at home with food, medical care, and other goods was always preferred by the people being aided. But for complex reasons, many American towns and cities expanded their poorhouses in the early nineteenth century, in part to save money, and in part to deter the less "worthy" from asking for any aid (Wagner 2005). As Irish immigrants without a legal settlement in a town (disqualifying them from outdoor relief), the Sullivan family was likely denied outdoor aid, and forced to send their children to the state almshouse for aid (the assumption is that Annie and Jimmie were the hardest to care for because of their disabilities).

Annie, at age ten, showed what would be a lifetime pattern of not accepting authority by refusing the almshouse's plan to split up her brother and her in different wards. Tying an apron on Jimmie, the almshouse staff placed the two in a women's ward because of Annie's objections. The two cut out pictures from newspapers and magazines and turned their living area into a bit of a picture gallery. Unfortunately, in what would hit Annie as the most significant abandonment since her mother died, Jimmie died three months after arriving at the almshouse.

Unquestionably, placing a ten-year-old with at least a thousand adults, including the ill and dying, pregnant women, and poor unemployed men, left a mark on Annie. One reminiscence was of the hospital:

[The] almshouse hospital [was] extremely depressing. The sick people were in one long ward. There was no classification according to age or disease or seriousness of the malady. The place was made more gloomy by having the windows on one side frosted, so that one could not see out of them, nor could they be opened for ventilation, there being the chance that some patients might attempt to escape. To aggravate the unpleasantness, the ward smelt like a sewage dump.... The stench drifted from end to end of the ward, and was the subject of unprintable remarks. (Braddy 1933b)

Later Annie was placed with the pregnant women, almost all of them young girls with children out of wedlock, probably denied hospitalization at places other than the almshouse:

> There was nothing I did not hear broadly discussed in gutter-language. From my earliest days I listened to talk upon every subject by persons whose experience had been such that they blasphemed against every respectability—talk which reached the climax in disgusting sex revelations ... the bawdy houses, seduction, about brothels and police corruption. The glimpses of promiscuity gained from those conversations sickened one,—trysting in dark courtyards, love-making in closets, drunkenness, amours of people that frequented sinister alleys like cats, and children begotten and abandoned on door-steps, or otherwise. (Nielsen 2009, p. 43)

Paradoxically, in many ways Annie Sullivan over her four years as an "inmate" grew to feel more comfortable among the poor, overwhelmingly Irish people at Tewksbury than she would later at age fourteen when she was transferred to the more affluent Perkins School for the Blind in South Boston. While at Tewksbury, Sullivan became close with many inmates, had other inmates read to her, and gained sympathy for the heroes of Irish Americans from Wendell Phillips to John O'Reilly of the *Pilot* (a Boston Catholic newspaper) to Charles Stewart Parnell. When she was transferred at her own request in 1880, she found that the students and teachers at the Perkins School made her feel her poverty.

Immediately upon entering the school as a charity case, she felt different. She did not know her birthday or how to spell her name. She was made fun of for having no toothbrush, hat, petticoat, gloves, or nightgown (Braddy 1933a, p. 64). The children made clear to Sullivan that they did not want to hear about her Irish heroes or stories of poor people. Suddenly she felt more abandoned by her father and her brother and from her home environment than ever before. Biographer Nella Braddy noted that "nothing had prepared her for this experience, always before she had been among Catholics, she had been among outcasts, now [she was with] the respectable, the girls were the daughters of ministers and teachers and dentists and druggists.... There was no common ground upon which she could meet any of them" (p. 66).

In what can serve as an explanation for how many poor people feel, Sullivan told biographer Braddy, "The essence of poverty is shame.

Shame to have been overwhelmed by ugliness, shame to be the hole in the perfect pattern of the Universe" (p. 62).

While Sullivan would surmount some of her problems at the Perkins School for the Blind, enough to be its valedictorian several years later, she never spoke (even with her lifelong companion Helen Keller) about her early years, including the years at the Tewksbury Almshouse. Being an inmate of a poorhouse was indeed a great shame at the time, and its association with all forms of problems (alcoholism, death, mental illness, out-of-wedlock pregnancy) as well as poverty likely made it far worse than, say, a homeless shelter today. Both her abandonment and institutionalization would strike her throughout her life despite its successes. As biographer Joseph Lash notes, "In later days, when she least expected it, memory would suddenly reach up and sweep her being with vague terrors, absurd insecurities, [and] violent rages" (1980, p. 13).

SEPARATION AND SHAME IN THEODORE DREISER'S YOUTH

Famous American novelist Theodore Dreiser (1871–1945) did not have quite as dramatically a bad childhood as Sullivan. However, the themes of separation and hurt and shame also marked his childhood.

Dreiser was born in Terre Haute, Indiana, the twelfth child of John Paul and Sarah, Moravian Germans. His father is described as a "morose, dour figure" who believed in a "punitive God who demanded nothing less than perfection" (Lingeman 1986, pp. 16, 20). His mother converted to Roman Catholicism and disapproved of her husband's efforts to constantly force religion down the children's throats. However, she was described as "histrionic" and often threatened the children with desertion. She would, for example, tell the children she was leaving, pack her basket, and even hide outside the house in an effort to frighten them (Loving 2005, p. 4). Dreiser, whose sister described him as a baby as "puny beyond belief," was always frightened of his mother leaving. Biographer Richard Lingeman writes that the "tactic left its mark—fears of abandonment ... haunted Dreiser the rest of his life" (1986, p. 29).

Dreiser's father had once been a manager of a mill, but a fire destroyed the mill and he was injured by a falling beam. He later lost his job and became chronically unemployed, not able to support his large family. When Dreiser was eight, his mother split up the family: Sarah took Theodore and the two other young sons, and the three older girls stayed with John Paul. Although the separation was ostensibly made for economic reasons, biographers have also cited the couple's differences on child-rearing, and Sarah's desire to escape "the general gloom" of her husband's punitive religious teachings (Loving 2005, p. 8).

Whatever impact his parents' separation had on young Theodore, his family's religiosity combined with his siblings' acting out made shame a constant fact of his childhood. His family moved frequently and at one point lived in a room above a firehouse where the fire chief allowed prostitutes to live. Theodore was fascinated, but his mother quickly packed up the family. Later his brother Paul, who had been involved with a prostitute, arrived back in the family with syphilis. His mother later took back in his brother Rome, described as a drunk "with nowhere to go" (Loving 2005, p. 14). The family's efforts to win respectability continued to fail when two sisters also had scandals, being pregnant out of wedlock.

These scandals added to the sense of shame that Dreiser recalls of poverty. He remembered being sent home from school for lacking appropriate clothes, including shoes. When his mother took in laundry, Theodore was ashamed of having to deliver the baskets of clothes, and took the "back-street routes" to do so. Lingeman describes the second winter away from his father as nearly putting the Dreisers in the poorhouse with nothing to eat but cornmeal (Lingeman 1986, p. 45). Dreiser described how for years afterward the sight of the neighborhood "filled [him] with an indefinable and oppressive dread ... thoughts and emotions which had a close kinship to actual and severe physical pain" (Lingeman 1986, pp. 45–46). In the biography of Dreiser by Loving, he cites Dreiser's leaving home at age sixteen to go to Chicago as "an escape from poverty and the stigma of [his] family name." He left with just one pair of underwear and socks, yet he saw the new freedom "as paradise" (Loving 2005, p. 26).

Dreiser's biography also reminds us that almost as keen as the experience of poverty is the experience of downward mobility that children can feel. Lingeman argues that the class-conscious writer Dreiser keenly felt his father's downward spiral and "his family's fall from grace." In fact, he argues "it also made him identify with the heroes in so many melodramas and dime novels of the nineteenth century [where] the young man or woman of good birth ... is plunged into poverty as a child" (Lingeman 1986, p. 26). The author of such classic American tales as *Sister Carrie* and *An American Tragedy* took his own "state of chronic foreboding" and lifelong deep anxiety about falling into poverty and put them onto the pages of his work (ibid.).

BASTARDY AND RESENTMENT IN JACK LONDON'S CHILDHOOD

The famous American writer, adventurer, and social critic Jack London (1876–1916) suffered an extremely unusual childhood, which involved his mother's illness and downward mobility, out-of-wedlock birth and scandal, and the beginning of an adaptation to life marked by machismo and struggle as much as the famous "wolves" of his own work.

London's mother, Flora Wellman, was the youngest child of a wheat merchant in Ohio. She was stricken at a young age by typhoid fever, "which not only ruined her looks and damaged her eyesight but stunted her growth ... the fever caused bouts of depression and left her permanently unhinged," notes biographer Alex Kershaw (1997, p. 11). The tiny woman left her family and became a spiritualist, playing piano to pay the bills. In California she got involved with an astrologer named William Chaney. When Flora became pregnant she was so depressed she twice tried suicide. According to biographer James Haley, a small mob tried to hang Chaney from a lamppost but he got away (Haley 2010, p. 12). Flora was nearly killed by the birth, and she saw her son Jack as a "badge of shame." An African American wet nurse, Virginia Prentiss, cared for him for some time. Virginia is seen as his savior considering his mother's grief and depressed state at the time.

Given both his temperament and the times, it is not surprising that when as a boy London found out the meaning of the term "bastard" and that he indeed was one, he immediately ran away from home for two days. Haley states that throughout London's life "the injured child would surface in sudden puerile, outbursts." He not only was ashamed of his illegitimacy but hid the facts from most accounts of his life.

Flora and Jack had a better start with his stepfather John London, whom Flora married not long after Jack was born. Jack got along well with his stepfather. But Flora's constant psychological problems and mood swings would continue to affect Jack. Her ordering John London to administer beatings to Jack was "unforgiveable" to him. Additionally, John London was missing a lung from the war, and though for a short time he was able to support the family by farming, eventually his efforts failed and the family moved further down the ranks of poverty (Kershaw 1997, p. 14). They finally lived in the poorest of the poor zones in West Oakland, California, near the docks, where London's family hated the new Italian immigrants and Chinese laborers (London would later become one of the few racist socialists in American history).

By his tenth or eleventh year, London went to work as part of a crew of child laborers who worked twelve hours a day at the Hickman's Cannery in Oakland. He was bitter that all his money went to support his family, and began developing his own style as a "wiry brawler ... a cunning fighter best left alone" (Kershaw 1997, p. 15). He sought according to Kershaw "to become a man among men ... he had to prove his masculinity not only by getting laid, but also by brawling, drinking, and standing up to any tough who threatened him" (p. 17).

Biographer Haley describes London as "raised but little loved, taught toughness by dockside brawling, taught that tenderness would be detected and attacked as weakness, assimilating that an intellectual curiosity only led to frustration in one fated to be a "work beast" [as London called himself], Jack London by age 15 already looked out on the world through the eyes of the wolf" (Haley 2010, p. 29).

By his teenage years, London had begun using alcohol in destructive ways. He had his first bout of severe alcohol poisoning after participating in a fire brigade parade. Later he would go off to sea to become a pirate, only later to turn around and police the pirates.

London's childhood suggests how complex difficulties confront people together not in separate compartments; here poverty accompanied mental distress and downward mobility, and shame accompanied deviance, and then in turn led to more troubles. London's "tough" adaptation of aggressive behavior differs from Sullivan and Dreiser but resembles quite a few of the subjects we will discuss. For many people raised in poverty and difficulty, the response is not carried inward as in depression or sadness but outward, in protecting and projecting yourself to others in an aggressive way. It is, of course, the macho way of handling difficult feelings and probably feelings of hurt and inferiority as well. Interestingly, London's written works as well as biographies do not mention the shame he felt at his illegitimacy and at his poverty; no doubt to a great degree it is because he turned it into anger that would mark his entire life.

CHARLIE CHAPLIN: LIVING THROUGH THE WORKHOUSE AND THE ORPHANAGE

Born in London in 1889 (died 1977) to two English vaudeville personalities, Charlie Chaplin not only endured a Dickensian childhood with repeated losses but went on to perfect the image of the "tramp" as the comedic and tragic symbol, in many ways a magnificent contribution of social class to public imagery.

Chaplin even many years later when working on his autobiography realized how deep were the blows and the losses he had suffered: "The rich and famous and fulfilled man whom the world sees still considers himself a victim maimed for life by the early catastrophic shock" (Chaplin 1964, p. 7). Chaplin and his brother Sidney would lose both parents—their father through drink and separation from their mother, and their mother to poverty, and then mental illness. Chaplin was only one year old when his father left them and went to live with another woman. Although Hannah, Chaplin's mother, went to the law courts to sue her husband, the case did not go well for her and she did not receive adequate support. Even prior to their outplacement, Chaplin presents a dark picture of his early life:

> Our house ... 3 Pownall Terrace, [was] a small garret with rickety stairs, the house was depressing with the air foul with stale slops and old clothes ... the room was stifling, a little over twelve feet square, and seemed smaller and the slanting ceiling seemed lower. The table against the wall was crowded with dirty-plates and tea-cups; and in the corner, snug against the lower wall, was an old iron bed which mother had painted white ... mother's hired sewing machine with which she struggled to support us had been taken away for owing back installments ... I was hardly aware of a crisis because we lived in a continued crisis ... [I] left home as much as possible, anything to get away from our depressing garret. (Chaplin 1964, p. 10)

Chaplin's mother found her voice cracked and she began to get booed at the theater. Unable to work, she got migraine headaches. Only later was his mother diagnosed as mentally ill. Chaplin quipped, "Picasso had a blue period. We had a grey one, in which we lived on parochial charity, soup tickets, and relief parcels" (Chaplin 1964, p. 23). When Chaplin was six years old, his mother, he, and his brother Sidney entered the Lambert Borough workhouse, hoping to gain some support for the family. Chaplin wrote of the boys having to separate from their mother and "the shock of seeing Mother enter the visiting room garbed in workhouse clothes" (p. 26). But things would get worse as the boys were sent to the Hanwell School for Orphans and Destitute Children, twelve miles from London, and further separated from each other as they were placed in different grades. Chaplin recalled,

> It was ... a forlorn existence. Sadness was in the air, how I dislike the walks [through the village] where the locals [were] staring at us! We were known as inmates of the "bobby hatch," a slang term for the workhouse. Then the punishment of offenses and boys marched military style to see the disciplining of boys by canes. The spectacle was terrifying. I remembered witnessing my first flogging and my heart thumping. (Chaplin 1964, p. 29)

At age eleven, Sidney joined the navy to get out of the workhouse, but Charlie was too young and spent the time back with his mother. Chaplin recalled that like a "game of draughts" the last move was always back to the workhouse (Chaplin 1964, p. 33). When he and his mother were readmitted, Charlie was told his mother was then in the Crane Hill Asylum. Hannah would be in and out of the asylum much of her life. Although there is some dispute as to her exact psychiatric condition, she was provided for by the sons when they did well living in the United States. "Forlorn and baffled," Chaplin was placed for a while with his father and stepmother, where he was mistreated, forced to scrub floors and clean knives. After the Society for the Prevention of Cruelty to Children visited because of allegations of violence in the household, Chaplin was able to go back to his mother (p. 39). Both shame and stigma were well known to Chaplin as a boy. In his autobiography, Chaplin revises Sigmund Freud as to what factors in life are most important: "Unlike Freud, I do not believe sex is the most important element in the complexity of behavior. Cold, hunger, and the shame of poverty are more likely to affect one's psychology" (Chaplin 1964, p. 206).

In a similar vein, he recalls,

> I was well aware of the social stigma of our poverty. Even the poorest children sat down to a home-cooked meal Sunday dinner. A roast at home meant respectability. A ritual that distinguished one poor class from another. Those who could not sit down to Sunday dinner at home were of the mendicant class and we were that. (Chaplin 1964, p. 50)

Although Chaplin would succeed beyond his wildest dreams, following a life his parents had encouraged in the theater (but moving quickly into the film business), his life would be marked by a melancholy pessimism that colored his thoughts. Quoting Joseph Conrad in his autobiography, he described how life made him feel like a cornered rat—ready to be clubbed. He added that the simile could be used to "describe the appalling circumstances of us all" (Chaplin 1964, p. 76). Chaplin among our other subjects shows how no degree of success—financial, public acclaim, or awards—can entirely reverse the harsh starts of poverty that affected the subjects.

EDNA ST. VINCENT MILLAY: ALONE IN A MAINE TOWN

The woman who would come to symbolize "the new woman" of the post–World War I period—independent, sexual, cigarette dangling from her lips—as well as the first "poetess" to win the Pulitzer Prize, Edna St. Vincent Millay (1892–1950), grew up minding her two sisters while her mother worked far away from home.

Not much is known about Edna's early years when her father, Henry, who had been a schoolteacher, was still around. Stories note his gambling difficulties and charges of irresponsible handling of school funds (Milford 2001, p. 27). When Edna was eight years old her mother, Cora, divorced him, and her father left for the northern Maine woods, where he frequently wrote that he was coming back "as soon as he could get enough money" (ibid.). Whatever the causes, the divorce left the family living in poverty in the rather middle-class town of Camden, Maine. When their house was sold from under them, Cora and her three daughters lived with a neighbor who had made room for them on one side of her house. Cora taught music lessons to pay the bills. But this did not keep the wolves at bay, and she took up nursing to live on. Her nursing duties took her all over the state, and while she was frequently away, Edna was left with the house and her sisters from a young age.

Not surprisingly, biographer Jean Gould notes that Millay "experienced a bewilderment and a feeling of abandonment which was to become outright skepticism toward the concept of enduring love between man and woman" (Gould 1969, p. 7) after her parents' divorce. She also notes that Edna had the "red-head's fiery temper, flare-ups that came and passed at the slightest provocation ... from this time on whenever crossed ... harassed or troubled by deep emotion, she could be contrary to the point of being utterly exasperating" (ibid.). Like Jack London in some ways, Millay's feelings of abandonment and fears took a more aggressive form, leading to a life filled with substance use and turmoil rather than a more inward depression or sadness.

The Millay children were looked down upon in Camden. Living among itinerant millworkers and with their mother away all the time, the children taught themselves to swim amid the colored dyes of the woolen mills. When one cold winter the family ran out of coal and money, the pipes burst and flooded the floors, turning the house into an ice-skating rink. The kids promptly converted it into exactly that. The neighbors considered the Millays "a harum-scarum gypsy household run by that strange red haired older daughter." They were criticized for their lack of a garden, for not suitably covering their house windows, and for not cultivating their plum trees but eating them green, calling them "mock olives" (Gould 1969, p. 20).

The Millay children certainly did gain more advantages than the neighbors saw. Cora was a bohemian and an intellectual, and the girls had the finest collection of books in Camden, even when the grocer or coal company was not paid (Gould 1969, p. 13). Early on Edna started doing art and writing poems. But her sisters also described Edna's "sudden rages" and wildness. She was also extremely aggressive to them. She was not liked in school. It seems the Millay family was on the borders of both poverty and art, and caught somewhere between the dominant norms and unconventionality. The loss of her father and no doubt most of her mother's time would leave Edna St. Vincent Millay's life troubled at the same time that she became one of the twentieth century's most famous women.

BABE RUTH: CHILDHOOD IN AN INDUSTRIAL SCHOOL

George Herman Ruth (1895–1948), the great baseball player, is a figure biographers wish they knew more about, particularly his childhood. He rarely talked much of himself except for baseball. His parents were long dead by the time he became famous. We know he was born the sixth of his siblings, all of whom died except for a younger sister. He was born in Baltimore, Maryland, on the seedy waterfront where his German-Irish parents had a sort of grocery store and saloon.

Whether through neglect, his father's violence, which his biographers hint at, or other causes, Ruth from an early age hung out on Baltimore's streets. Marshall Smelser, one biographer, talks of Ruth accumulating a considerable criminal record and "learning freedom, profanity, and larceny" on the streets (Smelser 1975, p. 3). Biographer Robert Creamer puts it more strongly, saying, "He hid in the alleys, ran with other tough little kids and became more difficult to control" (Creamer 1974, p. 28). Ruth is quoted as saying, "I learned to fear and hate the coppers and to throw apples and eggs at truck drivers" (Creamer 1974, p. 29).

Legend had it that he chewed tobacco, drank whiskey, and stole, and the odds are he dabbled in all three. "I was a bum when I was a kid," Ruth said curtly. He added he honestly did not know the difference between right and wrong.

When Ruth was seven years old, his parents got a Justice of the Peace to label him "incorrigible or vicious" and "beyond the control" of his family. He was sent to St. Mary's Industrial School in Baltimore, which was a combination of an "orphanage, boarding school, and detention center for adjudicated delinquents" (Smelser 1975, p. 362). No doubt Ruth did feel abandoned, and he ran away from the institution, for which he was punished. It was also a stigmatized setting that others felt shame to be in. Nevertheless, Ruth in his later life would have only positive things to say about the Xaverian Brothers who ran the school, particularly his mentor Brother Matthias. In many senses, Ruth enjoyed a postponed childhood there. Illiterate when he arrived, he learned tailoring—he could sew a shirt in less than a quarter hour (Smelser 1975, p. 16)—and before long he became the school's star baseball player. There are many stories of Ruth at the school, many extolling his generosity, such as his tendency to buy loads of candy at the store and distribute it to the younger children, particularly those who were orphans or who had no friends or relatives (Creamer 1974, p. 39). But he was also impulsive, unpredictable, and stubborn, characteristics he had his whole life, and which often would get him in trouble with managers, owners, and some fellow baseball players.

Ruth did go home for some of the twelve years of his youth. It is hard to tell how this combination of upbringing affected him. His mother was known to be ill for some time before she died in 1912, and he was not on good terms with his father. He always refused to go to school when on the outside, and this alone would be enough to put him back in the Industrial School for truancy.

Sheltered over his years in St. Mary's Industrial School, when Ruth came out to the farm teams of major league baseball in 1914, he was called "the Babe" in part because of his rube-like unfamiliarity with life in the real world, but also perhaps because his new friends thought he was a foundling in the Industrial School (Smelser 1975, p. 38). His biographers see him as greatly institutionalized, citing his unfamiliarity with money and handling emotions, for example, which led him into trouble as it would do for many years after. Both affable and generous, and yet greatly childlike and stubborn, Ruth's childhood would be reflected in his complex adult life.

Chapter 2

WILLIAM SAROYAN: THE BITTER FRUITS OF CHILDHOOD

Few of our subjects had as bitter an experience of childhood as Pulitzer Prize–winning playwright William Saroyan (1908–1981). The Armenian American author suffered not only his father's death and being placed in an orphanage, but a general rejection by his family.

Armenak, William's father, came to the United States in 1905 from Armenia on a promise of a missionary job at a church, a job that never materialized. He lacked any trade and tried to make a living for his wife, Takoohi, and the four children, of which William was the youngest child, by farming in the Fresno, California, area. He died in 1911 of a burst appendix when William was just three. Without any money and resources, Takoohi had to place the four children in Fred Finch's Orphanage in Fresno. Although biographers Lawrence Lee and Barry Gifford note the placement was supposed to be only temporary, evidently his mother's failure to secure enough resources from her work as a domestic servant kept the children in the orphanage for years (five in William's case) (Lee and Gifford 1984, p. 178).

The orphanage experience left Saroyan bitter. An oft-repeated story was that at Christmas, the young Saroyan told "Santa Claus" that what he wanted was his father back, to which the man playing Santa Claus assented. When he got a few blocks from Santa, "he felt he had been fooled, that his expectancy had been encouraged and then mocked" (Leggett 2002, p. 6). This hurt and bitterness stayed with him all his life. He remembered being taunted by a group of boys shouting "Orphan! Orphan!" at him (Lee and Gifford 1984, p. 180). At the same time, though, he was a favorite of the men and women who ran the orphanage, and he got away with a lot, from whistling in chapel to running away frequently starting when he was only five.

When William returned home, things were a bit better economically, but his relatives were hostile to him. He already had missed much of an upbringing, particularly in the Armenian culture and language. His relatives laughed at "his pitiful inability to speak the language" and his audacity (Lee and Gifford 1984, p. 184). He was seen as rebellious and engaging in purposeful joking. The family called him *tsoor*, which means "daydreamer" or "crooked" or "crazy." His uncle told him to walk through the alleys, not the streets, "that's where you belong, the streets are for people" (ibid., p. 192). Worse, when he got into the habit of reading, which was encouraged by a teacher, his mother greeted this with scorn. "Who did he think he was, Shakespeare?" (ibid., p. 199).

"Learn to pick up the broom and find your right place in life," she said. Despite his preciousness in learning, he was kicked out of school three times and never did graduate. He was too independent and rebellious during high school to continue, and again his family saw him as a "bum." When he later took to writing, his family once more responded with contempt and disinterest.

While some of the conflict no doubt represents the struggle of a more intellectual child in a traditional peasant-type family based on traditional authority, the anger and bitterness Saroyan would feel toward his family and the general world ran deeper. His son Aram speculated that Saroyan's stay in the orphanage may have frozen his emotional life (Lee and Gifford 1984, p. 181). He had anger at his father for not doing better, but this may also have been guilt, and "whether this is all true, Saroyan certainly felt abandoned by his family and was deeply ashamed of his period in the orphanage" and his hardships growing up. His success could not quite erase it, and when things became difficult for him later in his life, he became even more gloomy and depressed.

RICHARD WRIGHT: THE PAIN OF HUNGER IN CHILDHOOD

Poverty comes in different degrees, and our words often fail us in describing the sharp pangs and pain of its impact. Famed writer Richard Wright (1908–1960) provided the world a glimmer of the pain of hunger in childhood in his famous autobiographical novel *Black Boy*, written in 1945. Wright faced so much deep poverty, abandonment, hostility from his elders, and pain at the hands of whites in the South that it is truly amazing he succeeded in being one of America's first successful African American novelists.

Wright was born near Natchez, Mississippi, the oldest son of Nathaniel, an illiterate sharecropper, and Elaine, who had been a schoolteacher. Although both were of mixed black, white, and Indian blood, they were considered black, and Richard's grandfather had been a slave. When Richard was five years old, the boll weevil plague crippled the cotton fields, throwing his father out of work, and his mother was reduced to part-time work, finally only being able to work as a domestic. Although Wright tells a number of stories of physical and emotional abuse by his father, things became even worse when his dad left the family at this point, leaving his mother with two boys to support. In *Black Boy*, Wright discusses the new depth of hunger he was thrown into:

My mind was frozen with horror.... Hunger stole upon me so slowly that at first I was not aware what hunger really meant. Hunger has always been more or less at my elbow when I played, but now I began to wake up at night to find hunger standing at my bedside, staring at me gauntly.... Whenever I begged for food now my mother would pour me a cup of tea which would still the clamor in my stomach for a moment.... When my father had left I was happy but it had not occurred to me that his absence would mean that there would be no food.... Now whenever I got hungry I thought of my father with deep biological bitterness. (Wright 1989, p. 14)

A biography of Wright talks of dizziness, dim vision, and a lack of energy to play caused by hunger. Biographer J. A. Williams calls this "mis-meal cramps," as local African American people referred to them (Williams 1970, p. 7). At some point around this time, Richard and his brother were placed in an orphanage as Elaine took a domestic job out of town. Wright hated the orphanage, associating it forever with "the noise of screaming and crying children." Williams declares that Wright "would never again trust in grownups, he grew sullen and angry at [his] mother when she visited" (p. 16). He ran away but was quickly apprehended by the police. We do not have clear information as to how long Wright and his brothers were at the orphanage. Like other subjects, it seems shame mixed with hurt and sadness about his fate, particularly the perceived rejection by his mother.

Wright's childhood did not get much better after he was released from the orphanage. His mother moved the family to Arkansas where her sister lived. Wright hated it there in part due to the sternness of his aunt, a devout Seventh Day Adventist. Wright was constantly in trouble for his language, his refusal to pray, and other behavior. Even before he was a teen, Wright began to act out; he drank heavily, became familiar with all the houses of prostitution, and hung out with a local gang that fought the white children. Yet even though Wright was switched back and forth to different schools, he did extremely well there, and became the valedictorian of his ninth-grade class (as far as he was to go in school). His first completed story came the year before, when despite having to work in a brickyard and a restaurant to support his mother (who was now paralyzed by a stroke), he forced himself to write down his thoughts. A local African American newspaper published it. His grandmother reacted with rage, charging Richard had created a "bad reputation for himself, going around writing stories and also used curse words" (Williams 1970, p. 33). Like Saroyan's experience, many subcultures among the poor seem to have had hostility to intellects. (My own conjecture here, given the fairly limited evidence of all poor families discouraging education, is that certain religious views seem to have accentuated this tendency.)

Wright would leave the South as soon as he could. Not only did he hate the segregationist whites, but also he saw as passive and inert blacks' acceptance of their fate, and the lack of appreciation of any intellectual interests. He was an angry young man with a deep hatred for the society he was born into. Like some others we have explored (London, Millay, Ruth, and Saroyan) he dealt with his anger with aggression and arrogance, turning his feelings outward toward society.

JACKSON POLLOCK: THE UNHAPPY ARTIST-TO-BE

Few people had more unhappy (and short) lives than the famous abstract Expressionist artist Jackson Pollock (1912–1956). He was born the fifth and youngest son of Leroy and Stella, Scotch-Irish Presbyterians in Cody, Wyoming. Pollock was the victim not only of poverty but of extreme unhappiness, mental illness, and alcoholism. Given that the American National Biography Online (ANB) describes him as a "painfully insecure, irresponsible, and mentally conflicted young man, unsure of himself in social situations and impaired in his ability to verbalize thoughts and emotions" it is quite amazing that Pollock would become one of history's most successful artists (though much of his fame and even more of the money his paintings made would be posthumous).

Pollock's parents were both from stern stock, and both seemed chronically unhappy with themselves and each other. His mother left the Iowa town she was from in disgrace after having an illegitimate child, which she never told her new family about (Solomon 2001, p. 17). His father went from washing dishes to ranching to surveying to stone masonry, but seemed rarely to ever make a living. Shortly after Jack's birth, which was said to be a very difficult labor, Leroy, his father, became ill with rheumatic fever, and had to leave what had been a somewhat successful ranch in California to move south for the climate. When Leroy walked out on his wife and family, Stella refused to accept the separation (ibid., p. 28). As Leroy drifted from place to place, Stella followed with her children in tow, and they ended up in deeper poverty as they moved five times. As with other subjects, the departure of his father left Jack bereft:

> For Jackson whose itinerant youth had already deprived him of any semblance of community or continuity, his father's departure signaled the complete loss of childhood security.... [His] mother was incapable of providing [him] with the attention and affection he needed. A rigid woman ... she pulled deeper into herself ... internalizing the unhappiness and becoming a remote presence to her children. (Solomon 2001, p. 29)

As Jackson Pollock's mother became more depressed and was reduced to living on "occasional checks" from Leroy, biographer Deborah Solomon describes Pollock as having a "weak, uncertain image of himself and an unfathomable sense of loneliness" (ibid.). He was a poor student and so withdrawn he made few friends. Like London and Wright, he tried to compensate for his unhappiness and insecurity by being "'manly' aggressive and drinking," says biographer B. H. Friedman (1995, p. 8). Drink would become Pollock's lifelong solution to his shyness, insecurity, and inability to socialize.

Oddly Pollock first thought of being an artist because his oldest brother received praise for being interested in art. Pollock had little experience and no natural aptitude for drawing or other components of art. About the most helpful experience Pollock had as a youth was accompanying his father to the Grand Canyon area for a surveying job. This experience brought about his lifelong fascination with Native American art, colors, and form, which would influence his life. He then went to a Manual Arts High School in Los Angeles where he found a mentor who was an artist. Pollock never graduated the high school; he was expelled for passing out radical leaflets criticizing the school and faculty.

Pollock would grow to be internationally known, kind of "a hard-riding, hard-drinking cowboy from the Wild West," as he was known in Europe (Friedman 1995, p. 3). The art world too knew his reputation for drink, aggression, and unpredictability. Despite his personality and what many considered to be a bizarre way of painting, Pollock would be discovered by the post–World War II art world, which would be unalterably affected by him.

JOHN GARFIELD: THE TOUGH KID FROM THE LOWER EAST SIDE

It is hard to differentiate the early life of John Garfield (1913–1952, born Jacob Julius Garfinkle) from the famous actor's roles as a tough guy on the Hollywood screen, since Garfield portrayed similar characters in his acting career. Garfield may have embellished some tales of his childhood to fit his image, but nevertheless he too suffered poverty and abandonment and loss, and feelings of hurt, shame, and stigma.

John was the oldest child of David and Hannah Garfinkle, both Russian Jewish immigrants. His father worked as a clothes presser on the Lower East Side of New York, where he barely made enough to support his family. Julius grew up in a rat-infested slum tenement where there was no heat, and where pneumonia and consumption were common. After his brother Max was born in 1918, his mother became ill; she died in 1920. According to biographer Robert Nott the two boys became "unofficial orphans" from that time on (Nott 2004, p. 12). His father seemed to have no time or desire to raise the boys, and they were shunted to a host of relatives around the city to live temporarily. Feeling angry and abandoned, Garfield became at least something of a delinquent. "The streets were our playground and our jungle—and you behaved like an animal or you got your block knocked off," said Garfield (Nott 2004, p. 7). The street gang system in New York was organized ethnically, and each group was expected to fight to protect its turf. Moving constantly around the city from Brooklyn to the Bronx did not help his stability either, and he ended up in some neighborhoods where he was a distinct minority. He never got along with his father, and was not close to his brother, so he was very much a lone wolf.

Like others, Garfield benefited from the assistance of nonfamily members. He was sent to a public high school with a reputation for assisting "problem children." There Angelo Patri, the principal who would become a noted educator, took him under his wing. When Patri went to visit Garfield he found him sleeping in a hallway outside an uncle's house on a pile of coats (Nott 2004, p. 19). Taking him on as a project, Patri helped Garfield find possibility in acting, and helped him gain a scholarship to an acting workshop in high school. According to Nott, Garfield did not find the idea of "shedding himself" of his own character hard as "he did not like who he was" at this point (p. 21). His father disliked John's career choice, saying acting was for "bums" and not a real job. He dropped out of school in tenth grade, though he was able to find his way to the American Laboratory Theatre, where he would eventually be trained for Broadway.

Garfield would rise like a meteor in show business, yet always play the role of a tough working-class or poor character. He adopted the left-wing politics of the Great Depression and was later prosecuted harshly by the House Un-American Activities Committee for not cooperating in its hunt for communists. He would die of a heart attack at age thirty-nine in the midst of the McCarthy period.

BILLIE HOLIDAY: THE MAKING OF ONE TOUGH SINGER

More than even many other famous people, Billie Holiday's (born Eleanora Fagan in Philadelphia, Pennsylvania, in 1915, died 1959) life tends to be shrouded in conflict and different accounts. Holiday (she took the name for her singing career) was often known to stretch the truth in her own accounts, and her childhood was so bound to the streets and its culture that official records and clearly accurate accounts are rare.

Nevertheless, biographers agree she had a childhood marked by abandonment, violence and rape, and incarceration. Her mother, Sadie, from Baltimore, was working as a domestic in Philadelphia when she was seduced by Clarence Holiday, a musician. They neither married nor lived together, although Holiday did visit from time to time and occasionally gave Sadie money. Sadie returned to Baltimore but moved frequently with her young daughter. We know that Sadie married a Phillip Gough in 1920, who in turn abandoned them a few years later, and that they lived in poverty. According to an account by biographer Robert O'Meally, Billie Holiday was left with a cousin who beat her daily with a whip or a clenched fist because she was wetting the bed (O'Meally 1991, p. 75). New evidence also supports the fact that Billie was raped as a young girl (Blackburn 2003, p. 15). There is some conflict though as to whether her being sentenced to the Baltimore House of Good Shepherd for Colored Girls was because of truancy (Clarke 2009, p. 18) or was related to the rape. In one account (Blackburn 2003, p. 15) Billie was returned to the juvenile center as a witness against the man who raped her. Some accounts suggest Billie had lesbian experiences at the home (Clarke 2009, p. 19), but other accounts say she was depressed and talked to no one.

By the age of twelve or so Holiday began hanging around with an assortment of hustlers and pimps. She looked far older than she was, and left school in the fifth grade. Her mother had left her in Baltimore on her own while she moved to New York City to make more money. At around age fourteen (1929), Holiday joined her mother in New York and combined working as a maid, a prostitute, and a restaurant worker to earn money. She was arrested with her mother that year, and sent to Welfare Island (a house of correction) for a period.

Holiday clearly grew up adopting a "tough" attitude and a hostile attitude toward her mother, whom she would fight with all her life, sometimes to the point of physical altercations. O'Meally stresses the great guilt that Holiday must have felt being from a religious Catholic family:

> Billie Holiday's life was a tragic but unending quest for power. She sought the power to free herself from the narrow set of expectations offered her as a poor black girl born into a family where being a "bastard" was considered an embarrassment.... Abandoned by her parents, she was subjected to sexual mistreatment at the place she was expected to call home. She was served an unending round of punishments by her surrogate mother.... It is not surprising that this youngster, who was not exactly pious but who did attend church as often as her mother could make her go, figured that she was to blame for having been set adrift in an uncaring world. (O'Meally 1991, pp. 13, 77–78)

Biographer Donald Clarke focuses more on Holiday's rejection of outside convention and respectability since by a young age she had experienced so much rejection and hostility anyway, no matter what she did.

> She was the kind of person who thought "I'm gonna get cussed out anyways, so what's the difference? What the hell" ... She just went out and done what she felt like doing 'cause she was just don't care-ish ... she was young and rough in her way. (Clarke 2009, p. 27)

Billie Holiday was distinguished from all the poor girls on the street by her fantastic voice, which was immediately notable even when she was a preteen, and led her to gain club engagements and eventually to become one of the most famous singers in the world—and certainly the most famous voice of jazz and blues. Still, once she was famous the patterns of her life were greatly set, and these patterns included a number of destructive ones such as choosing men who would abuse her, fighting at times violently with many of those around her, and using substances to ward off the anxiety or depression she felt. Like other poor people with an awful childhood, she was haunted through her short life by the ghosts of her past, even though she would become a world-famous entertainer and recognized wherever she went. Like Jack London and Jackson Pollock, she would bring to her fame a series of missteps and aggressions that were clearly a downside (particularly as her life went on) to those in the music business who otherwise admired her.

Chapter 2

MALCOLM X: A PAINFUL CHILDHOOD POLITICIZED

Malcolm Little (1925–1965), later Malcolm X, is another famous figure who raises some historical controversy. The son of a Baptist preacher born in Omaha, Nebraska, his famous autobiography (1965, with Alex Haley) portrays his life as a kind of biblical "Saul to Paul" story of how he broke out of racial oppression to emerge as a militant hero (Wood 1992, p. 10). Some aspects of his narrative have been challenged as inaccurate over the years, yet the details do not seriously undermine either his accomplishments or the very real pain of his childhood.

Malcolm was one of eight children born to Earl and Louise, both of whom were active in Marcus Garvey's United Negro Improvement Association (UNIA). The family moved to East Lansing, Michigan, when Malcolm was four. Although an attack by the Ku Klux Klan on his house (as shown in the well-known *Malcolm X* film by Spike Lee, as well as written about in the autobiography) may not have happened (Wood 1992, p. 127), and his father's death in 1931 in a streetcar accident appears to have been just an accident, not a murder by whites as Malcolm suggested (Dyson 1995, p. 4; Wood 1992, p. 128), the decline in the family's fortunes was the result of his father's death. Malcolm did note that his father and mother fought physically with each other, and with the children, though, unlike the other children, he was not hit by his father (Wood 1992, p. 125). His autobiography had little sympathy for his mother, whom he characterized as looking "white" as compared to his "jet black" father (Malcolm X 1965, p. 64). Louise did mentally decompensate, though the timing is not totally clear. The ANB notes her mental downturn at the time of her husband's death, but Arnold Rampersan, a biographer and literary critic, points to Malcolm's statements about his family going on relief in 1934 and that "what he does not mention is that about this time his mother gave birth to another child; born out of wedlock.... Malcolm's silence about this child in the Autobiography may be a token of his sense of shame" (Wood 1992, p. 129). Certainly if this is true it would further explain his anger and contempt for his mother, who in 1939 was committed to a mental asylum. In his narrative, Malcolm is very much the successor of his father's blackness and militancy, and is negative toward his mother.

Malcolm was an excellent student. In his autobiography, he cites a white teacher warning him that his goal to be a lawyer was "not a realistic goal for a nigger" (Malcolm X 1965, p. 38). Malcolm's decline from here is placed in the context of anger at white authorities, but events are not as clear as they might be. He was declared "incorrigible" at some point and sent to reform school and various foster homes. We know he had to steal food to survive and to develop some of the skills at hustling that would characterize his life in his late teens and early twenties. He apparently was placed with neighbors first when he was twelve, and then sent to reform school at age thirteen. He left school in eighth grade.

Despite some unclarities, Malcolm seemed to have survived his early childhood intact. But by age six on, he faced the loss of his father, the mental decline of his mother, and the breakup of his family. Like others we have noted, Malcolm's story and presentation stress his macho ability to survive the harsh reality of these events caused by racism, poverty, and family-specific factors. He developed a narrative that, while based on facts, was also consistent with a political Manichaeism of the time dominant in the world of the Black Muslim Party (Wood 1992, p. 54). This reaction to some of what must have been the hurt and shame of his early life was turned to a different direction, helping him construct his political persona of the 1950s and 1960s.

MARILYN MONROE: POVERTY, SHAME, AND TRAUMA

Few famous people had as much going against them as Marilyn Monroe (1926–1962) the movie star and sex symbol. Born Norma Jean Mortenson (and also known as Norma Jean Baker) in Los Angeles, California, she was the daughter of a film cutter, Gladys Baker Mortenson, and an unknown father. Her mother gave up Norma Jean within two weeks of birth, feeling unable to care for her. She would spend very little time with her daughter, adding not only the feeling of abandonment and shame but a history of family mental illness to Marilyn's life (mental illness went back some generations in the Baker-Mortenson family, although this is contested by biographer Donald Spoto).

For much of the first seven years of her life she lived as a foster child with the Bolanders, a working-class to poor family with strict religious views. In her autobiography, Monroe noted,

> I thought the people I lived with were my parents. I called them mama and dad. The woman said to me one day "don't call me mama. You're old enough to know better.... You just board here"... the people I thought were my parents had children of their own. They weren't mean, they were just poor. They didn't have much to give anybody, even their

own children, and there was nothing left for me. (Monroe with Hecht 2007, p. 3)

When Marilyn grew aware of her real mother, she came to have a lifelong guilt and feeling of rejection. "I was probably a mistake. My mother did not want me. I probably got in her way, and I must have been a disgrace to her" (Spoto 1995, p. 17).

When Norma Jean turned eight, her mother signed guardianship over to her friend Gloria McKee, who also now had guardianship over Gladys Mortenson's estate when she was taken to a mental hospital. With a third mother figure now in eight years, Norma Jean got an entirely different sort of upbringing. Gloria wished to turn her into a movie star and by age eight had dyed Norma Jean into a peroxide blond and used makeup on her lips and cheeks. She would learn to be a young Jean Harlow or Clara Bow. She would later find sexuality to be her sole source of power. After Grace married, her new husband wished to be rid of Norma Jean, so she was placed in an orphanage. As Spoto notes, "Here was another relationship suddenly ruptured, and another promise broken; she was once again an unwanted commodity" (Spoto 1995, p. 43). Much of Norma Jean's memory of the orphanage is of depression and uniformity, particularly the blue dress and white shirtwaist uniform she wore.

Things did not get better when she came out of the orphanage; she was sent to live with various relatives and to nine different foster homes (according to her biography, Monroe with Hecht 2007, p. 14, there is again some contestation). It was in this period when a cousin forcibly sexually assaulted her, and another sexual incident occurred as well. As the ANB puts it, "given an insecure childhood that included the trauma of sexual molestation and early marriage arranged in part to prevent her return to the orphanage, it is a testament to her tenacity, personal strength, and resilience that she managed to achieve the heights she did."

Still, Monroe would carry with her a childhood of poverty, of maternal deprivation, a lack of stability of parents or adult role models, the shame of illegitimacy, and the history of mental illness. Biographers put it in different ways; Spoto notes "she was clearly scarred by psychological and emotional stress of her uncertain identity" (Spoto 1995, p. 19), while Barbara Leaming, another biographer, described her as having a "feeling of utter worthlessness" and her growing up "being told she was the embodiment of sin and evil" (Leaming 1998, p. 12). In her biography, Monroe talks about her childhood "character faults as a slightly overgrown child who stares and hardly speaks, and who expects one thing of a home—to be thrown out—[this] can seem like a nuisance to have around" (Monroe with Hecht 2007, p. 16).

Throughout her decade and a half of film success, Monroe carried all the guilt, shame, and grief of her childhood with her. Although her death at age thirty-six may not have been suicide, most around her were convinced it was.

STEVE MCQUEEN: BORN INTO BAD LUCK

The well-known actor and "king of cool" Steve McQueen (1930–1980) once said, "My life was screwed up before I was born" (Terrill 1993, p. 1). Indeed, few of our subjects were as deeply connected to a disreputable part of the poor as McQueen. Born in Beech Grove, Indiana, to a teenage runaway and alcoholic mother, Jillian Crawford, and William "Red" McQueen, a stuntman, he, too, was illegitimate. "What chance did a bastard child born on the wrong-side of the tracks in Indiana have in the 1930s?" McQueen queried (Porter 2009, p. 7).

According to one account (Porter 2009, p. 6) his father scraped together enough cash to open an illegal gambling joint in Indianapolis, and his joint and bordello flourished until police raided the building. Other accounts have his father simply deserting his mother by the time Steve was six months old (Terrill 1993, p. 2). His mother, reduced to working as a prostitute, left Steve with her parents in Slater, Missouri. His time there seemed somewhat better. Though his grandparents were highly religious disciplinarians, Steve was rewarded with a tricycle for his fourth birthday, and also had his own room as the grandparents had no other children. Just as he was adjusting, though, his mother returned to take him back to Indianapolis (Terrill 1993, p. 3).

As biographer Marshall Terrill notes, McQueen was "uprooted from the only stable home in his young life, Steve felt overwhelmed and he took the move ... very hard" (1993, p. 5). With no friends, he began roaming the streets and eventually got involved in a gang. McQueen stayed out all night, slept on the streets, and skipped school. School presented a great challenge to McQueen with his case of undiagnosed dyslexia as well as unrecognized hearing difficulties. Terrill notes that McQueen later confessed that his acting out "was a relief from boredom" (p. 6). When he was twelve years old, his mother wrote his relatives—with whom he was again living—that she had married again and was now living in the Silver Lake area of Los Angeles. She asked for Steve to come with her. Unfortunately her new husband, Berri, used his fists on Steve as well as his wife. Steve "ended up spending more nights on the streets than in the Berri household" (ibid.). Terrill says "he led the life of a young hobo. Sneaking on freight trains, hitchhiking, and eating around campfires were his way of life now." McQueen says, "I learned early in life not to trust anyone." He bore that mistrust toward everyone, says Terrill, and it carried into his adult life (p. 8).

McQueen then fell in with a gang that operated near Pershing Square in downtown Los Angeles. According to biographer Darwin Porter, "he stole purses from old ladies, ripped off hubcaps, and even hotwired a car or two" (2009, p. 21). He dropped out of school in the ninth grade, and was finally busted for shoplifting. His mother obtained a court order and Steve was sent to the Boys' Republic at Chino, a reform school.

Though McQueen began the Boys' Republic sullen and angry, he was taken under the wing of a Mr. Panter, a worker there (Terrill 1993, p. 10), and gradually came to be respected at the institution. He later said the Boys' Republic saved his life, and McQueen always gave fan mail from this institution priority over his other letters. When he was released at age sixteen, McQueen joined his mother in New York City, where according to biographers he was a prostitute, an alcoholic, and on and off homeless. It would still be about five years or more before acting became McQueen's calling.

McQueen is among our subjects who could directly use his life experience in his successful career. While McQueen matured in some ways, he was always also an aggressive and macho figure with relationship problems and substance use. His success in some ways legitimated his problems as well as showed his abilities.

RICHARD PRYOR: A CHILDHOOD THAT FUELED EDGY SELF-DESTRUCTIVE REBELLION?

In the words of biographer Audrey T. McClusky comedian Richard Pryor's unconventional and unstable youth can be seen as fueling Pryor's "brilliance and his edgy self-destructive rebellion" (McClusky 2008, p. 1). Born in Tupelo, Mississippi, Pryor (1940–2005) grew up in Peoria, Illinois, in a brothel run by his grandmother Marie Carter. His mother, Gertrude Thomas, was herself a prostitute there and his father, Leroy Pryor, was a former bartender and boxer. Pryor's family was "a hodgepodge of heritage, including part Native American" (Pryor 1995, p. 18).

Childhood Poverty

Pryor always acknowledged his bizarre childhood:

[In my] childhood so many things were impossible to understand that after a certain point you just quit trying. You dealt with the facts with survival. You didn't trust anybody! You watched your back.... On television, people talked about having happy lives, but in the world in which I grew up, happiness was a moment rather than a state of being. (Pryor 1995, p. 34)

Pryor talks of his early exposure to sex and his looking through keyholes to see what the adults were doing. But his parents struggled to provide him a normal religious upbringing and a good education. They placed Pryor in Catholic school, where he did well, getting straight As and impressing his teachers. Then his background came to haunt him: "Someone found out about the family business and that blew my chance. They gave me the boot. Kicked my ass out of school. I was crushed by this inexplicable rejection by people who professed love and forgiveness" (Pryor 1995, p. 40). He attended another school and did well for a while until he developed a crush on a little white girl and gave her a scratch board. Her father showed up the next day holding the toy, and yelling, "Nigger, don't you ever give my daughter anything!" (ibid., p. 43).

Meanwhile he was sexually abused, by his account at six years old (some accounts say by a Roman Catholic priest but this is not confirmed in his autobiography):

A sick pedophile turned me into a pin cushion for his perverted urges. I was paralyzed by terror and did not run. I felt violated, humiliated, dirty, fearful, and most of all ashamed.... I carried around that secret for most of my life, I told no one. (Pryor 1995, p. 28)

The "simmering rage in Richard Pryor that found its expression in his performance" as McClusky (2008, p. 2) says, has various roots. His sexual abuse, the general nature of the home he grew up in, the violence ascribed to his grandmother ("who would beat him for any eccentricities"), and the split of his mother and father at age ten, which forced young Richard to choose between them at an early age, were certainly among them.

When he was a young teen, a teacher named Miss Parker knew how to "handle" him. In exchange for doing his work, Miss Parker let him stand in front of the class each morning and tell jokes to his classmates.

He had "never thought of himself as having a gift" but he enjoyed hearing his classmates laugh (Pryor 1995, p. 47). Still, at age fourteen he was expelled from school for hitting a science teacher.

Pryor continued on the edge of falling into jail until well into his young adulthood. He spent much of his time in the US Army in the late 1950s in prison when he and some other black soldiers stabbed a white soldier who was racist. Early in his career he used a cap pistol to try to hold up the owners of a night club where he worked.

Just as Marilyn Monroe and Steve McQueen took their challenging youth and put their pains into entertainment, Pryor took his assortment of odd and wonderful characters from his youth and put them in his comedy act. As we shall see, like other subjects, he never "recovered" from his childhood and the conflict that enveloped him as a child. Rather, as famous as he got, the baggage of his emotions led to drug use, violent outbursts, and near suicides.

THE TRAUMA OF POVERTY IN YOUTH

Reading about the difficult and in some cases tragic youth of our subjects is meant to shed some light on the historic patterns of growing up poor. While these cases are too few and nonrepresentative to describe all poor childhoods (or all our subjects), they do reflect a very common pattern of poverty, drama, and pain that makes up too many people's early years.

To review briefly, virtually all those described in this chapter suffered some form of abandonment—the death of Anne Sullivan's mother followed by her father's placing her and her brother in a poorhouse; the splitting up of Theodore Dreiser's family; the desertion of Charlie Chaplin's father and then the placement of him and his brother in a workhouse and orphanage; the departure of Edna St. Vincent Millay's father and the physical absence of her mother through much of her childhood; the early death of William Saroyan's father; the desertion of Jackson Pollock's father; the early death of John Garfield's mother; the early loss of Malcolm X's father; and the split up of Richard Pryor's parents. Others who were "illegitimate" felt the stigma from the earliest they could become aware of it: Jack London, Billie Holiday, Marilyn Monroe, and Steve McQueen. Issues of illegitimacy in the family also affected Theodore Dreiser, Jackson Pollock, and Malcolm X.

Issues of loss and abandonment were compounded for nine of the subjects by placement in nonfamily settings that held considerable stigma.

Anne Sullivan and Charlie Chaplin went to poorhouses or workhouses; Babe Ruth to an Industrial School; William Saroyan, Richard Wright, Marilyn Monroe, and Chaplin spent time in orphanages; Billie Holiday, Steve McQueen, and Malcolm X were in juvenile homes or reform schools; and Malcolm X and Monroe were in foster homes. It is not the case that all such placements are negative or destructive—some placements both today and in years past were very helpful to poor people. Still, even at their best, given the high level of stigma present about both institutions and foster arrangements, we can expect exacerbation of previous childhood problems as well as bonding with other youth cut off from families.

Almost every other social problem reared its head in the fifteen cases we've looked at here. The mothers of Jack London, Charlie Chaplin, Jackson Pollock, Malcolm X, and Marilyn Monroe had serious mental health issues. Many of the subjects were abused physically or sexually, and others were very possibly abused. Biographers believe Anne Sullivan was abused, Richard Wright was physically abused, Billie Holiday was sexually abused, as were Marilyn Monroe and Richard Pryor; Steve McQueen suffered physical abuse at the hands of his mother's boyfriends. Charlie Chaplin tells of violence at the hands of his father and his new wife; biographers imply Babe Ruth may have been at least physically abused by his father.

Alcohol has an involvement with many of the parents and even in some cases the early lives of the children. Anne Sullivan's father was an alcoholic as was Chaplin's father, while Jack London, Babe Ruth, Richard Wright, Jackson Pollock, Billie Holiday, and Steve McQueen certainly took up drinking quite early. Gangs played a role at least in London's, Ruth's, Wright's, John Garfield's, and Steve McQueen's early years. Early sexuality and presence of prostitution occur in Theodore Dreiser's story as well as in those of Richard Wright, Billie Holiday, Steve McQueen, and Richard Pryor.

While we may find some of the stories exceptional, as noted in Chapter 1, poorer areas of our country have often been a breeding ground for social problems connected with poverty. Both the difficulty of surviving in poverty and the limited ways available to cope with such trauma (drink and gangs come to mind) as well as its dangers to sanity (mental illness) and presence of alternative ways of living (prostitution, for example) can all be expected to different degrees. In every case, what is perhaps most exceptional was the ability of the individuals to succeed in spite of these circumstances.

CHAPTER 3

HEDONISM, PAIN, AND SUFFERING IN ADULT LIFE

֎

Although our subjects all became famous and accomplished in many ways, none can be said to have escaped the extremely difficult childhoods they faced. Generally all were victims of degrees of poor judgment, personal pain or depression, and difficult personalities. One pattern that emerged in the biographies I studied was an aggressive, hedonistic, almost "bull in a china shop" type approach to life while, simultaneously, *even more commonly* a more depressed, sad, introspective, and worried personality prevented the subjects from fully enjoying their lives. Although a diagnostic approach in retrospect is not necessarily helpful, no doubt some of the first group would today be seen as having manic or manic-depressive characteristics. Others neither clearly depressed nor bipolar might be seen as having personality disorders today.

Two obvious variables affect these personality sets in this sample. One is gender. The history of American society is such that men are raised to be tough, "macho," strong, and to take advantage of situations to benefit themselves. What some sociologists and gender experts call *hegemonic masculinity*, a sort of stereotyped macho bravado (particularly within the lower classes), can be seen as reflected in showy sports stars such as Jack Johnson and Babe Ruth, adventurer and writer Jack

London, artist Jackson Pollock, the early life of singer Johnny Cash, comedian Richard Pryor, and to a large degree writer William Saroyan, actor Steve McQueen, and activist Malcolm X. Among women, only singer Billie Holiday, who was every bit as tough and aggressive as her male colleagues, and perhaps Edna St. Vincent Millay, who was capable of considerable highs as well as lows, come close. Although some males are in the more depressive realm—writer Theodor Dreiser, actor-director Charlie Chaplin, writer Richard Wright, and actor John Garfield—more women are here: "miracle worker" Anne Sullivan, birth control reformer Margaret Sanger, actress Marilyn Monroe, radical activist Elizabeth Gurley Flynn, and civil rights activist Fannie Hamer.

A second difference relates to the intellectuality of the subjects and the nature of their occupations. Writers like Dreiser and Wright and actor-director Chaplin were steeped in intellectual defenses and generally less likely to respond to events with aggression or react to personal setbacks or defeats as insults. Johnson and Ruth, on the other side of the spectrum, were expected to act like the tough sports figures they were and present a strong masculine front. But both the class nature of writers and intellectuals' positions and the norms of society would not find aggression acceptable in these areas.

After reviewing the difficulties some of our subjects faced in their lives, we will explore the differences in a sample I have drawn of mostly middle-class famous people, who appear to have far fewer personal and social problems than those from poor backgrounds.

"SHOW OFF" SPORTS STARS

Two great figures in American sports history—the first African American heavyweight boxing champion, Jack Johnson (1878–1946), and the most famous baseball player of all time, Babe Ruth (1895–1948)—appear as "larger than life" figures whose exploits dazzled the public but also provoked criticism from the press and parts of the national audience.

Jack Johnson was born in Galveston, Texas, to Henry, a janitor and former slave, and Tiny. At a time when African Americans were excluded from mainstream boxing, Johnson slowly worked his way up including participating in so-called battle royals, in which several black youth were placed in the ring together to knock each other out in a brutal free-for-all (Ward 2004, p. 24). As Johnson worked his way up the pecking order of boxing, each fight he qualified for drew a stream of racist invective and angry attacks on him, verbal and sometimes physical, from white spectators. Johnson's success was so great that his career caused a movement to end boxing, as well as added to Prohibition sentiment and antimiscegenation laws, all aimed at keeping people like Jack Johnson out of sports, from marrying white women, and otherwise threatening the color line.

Johnson, unlike other "firsts" later in sports, greeted white hatred with aplomb and resistance. He dressed in pink and other outlandish colors and was written about as a modern Beau Brummel (Ward 2004, p. 58). He had a love affair with new and fast cars, which he sometimes painted blue, cream, or brilliant red. Constantly in auto accidents and running afoul of the law with his driving, he also was prone to heavy drinking and gambling. But nothing would lead to more controversy than Johnson's penchant for white women. A source of deep hostility among many whites, and fear among some blacks who felt he was too provocative (and some who for political reasons disliked his penchant for white women), Johnson's actions led to the passage of the Mann Act in 1910, forbidding the transportation of women across state lines for "prostitution, debauchery, or for any immoral purpose." Conveniently at a time when the "great white hope" to defeat Johnson had not arisen, he was convicted and found guilty of violating the act, and fled to England in 1913. Having not succeeded in securing a white boxer who could defeat Johnson, the power structure found another way to remove him.

Unquestionably, it is impossible to not feel sympathy for Johnson as the great fighter provoked much of the negative reaction he did because of his race. As biographer Al-Tony Gilmore notes,

> At a time when black men could be lynched simply for looking at white women, Johnson caroused with and married them at will. He defied all of the degrading customs of America: he was rich when blacks were poor; free to do as he chose when blacks were forced to bear their oppression in silence ... but blacks were ambivalent about Johnson. Although he was their champion, they feared the white backlash to his escapades. (Gilmore 1975, pp. 3, 5)

Johnson, like other children of low-income people, would have had little experience in handling the dramatic levels of fame and attention he was suddenly subject to. Asked by a reporter about his fancy cars and speeding, he replied, "I always take a chance on my pleasures" (Ward 2004, p. 154). It seems along with Johnson's resistance was an aggression to capture all life's pleasures before they slipped away, sometimes impairing his judgment. Hence while his career provided a national hero for African Americans, it also became a cautionary tale for the future with those like boxer Joe Louis, baseball player Jackie Robinson, and others intentionally effecting a quite conservative self-portrayal of themselves outside both the boxing ring and the ballfield.

As Johnson lingered in Europe after escaping arrest in the United States, his physical shape declined, and he lost the world championship. He was forced to do vaudeville, play in films, try bullfighting, and even engage in comic fights in which he lifted people and other antics. He moved from Spain to Mexico, and in 1920 he returned to the United States to serve his one-year term. He would later divorce his wife and marry a third white wife. He became quite poor as he aged, and he would die in an automobile accident in which he was driving recklessly in 1946.

Babe Ruth was in many ways an even larger-than-life figure than Johnson. A man famous for his huge appetites for food, drink, sex, and fast cars, a biographer notes, "Ruth did not divide his life into parts but lived it whole. Baseball, food, drink, sleep were all of a piece. He behaved as if there was no life after baseball, no life apart from it" (Smelser 1975, p. 139). In fact, some biographers think Ruth even exaggerated his foibles. ("Ruth consciously tried to create the fable of Babe the Glutton. He often grossly overate when strangers or new friends were with him in order to keep alive his reputation as a greedy feaster," Smelser 1975, p. 140.) There was an aspect of folk hero in all this, that the greatest baseball player in the world "could flout every rule of conduct and still be a champion" (p. 142). Still, his behavior did not endear him with managers, coaches, and some fellow ballplayers (for example, Lou Gehrig). To them, he lacked qualities that they wanted: loyalty, conformity to authority, commitment to training rules, and trust in the orders of his managers. He often fell out with authority and over the years was suspended many times. As he aged, he also was denied something he coveted very much: a manager position. He and his family could never fathom their rejection by the Yankees from any position with the team, and this led to extreme bitterness in Ruth's later years. To those in Yankee authority, while Ruth was a talented commodity, he was a constant pain interpersonally with his behavior problems.

Ruth's behavior with women, driving fast cars, with binge eating and drinking became so legendary that the reality is hard to actually track and document. The New York Yankees as early as 1921 hired detectives to track Ruth's off-field exploits (Smelser 1975, p. 205). It is also unclear how intelligent Ruth was, as one biographer notes he "was equal to a child of nine, twelve and fifteen years (variously estimated)" (ibid., p. 146). Unlike Jack Johnson, whose race made his behavior astounding to white fans, Ruth was greatly forgiven his transgressions. "He was everybody's wayward boy so everyone forgave him" says biographer Marshall Smelser (1975, p. 259). Gradually, Ruth's second wife, Clare, and trainer Arthur McGovern in the mid-1920s to early 1930s were able to keep Ruth somewhat in shape, and away from too much alcohol, food, and sexual dalliances. The second part of his career was considerably steadier than the first.

Though Ruth stayed in good enough shape to perform his most famous and outstanding home-run hitting, the winding down of his career occurred with much bitterness toward the Yankees. It was as if as soon as Ruth was a spent force, he was let go. In part, Ruth and Lou Gehrig's mutual hostility was one cause of this. While friendly at first, the two stars were greatly opposite in style. Gehrig grew up poor as well, but he adopted a sort of stern German Puritanism and recoiled at Ruth's antics both off the field and on (with managers and so on). Eventually their wives also clashed and the couples both stopped speaking. The Yankees in 1935 passed Ruth on to the Boston Braves in a trade that looked good on the surface to Ruth, but that gave him no commitment to a manager's position. He was made assistant manager, which was a bit of a nonposition, and within a year, as his playing declined, he was eased out of baseball. During the remaining dozen years of Ruth's life, he and his (second) wife expressed great bitterness with baseball, and how little baseball management had ever done for one of its most famous sons.

On one level, Johnson and Ruth can be classified as hedonists who used their exalted status (for a period) to reap the rewards of fine cars, food, clothes, and sexual partners. Yet the desperation that accompanied at least some of the hedonism marks a strong discomfort that both sons of poor families must have felt in their elevated status. How much their actions were provoked by feelings of anxiety and aggression is hard to know.

FIVE BREAKTHROUGH ARTISTS WITH SEVERE PERSONALITY ISSUES

Five famous artists who made tremendous contributions to American history—writer and adventurer Jack London (1876–1916), painter

Jackson Pollock (1912–1956), jazz and blues musician Billie Holiday (1915–1959), singer Johnny Cash (1932–2003), and comedian Richard Pryor (1940–2005)—did so despite periods of excruciating suffering and personal distress. Although some might cite fame itself as a possible pathogen, in these cases, personal problems generally preceded by some time the actual period of breakout fame.

Jack London, a self-identified Nietzsche admirer, within his short life span tried to live several different lives: voyaging across the Bering Sea, covering the discovery of gold in the Klondike, tramping across America as a hobo, writing numerous books and newspaper articles, and traveling across the Pacific by boat. Biographer Alex Kershaw convincingly argues London was "wanderlust unequalled" (Kershaw 1997, p. xiv). As we saw in Chapter 2, London had a troubled childhood and struggled to fit in as an insecure man in a tough environment. Alcohol was always a key crux in London's ability to mount his courage. "He used alcohol as a means of fitting in with the other men, and also as a way of escaping circumstances, [he] also got into a lot of scuffles and bar fights when drinking with other men. He became known for being very tough and not to be messed with" (Haley 2010, p. 44).

But as much as London would become one of the most famous alcoholics of his time (captured in his 1913 book *John Barleycorn*), it was a deep ongoing depression (what London called his "long sickness") that always haunted him. As long as London could apply himself to his writing and political interests, he was tremendously productive, and would become the era's most productive and famous adventure writer. Kershaw notes, "The solitary comrade [was] still haunted by the fears of childhood, of being alone, unwanted, worthless. He had been hungry all his life; it seemed for affection and love" (1997, p. 109).

By the later years of London's life, his kidneys began to go, and he added a variety of painkillers such as morphine and opium to the mix. He also took to sleeping with a loaded pistol by his side. When he died at the age of forty, he was found with an empty vial of morphine beside him. Whether he killed himself has been, according to biographer James Haley, "a live and contentious [question] almost from the moment he stopped breathing" (2010, p. 310). London's short and dramatic life left behind, of course, his world-renowned books including *The Call of the Wild* and *White Fang*. Benefiting from what has been called the "Strenuous Age" (Kershaw 1997, p. 88), London's characters shaped by a Spenserian and Nietzschean worldview clearly met audience demand, particularly among young boys. Less successful and ultimately less coherent were his political views; despite being a radical socialist and anarchist, he eventually lost faith in the ability of the working class to make change, much less the parties that claimed to represent them. His constant racism against nonwhites also limited his legitimacy with his fellow radicals.

Jackson Pollock, though living a generation later than London, had a similar deep involvement with alcohol and chronic psychological problems that probably preceded his involvement with booze. He was described even as a young man as "shy, aloof, [and] somewhat threatening" (Solomon 2001, p. 52). Later in his life as he took up heavy drinking, his self-effacing behavior would alternate "unpredictably with hostile outbursts" (ibid., p. 54) Pollock's exploits are so many that they are impossible to verify as true. A friend spoke of his waking up with Pollock holding a drawn knife on him (Friedman 1995, p. 26), and he supposedly disrobed at a party at the house of his biggest promoter (Peggy Guggenheim), wandered naked, and urinated into the fireplace (p. 144). While a patient at Bellevue Hospital for alcohol detoxification, he allegedly smashed every window in the building (Solomon 2001, p. 99). But there was a key sense in which Pollock's introspection led to the radical disjuncture in art that his famous paintings marked. Pollock himself was greatly interested in psychotherapy, particularly the symbolic nature of Jungian and shamanistic representations of native peoples. Originally a student of the American Regionalist painter Thomas Hart Benton, a total representationist, Pollock broke with Benton first in eighty-three drawings he did in 1939–1940 for his own psychotherapy. In the 1940s, encouraged by Russian artist/entrepreneur John Graham, his partner painter Lee Krasner (who sacrificed a great deal of her own career to Pollock's), and the constant advocacy of *The Nation*'s art critic Clement Greenberg, Pollock moved to large canvases filled with color and shapes and a maelstrom of action. Like a lightning bolt, Pollock by the late 1940s and early 1950s had taken the art world by storm, despite the great (and continuing) skepticism about modern art among much of the populace. The mass coverage of his work included wonder and acclaim, but often implied head shaking and contempt that such artwork sold for so much.

Success did not have much positive impact on Pollock. Living in the small Hampton area town of Amagansett with Krasner, Pollock went through productive periods but then more unproductive periods when his drunken rages beset him. At the young age of forty-four, he crashed drunk at the wheel, killing himself and another passenger. Like

London (and Ruth for that matter as well) he shot like a comet and was gone before long.

Like London and Pollock, singer Billie Holiday became a breakthrough star, but she did so while enduring a life marked by physical abuse and substance abuse. Holiday first started singing as a young woman at jam sessions and speakeasies. By the mid-1930s she was playing the Apollo Theater in Harlem. In the later 1930s she joined Count Basie's orchestra and toured with the all-white Artie Shaw Orchestra, frequently being excluded from accommodations because of her race. In 1939 her act moved to the Café Society, a Greenwich Village "hangout frequented by an interracial audience of liberal intellectuals" (American National Biography Online). Here is where she sang her famous song "Strange Fruit" about southern lynching. As we saw in Chapter 2, Holiday was an abused and angry child. Throughout her life her domineering mother Sadie accompanied her everywhere and they fought bitterly, sometimes physically. One biographer describes Holiday as "fighting at the snap of a finger ... if anyone crossed her, she was really bad" (Clarke 2009, p. 79). No doubt some of the incidents were defending herself against racial epithets and some against rowdy men. Each of her boyfriends and partners appeared more violent than the last one, as biographer Robert O'Meally notes:

> Despite her showings of contrariness and her achievements as an artist, she was suicidally submissive to men. She had been a girl prostitute. She was controlled by one entrepreneur/lover after another, by drugs, and by drug-dealing entrepreneur/lovers who pimped her talent. Because she had been an abused child who grew up with violence all around her, she was drawn to the panther-pretty men in her life, the most brutal ones she could find. That is why when she chose women lovers, she preferred submissive ones, women whom—according to Buck Clayton and others—she herself would sometimes treat to a dose of violence. (1991, p. 172)

The biographies of Holiday review countless episodes of physical abuse by Holiday's boyfriends toward her, and considerable counterviolence by her. Additionally, by the early 1940s Holiday was using heroin and opium as well as marijuana. It was a well-known secret that Holiday was a user, and she entered a clinic to kick the habit in 1947. Federal agents were looking for a high-profile drug user to build their conviction rate and easily were able to bust Holiday. She spent a year in a federal reformatory. By the 1950s Holiday was in decline, looking considerably older than she was and unable to kick her drug habit. She collapsed in 1959 at age forty-four, fell into a coma, and died.

Holiday's life has been subject to some romanticization as a victim of a repressive, racist society, but her great talents and creation of great milestones in music stand for themselves, without necessarily mitigating how difficult Holiday's life was and how painful to her as well as others it apparently was.

Johnny Cash, the great popular singer and music icon, was born in the small town of Kingsland, Arkansas, in 1932. The son of a sharecropper, Cash began working the fields at age five. His childhood was a mixed one with a father who treated him hostilely, although he had a loving mother. The tragic accidental death of his older brother Jack when Johnny was twelve crushed him, and seemed to be a source of personal guilt through many years. After spending time in the service, selling appliances, and getting married and having children, Cash achieved his first successes in the 1950s with songs including "Folsom Prison Blues" and "I Walk the Line." However, in a parallel vision to Malcolm X's story, Cash's biographies and autobiography stress a period of sin and then redemption cast in terms of drugs and sin and Christianity (see essay by Held in Huss and Werther 2008).

Cash spent at least a decade in what he called "my affair with pills," which he combined with heavy drinking (Cash 2003, p. 23). Over the late 1950s to 1960s, Cash wrecked every car he had, antagonized the Grand Ole Opry by smashing out all its footlights, smashed up countless hotel rooms, set off cherry bombs in hotel toilets, and even triggered a mass forest fire when his truck caught fire due to an overheated wheel bearing. He was the only person successfully sued by the federal government for starting a forest fire (Cash 2003, p. 150). Although often thought to have been a prisoner himself because of his cultivated "outlaw image," he never served time behind bars other than for misdemeanors.

Cash attributes his change to his embrace of Christianity and his marriage to June Carter, to whom he remained married for thirty-five years. But besides these factors, Cash became a very different popular artist in the 1960s and 1970s. Interested in musical history and bringing forth America's excluded groups from Native Americans to prisoners, Cash as the "man in black" was a very different political and social symbol from the average country and western singer. While parts of his politics remained ambiguous, his popularity crossed all sorts of traditional lines in music and demographics.

Hedonism, Pain, and Suffering in Adult Life

Perhaps none of the five stars portrayed so far in this chapter had as equally a prominent professional and personal life as comedian Richard Pryor. As noted in Chapter 2, Pryor grew up in an environment where strange, bizarre, and eccentric characters surrounded him. Throughout his life, Pryor's fairly public deviance was well apparent, the most famous of which was his bursting into flames while freebasing cocaine and drinking 151-proof rum in 1980. As Mel Watkins, an analyst of black humor, notes,

> Pryor's turbulent personal life—his inflammatory public outbursts, his chaotic relations with women, his drug use, brawls, and run-ins with the law—have all been thoroughly documented.... Rarely has the age-old temptation to connect genius with neurosis been more overindulged. Few comedians have been subjected to the type of pseudo psychological, ad hominen interpretations that mark discussions of Pryor's life and work. (Watkins 1994, p. 530)

As troubled as Pryor's life was, Watkins is right that his accomplishment in bringing black street humor to American life was more profound. Even into the 1960s, strong rules of conduct marked black humor, and Pryor himself followed the traditions of Nipsy Russell, Geoffrey Cambridge, and Bill Cosby in both the content of his humor and his style. Humor avoided the intricacies of actual black life, particularly lower-class life, and the actual language of most African American people. A period of time Pryor spent with black radicals in the late 1960s in Berkeley, California, dramatically changed Pryor as a comic. His material, despite its shock, drew in whites as well as African American audiences, producing some of the most popular shows and records of all time. As Watkins notes,

> Volatile, yet vulnerable, crass but sensitive, streetwise and cocky but somehow still diffident and anxious, Pryor emerged at the right time and brought with him the incredible array of dramatic and comic talent fully needed to introduce and popularize the unique, previously concealed or rejected part of African American humor that thrived in the lowest, most unassimilated portion of the black community. Pryor drew from current street humor and ordinary folkways and attitudes of the people he grew up with and later, met in urban nightclubs and bars. (Watkins 1994, pp. 550–551)

Pryor left a huge influence on comedians both African American and not. These certainly include Eddie Murphy, George Carlin, Robert Townsend, Keenan Ivory Wayans, John Belushi, Jamie Foxx, Whoopi Goldberg, Steve Martin, Chris Rock, and Robin Williams.

DEPRESSION AND MORE INTROSPECTIVE CHARACTERS

As examples of our subjects who were born poor and achieved fame, but whose personalities were quite different than those discussed above, we can discuss five other well-known figures: author and father of the "Naturalist" school Theodore Dreiser (1871–1945); birth control activist and social reformer Margaret Sanger (1879–1966); film star and icon Charlie Chaplin (1889–1977); author Richard Wright (1908–1960); and movie star and popular culture icon Marilyn Monroe (1926–1962).

Theodore Dreiser, like some of his famous literary characters, seemed haunted, as biographer Jerome Loving notes, by "the thought that he was sure to fail" (Loving 2005, p. 89). Dreiser was able to leave his home area for Chicago, where he gained valuable experience as a reporter there as well as in New York, St. Louis, and Pittsburgh. This provided him a great deal of his experience with urban life, which he used in his novels. But he himself was caught in the depression of 1893, and Dreiser feared ending up as "one of the flotsam and jetsam" (ibid., p. 51) he saw on the park benches rather than being a success. He in the late 1890s began his career-making book *Sister Carrie*, but after the good news of being offered a contract, Doubleday and Company attempted to renege on it, calling it "immoral" because of its treatment of sex (and also its failure to punish his characters that were wayward, as was expected at this time). Doubleday's decision to essentially not promote the book at all sent Dreiser into a "nervous breakdown," which some analysts believed combined with his grief over the death of his mother. Dreiser was diagnosed with neurasthenia and put on opiates. In the three years of his breakdown, he came close to suicide by drowning himself in New York (ibid., p. 171).

While Dreiser would later achieve success—by way of a British publisher's putting out *Sister Carrie* to acclaim—and writing other renowned books like *The Financier*, *The Titan*, and *An American Tragedy*—his biographers agree that his life was marked by depression or possibly bipolar disorder. Loving argues that his "bad disposition contributed to his unhappiness all his life. He seems to have been almost genetically contentious, a quality enhanced by his having grown up with so many siblings and having had to fend for himself at such an early age" (p. 275). But Loving also argues at other periods of his life his mania lowered his inhibitions, and released his libido, as his sex life never could be contained in his marriages but burst forth in many settings. Biographer Richard Lingeman accents his depression more than possible mania. Noting "his constant moves as a child ... instilled in him a deep anxiety," later in life "he was unable to leave a place or a person he was close to without a sickening sense of doom and disaster" (1986, p. 55). Lingeman calls him "skittish and high-strung, more prone to pendulum swings of moods" (p. 85). Despite his material success and fame as a writer (and later as a political activist) Dreiser "demonstrated a tendency to melancholia, often accompanied by bouts of insomnia" (ibid., p. 344); he had an "utter sense of loneliness" and "few realized how the man suffered over [his] life" (ibid., p. 309).

Just as artists like Pollock and Holiday could amazingly channel their demons into art and music, Dreiser was able to use writing to effect great changes. How necessary personal suffering is to such achievement is an open question. In at least some cases, like Dreiser's writings, there is so much of his own biography, fears, hopes, and failures in his work that it is hard to see his work without his pain.

Margaret Sanger, the famous birth control advocate, was born in 1879 in Corning, New York, as Margaret Higgins to a large Irish family. One of eleven children, she attributed her mother's early death to the large number of children she had. Her father, a stone mason, did not work much, in part because he was a radical who was avoided by religious townspeople. Sanger, as captured best by biographer Ellen Chesler, was a contradictory figure: "a bohemian who loved money and things material. A confirmed sexual materialist who remained an incurable romantic. An adoring mother who abandoned her children. A socialist who became a registered Republican ... she often surprises, and yet there is a poignant, painful pattern to her life" (Chesler 2007, p. 18).

On the one hand, few can question her bravery and leadership in creating the birth control movement out of the 1910s socialist movement. While she did not credit others who worked in the same vein (for example, Emma Goldman; see Chesler 2007, p. 87) undoubtedly she became the major force behind birth control at a time when sending birth control information through the mail or in person was illegal. She garnered enormous enemies in her early years, and eventually fled the country for Europe to avoid jail (although she was later sentenced to the workhouse for again giving out birth control information).

However, her personal life was often dark and tragic, and the trajectory of her career certainly troubles some of her supporters. Sanger caught tuberculosis from her mother in her teen years, and Chesler sees Sanger's "first breakdown" as establishing "a pattern of stress, overwork, and illness that would repeat itself throughout her life" (Chesler 2007, p. 47). In part because of her fear of transmitting the disease to her children, she "was strongly indifferent to the responsibilities of motherhood." When her daughter Margaret died of polio in 1915, she could not forgive herself, and as many as two years later she would break into tears on the street when she saw a mother and child (Topalian 1984, p. 62). Chesler adds that the child's death "left a long legacy of resentment and remorse in the Sanger family. [Margaret] never stopped mourning her or exorcised the guilt for having been absent during the final year of her life [and] she had recurrent sleeplessness" (Chesler 2007, pp. 133–134).

Sanger was a dynamic leader and "not easily scorned ... those who disagreed with her quickly discovered her explosive temper" (Chesler 2007, p. 16). On the one hand, she pulled the movement out of the left wing, which with the decline of the socialist movement after World War I was no doubt strategically necessary. Yet in seeking mainstream allies, Sanger never repudiated racist and eugenicist versions of birth control. While she did not necessarily share these views, her failure to denounce them has created much controversy about the history of the birth control movement. Moreover, as the years went on, Sanger became more paranoid and anti–Roman Catholic (Chesler 2007, p. 338). She took the Church's opposition more than a little personally, and her anger at Franklin Roosevelt's alliance with Catholic ethnics may have held birth control back from New Deal reforms.

Sanger was no doubt a great figure but one plagued by personal issues in her own and family life, and which also intruded at times into the broader birth control movement. As she aged her increasingly conservative politics along with her dependence on drugs and alcohol made her a distant figure to those who were born in the new reform movement and who had at best mixed feelings about her (Chesler 2007, p. 417).

As noted in Chapter 2, Charlie Chaplin grew up in the deep poverty of the English workhouse and orphanage. Despite his dramatic success—he was no doubt among the most recognizable men of his era and one of the richest—a strong depression lingered throughout his life. Writer

Somerset Maugham captured well how class background can deeply shape and limit a person. Chaplin included,

> At the back of all is a profound melancholy ... his humor is lined with sadness. He does not give you the impression of a happy man.... I have a notion that he suffers from a nostalgia of the slums. The celebrity he enjoys, his wealth, imprison him in a way of life in which he finds only constraint. I think he looks back to the freedom of his struggling youth, with its poverty and bitter privation, with a longing which knows it can never be satisfied. (Chaplin 1964, p. 266)

As Chaplin goes through his life in his autobiography (praised as accurate by other observers), he marks almost every stage in his life with comments about melancholy and loneliness. When as a child star he first started touring with Fred Karno's group, "I was alone in the back rooms, never meeting anyone until evening.... I began to grow melancholy" (p. 82). Remembering his first fancy meal, he stated, "I felt it incumbent to order an elaborate meal which I really did not want. The dinner was a solemn ordeal. I was uncertain which implement to eat with" (p. 105). When he arrived in Los Angeles, "suddenly I was seized by shyness ... for two days [after] I arrived outside the studio, but I had not the courage to go in" (p. 142). Recalling other rounds of melancholy and introspection, he talks of his loneliness as an embarrassment: "Loneliness is repellent ... one feels slightly ashamed of it ... however, my loneliness was frustrating because I had all the requisite means for making friends: I was young, rich and celebrated, yet I was wandering about New York alone and embarrassed" (p. 180).

Chaplin noted he was by nature shy and not easily intimate with people: Douglas Fairbanks seems one of the few people to become close with him. Chaplin, like someone who fears bad luck will overtake the good, seemed always skeptical of his popularity, and he turned out to be right. By the 1940s, personal scandals and the beginning of a campaign that attacked Chaplin's politics and loyalty to the United States eventually led him back to England: "It is a mistake to dally long in the public's adulation; like a soufflé, if left standing, it bogs down. So with this welcome of mine: it suddenly cooled off" (p. 349).

Because Chaplin was so sensitive and lonely, the attacks on him took a toll that might well have been more than on other public figures. His reactions to his blackballing in the United States were also of profound sorrow and loneliness.

Chaplin may or may not have been judged depressed or impaired by a contemporary psychiatrist, but his deep expression of a life of loneliness and depression does remind us that poverty and social class last a lifetime in their effects (as well as other residues of his childhood with problematic parents). Success is not a tonic for it, even when material success is combined with positive relationships such as his fourth and longest marriage to Oona O'Neil.

Like Charlie Chaplin, a combination of an extremely difficult childhood and an intellectual countenance made author Richard Wright an introspective and at times morose person. Even in his autobiographical novel *Black Boy*, he comments,

> [A] somberness of spirit that I was to never lose … settled over me during the slow years of my mother's unrelieved suffering.… [It makes] me stand apart and look upon excessive joy with suspicion, that was to make me self-conscious, that was to make me keep forever on the move. The spirit I had caught gave me insight into the sufferings of others … it made me want to drive coldly into the heart of every question and lay it open at the core of suffering … it directed my loyalties to the side of men in rebellion. I still had no friends, casual or intimate. In all my life … I had not had a single satisfying, sustained relationship with another human being and, not having had any, I did not miss it. I made no demands whatever upon others. (Wright 1989, pp. 100–101)

In part, Wright stood out by his refusal to stand on simple truths. When he came to Chicago from the South, he became active in the Communist Party, which in many ways helped educate him and provided him a great opportunity to write. But Wright never trusted the party and its intentions toward African Americans. Upon becoming a famous writer he quickly moved out of the party orbit and criticized it, but he refused to serve the West either, even finding World War II hypocritical. He found himself alone in a bipolar world. In the 1950s, Wright became interested in Africa and spent time in Kwane Nkrumah's Ghana, one of the first postcolonial states. But he had trouble fully embracing African nationalism as well, and ended up criticizing the new state's complete embrace of traditional ways. He even wondered if it needed some sort of dictatorship to bring its people into the modern world (Rowley 2001, pp. 417–435). Earlier he got in trouble with his criticism of Southern blacks, who he remarked often "lacked real kindness." He argued that he "was reacting to the legend that all Negroes are kind and love animals and children" (Levy 2008, p. 97).

Biographer Deborah Levy summarizes that Wright received very little encouragement from anyone and had to make his way on his own—others had factional and other alignments that prevented them from fully aiding him. She quotes Wright as saying, "I declare unabashedly that I like and even cherish the state of abandonment, of aloneness" (Levy 2008, p. 142).

While Chaplin and Wright, for example, can be said to be depressed, they clearly functioned adequately in the world to achieve their fame in film and books. Marilyn Monroe, as we saw in Chapter 2, had such a difficult childhood and was in such constant emotional pain that her depression and anxiety constantly interfered with her performances despite her great stardom.

In an autobiography not published until the 1970s, Monroe shared how deeply hurt she was from childhood. "I often felt lonely and wanted to die ... I never dreamed of anyone loving me as I saw other children loved," she remarked (Monroe with Hecht 2007, p. 13). Commenting on her adulthood she remarked, "This sad, bitter child who grew up too fast is hardly ever out of my heart" (ibid., p. 33). She told Ben Hecht, who helped with the autobiography, "Yes there was something special about me, and I knew what it was. I was the kind of girl they found dead in a hall bedroom with an empty bottle of sleeping pills in her hand" (ibid., p. 79).

Other biographers point out how Monroe could not adapt to the constant attention and pressure of a movie career as much as she felt she wanted it. On the one hand, as Donald Spoto points out, "so limitless was her need for the kind of approbation promised by celebrity, so bereft of the supports of normal life, and so primed was she for the acting profession, that she was willing to sacrifice almost anything for it" (Spoto 1995, p. 166). Yet "the paradox of her career, the professional means to raise her self-confidence had the opposite effect, she became even more self-conscious and unfree in acting and effected a kind of paralysis ... with each project she became more frightened, an anxiety-ridden performer" (ibid., p. 190). Monroe became incredibly anxious with each rehearsal or performance, relying more on drugs, but still being unable to learn her lines or appear at the studios anywhere near the correct time. Her own fears of failure led to the very anxiety that hurt: "She would break out in rashes, vomit, and revert to [her] childhood stutter" (Leaming 1998, p. 31). Leaming argues Monroe "experienced violent mood swings, veering between depression and intense bursts of energy ... she had bouts of sleeplessness" (p. 68).

To this day much controversy surrounds Monroe's death and many of the details of how her handlers, therapists, and others may have themselves been at fault in their taking advantage of Monroe. Still whether Monroe killed herself or would have done much better with a different set of companions, she remains one of the saddest people who went on to win fame, since the fame did not appear for the most part to bring her any joy.

COMPARING OUR SUBJECTS WITH ANOTHER SAMPLE

Both because our sample is small and because it is tempting to imagine that fame breeds difficulty and problems, it is of interest to compare our study briefly with another sample I drew from the American National Biography Online (ANB). This biographical database contains many thousands of Americans whose fame comes from a wide variety of sources. I randomly selected 100 names fitting two criteria: First, as with my study I wanted the sample to be somewhat modern, and hence included only those born after 1865 (the ANB includes only deceased people). Second, I wanted the sample to include middle- and upper-class individuals, which they primarily are, with a few working-class people. This gives us some idea of the nature of fame for other Americans.

Once having drawn the sample, I explored the biographies to review the individuals' histories particularly in terms of obvious pain and problems such as alcohol or other substance abuse, depression or psychiatric problems, and so on. While recognizing this review could hardly constitute the kind of analysis reading full biographies would, still the two- to three-page synopsis of subjects' lives in the ANB does provide us some degree of detail. Of the 100 people listed below (their fathers' occupations are listed beside them, followed by their own occupations) only fifteen or about one in seven were found to have a clear personal problem.

We note first that out of a randomly drawn group of 100, only fifteen individuals, a fairly small percentage, had serious personal problems (Agee, Alexander, Barrymore, Beers, Davis, Fitzgerald, Forrestal, Frost, Hayden, Leigh, Lewis, Lindsay, Lowell, Plath, and Sexton). This compares with a conservative count of 70 percent of our small sample (fourteen out of twenty), in which Sullivan and Dreiser would likely be counted as suffering psychiatric problems; London from drug, alcohol,

Table 3.1 Middle-Class Sample Drawn from American National Biography Online

Name	Dates	Parents	Occupation	Age at Death
1. Abernathy, Ralph	1926–1990	large farmers	civil rights leader	64
2. Acheson, Dean	1893–1971	father a minister	political figure	78
3. Addams, Charles	1912–1988	manager of a piano company	cartoonist	76
*4. Agee, James	1909–1955	father construction employee	writer [alcohol and drug use]	46
*5. Alexander, Grover	1887–1950	farmer	baseball player [alcohol]	67
6. Allen, Frederick Lewis	1890–1954	clergyman	historian	64
7. Alinsky, Saul	1909–1972	tailor	community organizer	63
8. Babbitt, Irving	1865–1933	physician/writer	critic	68
9. Baker, Home Run	1886–1963	butcher/farmer	baseball player	77
*10. Barrymore, Lionel	1878–1954	father actor	actor [had nervous problem for a while, later in life morphine addiction]	76
*11. Beers, Clifford	1876–1943	father a produce merchant	founder of the mental hygiene movement [mental health]	67
12. Belli, Melvin	1907–1996	banker/rancher	lawyer	89
13. Bellows, George	1882–1925	builder/contractor	painter	43
14. Bombeck, Erma	1927–1996	laborer	humorist	69
15. Bono, Sonny	1935–1998	truck driver/beautician	entertainer	63
16. Breckinridge, Sophonisba	1866–1948	lawyer and US congressman	social service reformer	82

Table 3.1 Middle-Class Sample Drawn from American National Biography Online (continued)

Name	Dates	Parents	Occupation	Age at Death
17. Brice, Fanny	1891–1951	bartender	comedian	60
18. Bunche, Ralph	1904–1971	barber	diplomat	67
19. Cage, John	1912–1992	inventor/reporter	musical composer	80
20. Caldwell, Erskine	1903–1987	minister/teacher	writer	84
21. Carmichael, Stokely	1941–1998	carpenter	civil rights leader	57
22. Carvel, Thomas	1906–1990	wine chemist	businessman	84
23. Celler, Emanuel	1888–1981	liquor and wine merchant	lawyer and politician	93
24. Chancellor, John	1927–1996	hoteliers	journalist	69
25. Chayefsky, Paddy	1923–1981	executive	writer	58
26. Cooke, Terence	1921–1983	chauffeur	archbishop	62
27. Croce, Jim	1943–1973	"middle class"	musician	30
28. Cousins, Norman	1915–1990	owner dry goods store	magazine publisher	75
29. De Mille, Cecil B.	1881–1959	playwright/minister	filmmaker	78
*30. Davis, Miles	1926–1991	dentist	musician [heroin addiction]	65
31. Dewey, Thomas	1902–1971	newspaper editor/politician	lawyer	69
32. Disney, Roy	1930–2009		businessman/entertainment	79
33. Drysdale, Don	1936–1993	repair supervisor	baseball player, management	57

Table 3.1 Middle-Class Sample Drawn from American National Biography Online (continued)

Name	Dates	Parents	Occupation	Age at Death
34. Earhart, Amelia	1897–1937	railroad clerk/lawyer	aviator	40
35. Eddy, Nelson	1901–1967	electrical engineer	radio/TV personality	66
36. Ellington, Duke	1899–1974	butler/waiter	musician	75
37. Fadiman, Clifton	1904–1999	pharmacist	entertainer	95
38. Fenwick, Millicent	1910–1992	financier	politician	82
*39. Fitzgerald, F. Scott	1896–1940	businessman	writer [alcohol, depression]	44
40. Fonda, Henry	1905–1982	printer	actor	73
*41. Forrestal, James	1892–1949	construction contractor	secretary of state [committed suicide]	57
*42. Frost, Robert	1874–1963	teacher/newspaper man	poet [some history of depression]	89
43. Gardner, Erle Stanley	1889–1970	civil engineer	lawyer and popular writer	81
44. Garson, Greer	1904–1996	clerk	actress	92
45. Getty, J. Paul	1892–1976	attorney/oil investor	businessman	84
46. Gould, Stephen Jay	1941–2002	court stenographer	academic	61
47. Gwynne, Frederick	1926–1993		actor	67
48. Hackett, Buddy	1924–2003	furniture upholsterer	entertainer	79
49. Hampton, Lionel	1908–2002	railroad worker	entertainer/musician	74
*50. Hayden, Sterling	1916–1986	newspaper salesman	actor [alcohol]	60

Table 3.1 Middle-Class Sample Drawn from American National Biography Online (continued)

Name	Dates	Parents	Occupation	Age at Death
51. Hoover, J. Edgar	1895–1972	printer	FBI head	77
52. Huston, John	1906–1987		actor, film director	81
53. Johnson, Howard	1896–1972	cigar wholesaler	businessman	76
54. Johnson, James Weldon	1871–1938	headwaiter	civil rights activist	67
55. Kaufman, Andy	1949–1984	jewelry business	comedian	35
56. Kaufman, George S.	1889–1961	small businessman	playwright	72
57. Kempton, Murray	1918–1997	stockbroker	journalist	79
58. Kubrick, Stanley	1928–1999	physician	entertainment/film	71
59. Kuhn, Bowie	1926–2007		fuel company executive lawyer and baseball commissioner	81
60. Landon, Michael	1936–1991	manager of movie theaters	actor	55
61. Ring Lardner	1885–1933	writer/journalist	writer	48
*62. Leigh, Vivien F.	1913–1967	father in brokerage firm	actress [psychiatric problems]	54
*63. Lewis, Sinclair	1885–1951	physician	writer [drinking]	66
*64. Lindsay, Vachel	1879–1931	physician	poet [near end of life had mental problems and committed suicide]	52
65. Lippmann, Walter	1889–1974		journalist	85
*66. Lowell, Robert	1917–1977	engineer	poet [bipolar]	60
67. Luce, Henry	1898–1967	missionary/educator	businessman	69

Table 3.1 Middle-Class Sample Drawn from American National Biography Online (continued)

Name	Dates	Parents	Occupation	Age at Death
68. Malamud, Bernard	1914–1986	grocer	writer	72
69. March, Fredric	1897–1975	manufacturer	actor	78
70. Meadows, Audrey	1922–1996	minister	actress	74
71. Mills, Wilbur	1909–1992	general store owner	politician	83
72. Mingus, Charles	1922–1979	postal worker	jazz musician	57
73. Moses, Robert	1888–1981	department store owner	politician	93
74. Mumford, Lewis	1895–1990	businessman	social historian	95
75. Nelson, Ozzie	1906–1975	banker	actor	69
76. Newman, Paul	1925–2008		actor	83
77. Niebuhr, Reinhold	1892–1971	clergyman	theologian	79
78. Norris, Frank	1870–1902	jewelry merchant	writer	32
79. O'Connor, Carroll	1924–2001	lawyer/businessman	actor	77
80. O'Connor, Sandra Day	1930–2009		supreme court justice	79
81. O'Neill, Thomas "Tip"	1912–1994	city official	politician	82
82. Ovington, Mary	1865–1951	china and glass importer	civil rights leader	86
83. Parks, Rosa	1913–2005	carpenter/stone mason	civil rights activist	92
84. Paul, Alice	1885–1977	banker/businessman	women's rights advocate	92
85. Perkins, Anthony	1932–1992	actor	actor	60

Table 3.1 Middle-Class Sample Drawn from American National Biography Online (continued)

Name	Dates	Parents	Occupation	Age at Death
*86. Plath, Sylvia	1932–1963	professor	writer [psychiatric problems]	31
87. Rand, Ayn	1905–1982	chemist	writer	77
88. Reiner, Fritz	1888–1963	textile merchant	conductor	75
89. Rockwell, Norman	1894–1978	manager textile firm	illustrator	82
90. Roper, Elmo	1900–1971	banker	pollster	71
91. Rogers, Fred	1928–2003	brick manufacturer	entertainment	75
92. Saltonstall, Leverett	1892–1979	attorney	politician	87
93. Sellers, Peter	1925–1980	pianist	actor	55
94. Serling, Rod	1924–1975	grocer/butcher	writer	51
*95. Sexton, Anne F.	1928–1974	woolen manufacturer	poet and playwright [suicide, psychiatric problems]	46
96. Shepard, Alan	1923–1998	army colonel	astronaut	75
97. Simmons, Jean	1929–2010		actress	81
98. Sinatra, Frank	1915–1998	firefighter	singer	83
99. Siskel, Gene	1946–1999	middle class	film critic	53
100. Smith, Roger	1925–2007		businessman	82

* Recorded as having personal problems.

and psychiatric problems; Jack Johnson at least from alcohol problems; Millay from psychiatric and substance use problems; Ruth also from alcohol problems; Saroyan from alcohol and gambling addictions; Pollock from alcoholism and psychiatric illness; Holiday from substance use and psychiatric illness; Malcolm X from drugs and other problems in adolescence; Monroe from drugs and psychiatric problems; McQueen from psychiatric and substance use; Cash from substance use; and Pryor from substance use and psychiatric problems.

One interesting finding is if the random 100 are broken down into their careers, we do find one broad field—art, writing, and acting—that has a far more substantial number of people with personal problems, bespeaking either that such fields attract people with emotional issues or that the process of art is such as to put people at risk for emotional problems.

One other interesting fact is that the high mortality rate in our own small sample is not seen in the random ANB one. A full half of our subjects died before the age of sixty: Marilyn Monroe and Malcolm X at thirty-six; John Garfield at thirty-nine; Jack London at forty; Billie Holiday and Jackson Pollock at forty-four; Steve McQueen at fifty; Babe Ruth and Richard Wright at fifty-two; and Edna St. Vincent Millay at fifty-eight. In the ANB sample of 100, a more modest twenty-one died before age sixty.

Table 3.2 Careers and Personal Problems among Randomly Selected ANB Sample

	Total	Number with Personal Problems
Politics or Office Holding	18	1
Minister	2	0
Artist/Writer/Actor	38	11
Sports	3	1
Comedian	2	0
Academic	4	0
Musician	9	1
Critics	3	0
Businessmen	9	0
Lawyer	1	0
Miscellany	11	1
Total in Sample	100	15

This comparison suggests that a broader study either of the famous per se (to which I have no knowledge of any references) or of a large sample of people from different social classes would need to be undertaken. Of course, the comparison supports my argument in Chapter 1 (and the bibliographic essay) that poorer people suffer more from the great variety of social problems such as substance use, mental illness, and earlier deaths.

Earlier in the chapter I had noted the high number of people in the small sample who had suffered from personality problems of various kinds. Although it is a question as to which figures might be diagnosed as being "psychiatric cases" it is not a question with any answer because social norms change over time and psychiatry and other labelers have as well, so there is not a conceivable answer to that question. Rather than use retrospective psychohistory, the chapter presented qualitative evidence that shows the vast majority of the group had suffered from high levels of personal pain and suffering throughout their lives.

CHAPTER 4

CLASS CONSCIOUSNESS

No person studied in this group lacked class consciousness. Whether it is as true today as in 1880 or 1940 or not, for these subjects growing up poor, each recognized and identified with their own social class, tended to prefer the company of people similar to them than those higher in class, and at least to a great degree much of their behavior represented their own particular backgrounds. The social environment of their times forced them to acknowledge their differences from others, and, as we shall see, for many their very success or fame was in conflict with their class background.

Having said this, not all subjects saw class consciousness in a political or Marxist way. Interestingly, the vast majority of our subjects did spend some years coming in contact with the political left. However, for a variety of complex reasons, actual involvement in the political left was more limited. One way to put it is almost all subjects confronted the dilemma of being anti-authoritarian and rebellious while not necessarily being class conscious in an organizational way. In my view, "class consciousness" does not mean an agreement with what some observers or others feel is in the "ultimate interest" of a class, nor does it mean (as we shall see) that poor people are likely to necessarily support middle-class and other nonpoor leaders (whether they are on the left or right or center).

Chapter 4

CLASS CONSCIOUSNESS AND POVERTY

There are, of course, many American scholars who throughout at least the twentieth century denied Americans had very much class consciousness, particularly compared with other societies (Sombart 1906; Perlman 1928; Hartz 1955; Lipset 1963; Hochshild 1981). Interestingly, survey research has found many Americans do strongly identify with such descriptors as "working class," according to at least one major study (Vanneman and Cannon 1987) as much as workers elsewhere (see also Jackman and Jackman 1983). *This is often obscured by the press and politicians' constant use of the term "middle class" to apply to all but the very rich and a few very poor.* For some Marxists, descriptors or perceptions are not sufficient because classes form historically and in action, and so surveys and other individually obtained measures of class do not prove much (Fantasia et al. 1991).

These arguments press me to make clear what I mean by "class consciousness." Part of the difficulty is that to both some conservative and Marxist critics, class consciousness carries a political weight based on Marx's notion of a class "in itself" becoming a "class for itself" in which structured action flows from consciousness. But it seems to me there is also a very important sociological concept being carried by the name "class consciousness," as follows:

1. The identification of a person, group, or family with a label and experience.
2. A feeling of solidarity with others who grew up with (or currently hold) the same position.
3. A tendency toward discomfort and sometimes hostility to interaction with people in very different classes from themselves.

It seems important that whether we need different names to separate this concept from class consciousness or whether we mean different degrees of class consciousness, we still need a term that speaks to the above experience.

In this study—and it is one of the few examining people born poor—the subjects greatly adhered to a class-conscious life even when their circumstances may have allowed them to escape to a more wealthy life *and hence higher class identification.* Perhaps this is most visibly true not just for those portrayed above, but for a few of the subjects who might be argued to have to some extent tried socially escaping more.

For example, biographer Ellen Chesler is critical of Margaret Sanger's upward movement in class, particularly seeking after 1919 a more powerful group of sponsors for the birth control movement. But she quickly notes that Sanger was unable to ever get comfortable with those who came from wealthier backgrounds, and often they did not feel comfortable with her (Chesler 2007, pp. 238–240). This suggests it is not a momentary conversion or mere wishing to be different that affects class consciousness, but something far deeper. Babe Ruth provides another example. In moving up in fame, and to some degree, wealth, Ruth was at one point put in contact with many wealthy people; however, his conduct was deemed too crude at these events, and as a result he seems to have quickly stopped attending these events (Creamer 1974, p. 186). Nor is it a matter of just taking enough charm classes, as Ruth's hostility to Yankee and baseball management never made him a "team player" despite the salary he earned.

Class consciousness is an important subject to study both for its own sake and for the light it shines on social class as a powerful social psychological influence over life. It has a very different influence than simple amounts of salary or wages or other superficial measures of class and status. I argue here for a broad influence of social class that seeps through one's entire life; and while it can change, such changes are not easy.

THE REBEL GIRL, MALCOLM, AND FANNIE LOU HAMER

For Elizabeth Gurley Flynn (1890–1964), who served as an organizer for the radical Wobblies (and later in her life was part of the leadership of the Communist Party), class consciousness and organization were always central to her life. A class-conscious radicalism different from the leadership of the mainstream civil rights movement also characterized Malcolm X (1924–1965) and Fannie Lou Hamer (1917–1977). In contrast, for those who were intellectuals—Anne Sullivan, Theodore Dreiser, Jack London, Edna St. Vincent Millay, and Richard Wright, for example—a tension was always present between left groups and their own individualism and personal freedom. We will also discuss those subjects who were not connected with any organizations but *still* expressed class consciousness, such as Johnny Cash, Charlie Chaplin, and Jackson Pollock.

Elizabeth Gurley Flynn, born in 1890 in Concord, New Hampshire, to a radical family, came to her nickname as the "Rebel Girl" quite naturally. Malcolm X (Little) also was born to activists, although Fannie Lou Hamer (1917–1977) did not come from an activist family and joined the civil rights movement only in middle age.

Flynn's parents, particularly her father, were quite radical. They associated with radical Irish nationalists, populists, and then socialists. Her father has a mixed reputation in the literature (quite similar to Margaret Sanger's father) in that he is said to have rarely worked, which may have helped keep the family poor (Baxandall 1987, p. 4). He had been a stone cutter in New England and was injured, and then trained as an engineer for a while until an illness in his family cut that short. Flynn's mother, an ardent feminist and Irish nationalist, seems to have held the family together. In the early 1900s the family moved to the Bronx, where they were active socialists. By age fifteen, Elizabeth Gurley was mounting the soapbox and rallying the crowds. She was arrested along with her father, but after the judge released her, she was suspended from school. A newspaper headlined her early on as "Mere Child Talks Bitterly of Life," and Theodore Dreiser called her the "East Side Joan of Arc" (Baxandall 1987, p. 2). Although the initial impulse came from her family, her school awards and tremendous praise as a speaker were tributes to her own abilities, and also to the lack of other well-known female activists in the movement, allowing her the special attention as the "Joan of Arc."

Unlike her parents, she gravitated to the Wobblies (the International Workers of the World, IWW), who were more anarchist, specifically syndicalist, than socialist. Interestingly, the Wobblies were the most working-class based organization in the US twentieth century (perhaps more so than the 1930s Communist Party) and attracted a number of our subjects, including Dreiser, London, Sullivan, and Millay. The IWW glorified direct class action, not politics or elections, and saw working-class power as coming through syndicates or large unions that would use tactics such as the general strike and sabotage to defeat capitalism. The Wobblies organized where the American Federation of Labor had failed to, including the well-known Lawrence (Massachusetts) textile strike, the Paterson (New Jersey) silk strike, and the Masabi range mine strike. Not only were the Wobblies repressed by police and troops, but they had (to put it mildly) an uneasy relationship with socialists and liberals and affluent supporters. Flynn, for example, like Anne Sullivan (and famous agitator Mother Jones), found the women's suffrage movement of the time to be bourgeois and did not believe women voting would change much of anything (Camp 1995, p. 13;

Wagner 2012a, pp. 123–124 on Sullivan). Flynn talked of the Socialist Party as "stodgy" as well.

The admiration of at least some of the poor for the IWW makes one wonder how a countervailing thrust of American radicalism existed separately from the groups usually listed as the primary left-wing groups. For example, the Socialist Party of the first two decades of the twentieth century, despite the great appeal (and relative success) of Eugene V. Debs, was not as based in the working class as the IWW. In a similar way, we will see that Malcolm X and Fannie Hamer's appeal was to different parts of the African American community than the mainstream civil rights movement. The examples raise questions about how traditional parties, whether of left or center or right, appeal to poor people, and whether the standard tactics of legislation, lobbying, and campaigning have as much appeal to them as they do to middle-class people (see Croteau 1995 for a good discussion of working-class politics versus middle-class politics even at a "radical" level).

Flynn in the 1910s became a "secular saint," a "mythic hero" who traveled the country to rouse the masses. She perfected a simple style of speech accessible to immigrant workers. Biographer Helen Camp discusses how the IWW constructed Flynn's gender role carefully so as to not antagonize its working-class supporters:

> IWW adored her, calling her Gurley or more mischievously "Girlie." They liked to boast that she was as safe with them "as if she was in God's pocket." They cultivated her reputation as a lady, she wore a full-length, red wool cape; this young, small, intense, Irish woman with the leather lungs also fascinated the press. (Camp 1995, pp. 17–18)

However, Flynn's activism did come at some personal cost: she had a brief marriage to a western miner, Jack Jones, and lost a baby prematurely. The love of her life was Carlos Tresca, the Italian Wobbly, who with his friends Joe Ettor and Arthur Giovannati, were also friends with Anne Sullivan and Helen Keller. Flynn and Tresca had an affair for a decade and a half. The two cut a dashing figure of radical anarchists in love. However, in the mid-1920s when Flynn had a nervous breakdown, one factor was the revelation that Flynn's sister Bina had had a long affair and a child with Tresca (Baxandall 1987, p. 30).

Flynn's ten-year collapse occurred when she lived with Dr. Marie Equi, an activist in Oregon who was a women's rights leader and lesbian. Most biographers see Flynn's collapse as having physical and mental aspects to it. She had developed an enlarged heart and a severe infection of the teeth. But also at this time was the collapse of her relationship with Tresca and the collapse by the mid-1920s of not only the IWW but much of the Left. Equi was ill herself, and a kind of symbiotic relationship developed between them in which Flynn felt that despite entreaties by her family, she could not leave Equi, and evidently Equi blocked access to others even by mail (Baxandall 1987, pp. 30–34).

After a ten-year hiatus surrounded by some mystery, Flynn returned to New York and joined the Communist Party, where by the early 1940s she was placed on the party national commission. Rosalind Baxandall describes many of her friends, particularly socialists, Bohemians, and feminists, as "dismayed and saddened" by her decision to join the Communist Party (p. 36). For Helen Camp, however, Flynn's decision made sense as the Communist Party was the major organ of the left-wing working class at the time:

> She had become an activist without a movement. Her deepest passion was to stand on a platform, surrounded by a sea of humanity straining forward to catch her words ... the class struggle was dear to her, ideology was only an afterthought and she had some stars there too; the second thing was that she had come from the working class ... and it was that identity, I think, that made her feel the Communists were the truest representatives. (Camp 1995, p. 120)

While Flynn was the subject of much notoriety in her remaining years—a major battle in the late 1930s and early 1940 to remove her from the American Civil Liberties Union because of her Communist Party membership; her jailing under the Smith Act in 1954; and her burial in the Kremlin along with Americans John Reed and William Haywood—for those who are critical of the party's many twists and turns, she did not publicly criticize them but stayed silent. While her writings reveal many criticisms in retrospect of the Communist Party in the 1940s and 1950s, Flynn, quite different than many other members of our sample, was not a critic or anti-authoritarian in the second part of her life (see Flynn 1955). For whatever reason of personality, she chose to remain a loyalist in the last nearly three decades of her life.

Both Fannie Lou Hamer and Malcolm X were more like the "Rebel Girl" of Flynn's youth throughout their lives in presenting a poorer persona to African American leadership, which was often explicitly critical of the mainstream civil rights leadership.

Malcolm and Fannie Lou were raised in poor households and their life experiences differed considerably from the black middle-class leaders of the civil rights movement. After a spell in foster homes and orphanages, the young Malcolm X moved to Boston, where he lived the hustling life of petty crime, zoot suits, and conk hair, and eventually wound up in prison. In his autobiography, Malcolm shares how his view was from the bottom of society:

> I believe that it would be almost impossible to find anywhere in America a black man who has lived further down in the mud of human society than I have; or a black man who has been any more ignorant than I have been; or a black man who has suffered more anguish during his life than I have. But it is only after the deepest darkness that the greatest joy can come; it is only after slavery and prison that the sweetest appreciation of freedom can come. (Malcolm X 1965, p. 379)

Recent literature agrees that Malcolm was shaped by his poverty and street life, in fact, far more than he perhaps was willing to admit at the time of his Muslim identity. Robin Kelley in an anthology on Malcolm X notes,

> It is my contention that his [Malcolm's] participation in the underground subculture of black working-class youth during the war was not a detour on the road to political consciousness but rather an essential element of his radicalization.... [This] unique subculture enabled him to negotiate an identity that resisted the hegemonic culture ... when [he] arrived in Boston he found he had little tolerance for class pretensions of his [more affluent] neighbors. (Wood 1992, pp. 157–159)

A collection by Michael Dyson (*Making Malcolm*) similarly argues that for the black masses, it was not necessarily Malcolm's Nation of Islam affiliation that was important, but that at a time when "so few resources [were] available to blacks before ... Malcolm's oversized and defiant rhetoric rallied black rage and anger to their defense," and it was Malcolm's whose "life was itself an accusation—a passage to the ninth circle of that black man's hell and back [was] the real meaning" (Dyson 1995, p. 47). Malcolm stood in opposition to Martin Luther King's understanding of America; he called for a rejection of America's public morality, not its usage to expand democratic rights (p. 46).

Whether embraced in such well-known slogans as "No Sellouts!," "By Any Means Necessary," or "The Ballot or the Bullet," what Malcolm communicated was a frustration with the slow and peaceful, often seen as collaborative leadership of the civil rights leadership. To take just two further examples, Malcolm did not hesitate to criticize the black leadership:

> Even so, my bitterness was less against the white press than it was against those Negro "leaders" who kept attacking us.... The press and others continued to criticize their work, but instead of abating, the black puppets continued ripping and tearing at Mr. Muhammad and the Nation of Islam—until it began to appear as though we were afraid to speak out against these "important" Negroes. That's when Mr. Muhammad's patience wore thin. And with his nod, I began returning their fire. (Malcolm X 1965, p. 243)

In another quote, Malcolm took on the white liberal, the cornerstone of the alliance for civil rights:

> The real criminal is the white man who poses as a liberal—the political hypocrite. And it is these legal crooks, posing as our friends, [who are] forcing us into a life of crime and then using us to spread the white man's evil vices among our own people. Our people are scientifically maneuvered by the white man into a life of poverty ... the only person who can organize the man in the street is the one who is unacceptable to the white community. (Dyson 1995, pp. 170, 175)

None of this is to argue that Malcolm's foreshortened life gave enunciation to a complete program for African American liberation, much less an alliance with other groups. His views were in the process of rapidly changing the year before he was assassinated, and they have been given many interpretations, in part because his views were so inchoate. His name remains a rallying point for militants of varying sorts who take his oppositional statements and gestures as symbolic points of reference.

Although she was less well known than Malcolm X, Fannie Lou Hamer (1917–1977) presents another example of how class split the modern civil rights movement. Hamer was born in Montgomery County, Mississippi, the twelfth child of sharecroppers. Raised in abject poverty, she suffered a forced hysterectomy at a local hospital (a fate many other African American women in the South also suffered). Hamer became active when the Student Non-Violent Coordinating Committee (SNCC) came to her rural part of Mississippi in 1962 to organize blacks to vote. Hamer, who had advanced to a timekeeper in the cotton fields, had considerable leadership potential, and as the activists were continually attacked violently, all her capabilities were soon tested.

Out of the two-year drive to integrate Mississippi voters came the Mississippi Freedom Party (MFP), which at the 1964 Democratic Convention led by Hamer challenged the official all-white delegation to the convention. Despite tremendous public sympathy and media publicity, Lyndon Johnson did not want to risk the Southern vote by pursuing anything but a token settlement of the dispute. Hamer and others rejected the efforts of the dominant civil rights leaders to persuade them to accept two seats instead of blocking the entire segregationist delegation. According to a biography of Hamer, Roy Wilkins of the National Association for the Advancement of Colored People (NAACP) told her, "You are all ignorant. You made your point. You should just pack your bags and go home" (Lee 1999, p. 100). Hamer immediately stopped paying her dues to the NAACP, which she would later refer to as "the National Association for the Advancement of Certain People." In contrast, Bob Moses of the SNCC recognized that Hamer's popularity in Mississippi's rural areas was directly related to her "ideological and organizational distance from the middle-class established leaders and politicians" (Lee 1999, p. 72).

From 1965 until the mid-1970s, Hamer was a grassroots activist who ran for office several times in Mississippi, helped organize migrant and farm workers, and developed a large Freedom Farm Cooperative. She was also one of the few African Americans active in the early women's movement.

Throughout those years, Hamer, unlike others, was perfectly willing to criticize the leadership of the African American movement, as apparently they criticized her as well. Coretta Scott King at least on one occasion would not share a platform with her (Mills 2007, p. 248), and leaders of the Southern Christian Leadership Conference (SCLC) reputedly said, "local people in Mississippi need someone to think for them" (Lee 1999, p. 116). In turn, Hamer did not attend Martin Luther King's funeral because she "couldn't remorse around the hypocrites who were there" (ibid., p. 100). Hamer criticized "the preachers and teachers [who] look down on the little people, but now these little people are speaking up" (ibid., 116), and at another time said, "these bourgeoisie Negroes aren't helping. It's the ghetto Negroes who are leading the way" (Mills

2007, p. 157). The media in turn criticized her as "unwise, impatient and irreverent," with *Newsweek* magazine saying she had "disturbingly demagogic tendencies, attacking middle-class Negroes and whites, American policy in Vietnam, and Martin Luther King" (Lee 1999, p. 118).

Of course, it is important to remember the context of the 1960s and 1970s, which lately have been reduced to simple recitation of Martin Luther King Day speeches. As important as the role of King and his SCLC and NAACP and other allies were, the civil rights period was marked by radical SNCC activists who led the Southern sit-downs, by ghetto riots that occurred nearly every summer during the 1960s, and by the emergence of African American radicalism such as the Black Panther Party and the Black Muslims. There is, of course, not a parallel in each case between class and politics. However, as a generalization, particularly as the years went on, many poor and working-class African Americans were more skeptical of nonviolence, of church leadership, of conventional politics, and of rights rhetoric divorced from economic and social change. It is important to also keep in mind that those who raised their voices in dissent paid a penalty. For example, Chana Lee notes that the more respectable leaders regarded Hamer "as abrasive" and "an embarrassment," and this in turn "left her angry, unfulfilled, wanting and confused" (Lee 1999, p. xi). Hamer and others were also sensitive people, and particularly among those who came from backgrounds without validation for speaking and leading, rejection did enact a painful price, even though militants may intellectually have expected it.

CLASS-CONSCIOUS INTELLECTUALS: SULLIVAN, DREISER, LONDON, MILLAY, AND WRIGHT

One group that was present in the late nineteenth and early twentieth centuries, but seems to have declined later on in American history, were class-conscious intellectuals who came from poor backgrounds. As I have noted, given the amount of economic resources required for higher education and human capital necessary for success in many fields, it is not surprising that few poor people make it to the level of being considered "intellectuals." Clearly, people like Anne Sullivan, Theodore Dreiser, Jack London, Edna St. Vincent Millay, and Richard Wright were quite unusual for their times. As far as I can tell, people like them have become even less common in days since (at least judging by databases on births since 1940 and the number of famous people from poor backgrounds, which include primarily entertainers and sports figures; see Chapter 7).

Their presence represents, on the one hand, the wider acceptance of socialist and other radical ideas in the late nineteenth century and early twentieth century than in many ways they would be afterward (the 1960s–1970s period was quite the reverse, at least among whites, with leaders of social movements being greatly from middle-class sectors of society), and, on the other hand, the ability of a small number of the poor to access books and even some college at the time.

Edna St. Vincent Millay represents the most dramatic educational achievement in that an award-winning poem she wrote in high school led her to be noticed by philanthropists and financed through Vassar College in the 1910s. Theodore Dreiser was helped by a teacher to attend a year of Indiana University at Bloomington, and Jack London took some classes at the University of California–Berkeley and passed the admission tests (though he did not continue his education). Anne Sullivan attended Radcliffe with her mentee Helen Keller, and interpreted nearly every word she read or that was spoken to her, though she did not formally receive a degree until 1932, when Temple University awarded her an honorary degree. But London, Sullivan, Dreiser, Wright, and Chaplin managed to read a huge amount of material and become familiar with major literary, philosophical, and political debates. Except for Millay, the figures became bona fide intellectuals without the benefit of graduating college.

Anne Sullivan was a reluctant public figure who, after becoming famous for teaching Helen Keller, often tried to avoid the limelight. Sullivan was placed in a no-win situation because so many people refused to believe Keller and Sullivan could have separate ideas and opinions. When Keller took controversial stances (such as becoming an open socialist in 1911), much of the public blamed Sullivan (and her husband at the time, John Macy). Interestingly some biographers have gone to the opposite extreme and presented Sullivan as a kind of empty vessel in order to somehow emphasize Keller as the more prominent figure. But based on historical evidence, Sullivan was perhaps more intellectual than Keller and was dramatically more well read and versed in education, literature, politics, and philosophy. Much of her impact comes now to us secondhand through her own writings, and through some of her letters to Keller. Major figures in American history from Alexander Graham Bell to Mark Twain to Charlie Chaplin (who met her and became quick friends in 1919) saw Sullivan as a great intellectual figure that had considerable radical ideas on education and in other areas. Many urged her to open a school or teach other children.

As was noted in Chapter 2, Sullivan grew up in a poorhouse and was acutely conscious of both her class and her Irish ethnicity from her experience there, and the contrast that the more affluent Perkins School for the Blind provided her. How brilliant a young person Sullivan must have been is illustrated by how she entered Perkins as a poorhouse inmate who had no toothbrush and did not know her birthday and left as valedictorian of her class only a few years later. After her famous teaching of Keller, the two became involved in Massachusetts politics in the 1900s, favoring a more self-help and disability rights approach to the blind than did the philanthropic elite of Boston (see Wagner 2012a, chapter 5). In the 1910s, Sullivan and Keller, both of whom had leaned to the left, gradually came to champion socialism and syndicalism. After publicly supporting the 1912 Lawrence textile strike, they became friendly with Wobblies such as Carlos Tresca, Joe Ettor, and Arthur Giovannati, who became frequent houseguests at their Wrentham, Massachusetts, home. Although Sullivan and Keller were strong supporters of Eugene V. Debs, Sullivan in a series of letters to Keller in 1917 from Puerto Rico denounced the "parlor socialists" who had supported Woodrow Wilson and World War I:

> I am not influenced in the least by Upton Sinclair's faith in President Wilson. Sinclair is one of those parlour socialists that Joe Ettor despises. He would be just the one to be caught by Wilson's verbiage. No, no! Wilson is a not a great humanist. All his words and acts are controlled by a fixed idea.... One thing is certain, everything he does will be for the world's supreme good. Exploitation is always benevolent—it is the Christian pose. I am afraid nothing short of a revelation from above could open my mind and heart to see anything approaching altruism in President Wilson's deeds and many words. I guess I'm one of those people who can't expand. (American Foundation of the Blind, Letters between Helen Keller and Anne Sullivan Macy)

Sullivan would question how "civilized" the West really was, and favorably quoted the Wobblies' "Big Bill" Hayward:

> Yet it is unthinkable that anything so infamous (the war) should happen in the age we have been living in and called enlightened and civilized. You can understand now why Bill Haywood derided the idea that any

country is civilized. I remember his saying that our high refinement was a thin veneer concealing liars, swindlers, and murderers. I thought at the time he was talking rather wildly, but now the abominations of this war make his statements appear mild. How easily European nations have chucked their Christianity, their international friendships, their philosophy and humanity, and assumed the spiritual garb of savages! Truly, "where are the great ones of the earth?" It seems to me, they are all active for evil. (American Foundation for the Blind, Letters between Helen Keller and Anne Sullivan Macy)

Sullivan acted as a "beyond the scene" analyst for the more openly political Keller, who was from the middle class and often more sympathetic to reformers than Sullivan was. What separated them was a style of a middle-class "claimsmaker" that Keller adopted, sharing with the media and public her many thoughts. Sullivan, who had been burned by an encounter with the press and felt more vulnerable, was just as happy to write her thoughts and communicate to Keller. Both Sullivan and Keller were crushed when many socialists across the world supported the war, and they soured on organized politics at least for a while. But Sullivan's writings show a continued loyalty to Debs's socialism and an interest in the Russian experiment.

Theodore Dreiser came to his class consciousness through his own experience. Biographer Jerome Loving talks of how Dreiser's first job at a wholesale hardware concern put him in contact with industrial spies and "the sissy" rich boys that his brother Rome had warned him of. When Dreiser became a reporter, he found himself sympathizing with the strikers he covered for the newspapers rather than being neutral (Loving 2005, p. 74). But as biographer Richard Lingeman notes, it was his own fears that propelled his sympathies: "He was haunted by the fear of slipping off an economic treadmill" (Lingeman 1986, p. 126) and in his own fears of falling helped create the famous character of Hurstwood in *Sister Carrie*, of someone who falls all the way down. Loving summarizes, quoting novelist Robert Penn Warren, that what shocked people about *Sister Carrie* "was not so much the things he presented as the fact that he himself was not shocked by them." Rather, says Loving, Dreiser "was the first great American novelist from the wrong side of town" (Loving 2005, p. 92).

Dreiser's constant battles with the censors on most of his books put him quickly in a political alliance with other authors and intellectuals who leaned left. His move to Greenwich Village in the 1910s also put him in contact with radicals like Floyd Dell, Sanger, Max Eastman, and John Reed. He supported the birth control movement, wrote an antireligious play, and began to fight the United States' entrance into the world war. Dreiser began denouncing America as a culture from its destruction of the Native Americans to its "commercial oligarchy" to the fact that unlike Europe, America had "produced no philosophical or literary greats," mostly because of its censorship (Loving 2005, p. 271).

Dreiser did not necessarily have a total sense of ideological coherence. In 1927 he accepted an invitation to visit Russia on a delegation with a clear statement that he was an individualist at heart (ANB, p. 5). By the early 1930s when the Great Depression hit, he more and more supported Marxist ideas. He became active in the League of American Writers and the National Committee for the Defense of Political Prisoners. He was indicted for criminal syndicalism when he organized a committee to investigate the conditions of the striking miners in Harlan, West Virginia. Later he wrote the book *Tragic America*, which put together a massive amount of data about corporations and American power elites generally. By the late 1930s he had clearly moved closer to the Communist Party of the USA, although he did not officially join the party until July 1945, only five months before his death.

Regardless of his exact ideology in any given year, Dreiser had spent most of his life as a class-conscious ally of the downtrodden who, despite his own success (which did not come easily), identified with his own origins and the millions of people who had similar origins to him.

Like Dreiser, Jack London (1876–1916) sought to be an intellectual of the working class. Biographer Alex Kershaw remarks that London "did more to increase class consciousness than any other writer of his time" and that "he had become the first working-class writer in America whose books were read by his own class" (Kershaw 1997, pp. xiv, 282). Perhaps London's most important experience was his joining, at age eighteen, a local wing of "Coxey's Army," a group of tramps then marching in protest to the nation's capital. He was impressed with the intelligence of his fellow marchers and became a convert not only to this cause, but to the socialist and syndicalist movements. He began going to the "speaker's corner" in Oakland and speaking for socialism. He became known as the "boy socialist" and was arrested to protest the lack of free speech. He was arrested for vagrancy and beaten on the head with a night stick when he was tramping in Niagara Falls, New York, and this too was an experience he frequently cited as helping him understand the daily experience of the working class.

Of course, much of Jack London's writings were fiction aimed at adventure, though several works he wrote were more political. He spent time with the poorest of the poor in London's East End and wrote *The People of the Abyss* as a tribute to those who could survive capitalism's worst onslaughts. He wrote about his own experience with child labor, recounting his work as a youth in a jute mill in "The Apostate" for the *Women's Home Companion* in 1906, which wielded much influence in the debate over child labor.

London was always subject to some idiosyncrasies, however. He seemed to invest class and socialist ideas with a kind of hyper-masculinized idea of racial superiority and also support for war. His interest in Nietzsche and Spencer seemed to combine with his interests in socialist and syndicalist ideas. More and more toward the end of his short life, he distanced himself from the movement, resigning from the Socialist Party, which he found had lost "its fire and fight." As Kershaw notes, "He began to rant about his current pet peeve: East Coast socialists, the bleeding-heart liberals wearing their social conscience on their starched sleeves, whose beliefs now taste like ashes in his mouth" (Kershaw 1997, p. 8). London, like Sullivan and Keller, was in part reacting to the takeover of most of the socialist parties of the world by safe parliamentarians who eschewed more radical goals and struggles, but it is also possible that London's own odd amalgam of ideas might have led him away had he lived longer.

Both Edna St. Vincent Millay (1892–1950) and Richard Wright (1908–1960) had complex roles as intellectuals since they also were taken very much as representing women (for Millay the "new woman" of the 1920s) and African Americans (for Wright) as well as their class background. Yet both were highly class conscious and oriented toward the left wing in general. With her poor background, Millay clearly felt like a "stranger in paradise" when she arrived at Vassar College. Biographer Nancy Milford talks about her "as being in disguise" (Milford 2001, p. 109). She disobeyed every rule she could at Vassar, from smoking on campus to leaving campus without permission. Faculty found her "saucy" and "marked by cheek and ignorance." She was nearly expelled, narrowly avoiding it by a petition signed by students and some faculty. A great deal of her discomfort was no doubt due to class. She describes a luncheon at Barnard College that gives some sense of her awkwardness:

[I was] let in by a butler and ushered and announced [and] I could barely touch my food, I was so nervous that I couldn't hold anything in my fork, but I could manage a knife so I buttered my muffin and ate that ... and so help me that's all I could get, but I strategized and toyed with my food and anyway it's classy not to eat any-thing. (Milford 2001, p. 110)

Millay after college found the radicals of Greenwich Village and began hanging out with the Provincetown Players and the editors of the socialist newspaper *The Masses*. She in fact had an affair with and lived together with Floyd Dell. Here too she knew Max Eastman, John Reed, Edmund Wilson, and the other radicals. Late in the war years she attended the sedition trial of *The Masses* and later wrote an anti-war play, *Aria da Capo*.

As a poet who smoked when women did not, and with poetry and a lifestyle that seemed to promote bohemianism and free love, Millay became wildly popular in the 1920s. J. Gould notes that "she was known as the poet laureate of the 1920s, the spokesman for the new woman, [with a] flippant attitude toward life and love" (Gould 1969, p. 123). Cleverly, Millay did not take time to dispel any rumors or readings of her poems that attributed unconventionality to her; she accepted any interpretation of them.

Politically, in 1927 she took an active role in the Sacco and Vanzetti defense and was arrested at the "death watch" for them. She wrote a well-known poem, "Justice Is Dead in Massachusetts," about the trial. In the article "Fear" she condemned Americans' "indifference toward injustice" and called the real criminals "greed and blind prejudice" (Gould 1969, p. 187). Asked if she supported the profit system, she replied she did not but supported a world in which all were guaranteed jobs and leisure and other necessities of life. Milford notes the FBI "became more alert" to Millay after this interview.

Millay continued to write against war in the 1930s, although eventually she supported World War II and wrote the famous "Lidice" poem about the village in Czechoslovakia destroyed by the Nazis, which was read to a wide audience on the radio. Mostly, though, Millay's poetry was about love, freedom, happiness, and unhappiness, and it included frequent references to her poor family.

As one of the best known poets and women of the twentieth century, Millay was greatly torn about fame and wealth. She married a rich businessman, Eugene Boissvain, who was a feminist and agreeable to an open marriage. He was also willing to devote himself to home and details that Edna was not. She remained uncomfortable with money, and they eventually lost the money they had, leaving her fairly poor at the end of her life. She complained about "prostituting" herself by selling her poems and charging for readings. Being famous and wealthy was psychologically a problem to her as well as a benefit, and the difficult time she had in her adult life with depression and substance use is no doubt a part of that.

Not surprisingly, Richard Wright expressed a similar ambivalence about fame. After the publication of his book *Native Son*, Wright for a while became the most acclaimed African American writer in the United States. He was asked to join many boards (joining Dreiser, for example, on the *New Masses'* editorial board), he became the first black writer to be chosen for the Book-of-the-Month club's selection, and Orson Welles wanted to do a play of his book. However, as biographer John Williams described,

> The fame made Wright somewhat uncomfortable; it seemed to him to be so exaggerated as to cheapen the book. His concern for the ghetto dweller was real; his condemnation of the system capable of producing Bigger Thomases [the lead character in *Native Son*] did not warrant all the money, all the acclaim. (Williams 1970, p. 73)

This quote aptly sums up the mixed feelings of many of our sample toward fame: fame as a commodity accrues to an individual—it escapes the issues or concerns that books or plays or poems or even comedy acts are about. In particular for a political and class-conscious actor, the broader mass is lost to fame, and the author is stripped from his context that he or she wrote about and tried to get across to the public.

Moreover, for some people—Wright and Anne Sullivan would be good examples—loyalty to principles does not necessarily win popularity contests in an often polarized world. As we saw, Wright joined the Communist Party as a young man and was afforded considerable opportunity in it for his advancement. But he was unable to stay in the party with his doubts about its sincerity as well as his preference for writing over organizing. When Wright came in contact with the more middle-class African Americans of the Harlem Renaissance, he had the opposite problem. Williams quotes an account of a party Wright attended in which W. E. B. Du Bois reigned in a place of honor "surrounded by admirers" while Wright felt "practically ignored by the gathering of intellectuals and middle class matrons, and he was antagonistic and resentful" (Williams 1970, p. 81). The sense of not "fitting in" may well be an occupational hazard for these poor people who moved up some in the world but throughout their lives did not feel at all comfortable in middle-class environments. The poor turned more middle class or fit nowhere.

These encounters are not at all limited to political environments. Williams argues that when Wright traveled to Mexico for the first time, he was uncomfortable with the luxury he was exposed to in Cuernavaca, and "empathized with the servants." He quickly became distant from his new wife (his marriage did not last long), whom he regarded as too "bourgeois" for her love of parties and having servants waiting on her. Accounts of Sullivan's life similarly talk of parties of the higher classes of Boston that she skipped or left early, and a lifelong discomfort with contact with the philanthropic elite who for a time financially supported her and Keller. Charlie Chaplin, too, expressed his views that inside he felt like the tramp character, not the more affluent person he became.

CHARLIE CHAPLIN, JACKSON POLLOCK, AND JOHNNY CASH

One need not be a political leader or a traditional intellectual to show class consciousness. The range of years between Chaplin's life (born 1889) and Cash's (1932–2003) shows how class consciousness may have changed some in historical context.

Charlie Chaplin by his own description never joined an organization, and at one point he affirmed he had not voted either, but his autobiography, as well as other accounts, is full of working-class/poor-class consciousness. Not surprisingly for someone who grew up in a workhouse and a related orphanage for the poor, he always felt himself on the defensive. He gives an example early on in his autobiography, when he discusses his passion for self-education. Rather than cite noble reasons or even upward mobility, Chaplin states, "I wanted to know, not for the love of knowledge, but as a defense against the world's contempt for the ignorant" (Chaplin 1964, p. 5). He recalled his first venture into a restaurant on an early date in his late teens: "As we were occupying a whole table in a very posh restaurant, I felt it incumbent to order an elaborate meal which I really did not want. The dinner was a solemn ordeal: I was uncertain which implement to eat with!" (p. 105).

His likes and dislikes even as an older adult were intertwined still with class. When discussing sets and theater, Chaplin revealed his bias against Shakespeare:

> Moreover I dislike Shakespearean themes, including kings, queens, august people and their honour. Perhaps it is something psychological within me, possibly my peculiar solipsism. In my pursuit of bread and cheese, honour was seldom trafficked in. I cannot identify myself with a prince's problems. (Chaplin 1964, p. 253)

To take still another example, Chaplin was reportedly angered at an American actor who was "slumming" near his old London neighborhood:

> I told him that it was very fine for well-fed, overpaid actors flaunting toughness at these deprived people, who are gentle and nice and if ever tough, only because of environment. I asked him just how tough he would be if he were living the life that some of these unfortunate families must live. (Chaplin quoted in Robinson 1994, p. 284)

Chaplin's very creation of his alter ego, the tramp, was a tremendously creative way to introduce a class icon who could also be identified with the vast majority of people at the time. Chaplin discusses how the pursuit of the tramp by higher class figures whom he interferes with is part of the joy of his films:

> The delight that the average person takes in seeing wealth and luxury in trouble ... people get a satisfaction from seeing the rich get the worst of things. The reason, of course, lies in the fact that nine-tenths of the people in the world are poor, and secretly resent the wealth of the other tenth. (Chaplin quoted in Robinson 1994, p. 203)

The class-based humor of the films did not escape everyone's attention, and just as there was opposition in many quarters to the rise of film as a medium generally in the first decades of the twentieth century, some protested Chaplin's films in specific. A speaker at the Women's Alliance at a Unitarian Church in Brooklyn called him "a moral menace. His is a low type of humor that appeals only to the lowest type of intellect. I cannot understand how any resident of Flatbush can go see [the films]" (Robinson 1994, p. 213).

This does not by any means presume that the tramp was *only* a lower-class street figure. The empathy people felt for him came greatly from his malleability. As Chaplin describes the early invention of the tramp in his career, he notes, "You know this fellow is many-sided, a tramp, a gentleman, a poet, a dreamer, a lonely fellow, always hopeful of romance and adventure. He would have you believe he is a scientist, a musician, a duke, a polo-player." Yet he adds quickly in his autobiography, "However, he is not above picking up cigarette-butts or robbing a baby of its candy. And of course, if the occasion warrants, he will kick a lady in the rear—but only in extreme anger." It seems as if primarily his heart was most in the tramp as a loveable everyman who was out of place in society: as his first demonstration of the tramp, he "found [himself] in the hotel lobby [and] I felt I was an imposter posing as one of the guests, but in reality I was a tramp just wanting a little shelter. I entered and stumbled over the foot of a lady. I turned and raised my hat apologetically, then turned and stumbled over a cuspidor" (Chaplin 1964, p. 146). The funny, stumbling figure, taken along with most of Chaplin's autobiography, shows how the tramp mirrored Chaplin's discomfort with all forms of higher society.

Interestingly, while Chaplin's biographers are comfortable describing Chaplin as a "red" or anarchist at heart despite his lack of organizational contacts, Jackson Pollock's biographers are somewhat at pain to describe Pollock as nonpolitical despite a much more extensive contact with the Left. Again, some of this represents a confusion between class consciousness itself as a poor person or worker, which all our subjects had, and a sympathy with the ideas of the Left, which most of our subjects who lived through the 1930s also had. It is not to indicate except in the cases noted—Flynn, Wright, and (briefly) Dreiser—that the individuals were members of a left-wing party.

Pollock from his youth had a strong class consciousness, and at least on-and-off (if not more) contact with the Left. One story told about his father, Leroy, was of his anger when a neighbor or acquaintance "denigrated [the] IWW." Leroy was not a political activist, but he identified with labor's struggles and was acutely sensitive to any form of injustice (Solomon 2001, pp. 23–24). This recollection may apply to Pollock as well. Early in his life, while still a high school student, Pollock played the school subversive. He grew his hair long and renamed himself "Hugo" after Victor Hugo, and he and two other students in art class published a newsletter called the *Journal of Liberty*. It was "flagrantly subversive, extorting the student body to 'awake and use your strength.'" He was discovered trespassing after school putting papers under doors and was suspended from school for the remainder of the year (Solomon 2001, p. 42). While still a youth, he was introduced to the radical Mexican muralists led by Diego Rivera, and while biographers emphasize the artistic influence again more than the political, Pollock was clearly getting familiar with radical politics.

Pollock spent part of the 1930s hoboing and tramping, hopping trains. Biographer B. H. Friedman talks about how influenced Pollock was by the bums he met, and by being thrown in jail for hopping trains. He also notes how "the grinding poverty" he saw in his trips across the country influenced him and pushed him toward the Left (Friedman 1995, p. 29). Biographer Deborah Solomon notes that the first painting of Pollock ever displayed was at the John Reed Club, a center for radical art and politics (Solomon 2001, p. 73). While working in New York City in the Works Progress Administration (WPA), he got to know and paint with another radical Mexican muralist named David Siquerios, and later got in trouble (along with his new girlfriend and future wife Lee Krasner) for signing Communist Party–backed petitions. No painting, says Deborah Solomon, was more pivotal in Pollock's development than Pablo Picasso's *Guernica*, recounting the bloody fascist attack on Republican Spain, which was shown in New York City in 1939–1940. Still another unremarked aspect of Pollock's travels with the Left was the influence of Clement Greenberg, the critic who helped "make" Pollock, who was a self-described Marxist. Though the subject of art appreciation and politics is a complex one, and one in which other radicals and Marxists would not necessarily agree to salute Pollock's work, it is still interesting that Greenberg saw Pollock's work as a key paradigm shift in art, and the breaking into a truly "American" style of art, a mark of dialectical progress.

Beyond Pollock's peripheral association with the Left, though, Pollock was also a distinctly class-conscious man. Some of his actions cause some head scratching, such as his yelling at a wealthy-looking man with a dog and getting down on all fours and barking, saying "you feed that dog while I am starving" (Solomon 2001, p. 67). But other actions were similar to those of our other subjects. Friedman describes Pollock "as uncomfortable with cultivated people," which became even worse when he became famous (Friedman 1995, p. 137). The world of critics, dealers, collectors, and lawyers was a "world in which Pollock felt inadequate, as expressed sometimes in his regrets at not having gone to college" (ibid., p. 103). Pollock also, like many of our subjects, felt uncomfortable with fame. When *Life* magazine profiled him in the late 1940s and early 1950s, Pollock felt uneasy. He had always prided himself on his independence, and why was he not appealing to middle-class America? (Solomon 2001, p. 195). Pollock's ambivalence about success may well have caused him either to slow down his painting or to change his painting to not suit the market (both of which happened in his later years).

Johnny Cash was born to sharecroppers in rural Arkansas in 1932 and certainly seems to have spent most of his life as a class-conscious person despite his fame as a world-renowned singer. The first song he remembered hearing on the radio was Jimmie Rodgers's "Hobo Bill's Last Ride." He recalls in his autobiography how "the image of a man dying alone in a freezing boxcar felt so real, so close to home" (Cash 2003, p. 50). Throughout his autobiography, he often assesses people and groups based on how they measured up to his background. One example is the country music world, with which he was on bad terms most of his life and which rejected him from affiliation early on his career:

> The "country" music establishment including "country" radio and the "Country" Music Association, does after all seem to have decided whatever "country" is, some of us aren't. I wonder how many of those people ever filled a cotton sack. I grew up in a bare-bones kind of place, three rooms in a row, the classic shotgun shack. It shook like the dickens every time a train went by … it wasn't the worst, my grandfather's house had no windows, in winter my mother hung blankets of whatever she could find. (Cash 2003, pp. 13–14)

When he speaks favorably about people such as John Rollins, he comments that "they took to each other in the first meeting. Being of … similar roots. He too came from the cotton fields" (p. 32).

Late in his life he and his famous wife, June Carter, had a home on the island of Jamaica. He suffered a major robbery of the house, yet in his autobiography he refused to blame those found guilty: "My only certainties are that I grieve for desperate young men and the societies that produce them and suffer so many of them, and I felt that I knew these boys. We had a kinship, they and I" (Cash 2003, p. 41).

Cash not only had his outsider status as the "man in black" that caused his identification with his perpetrators, but according to biographer Michael Streissguth he had a "robin hood" enterprise going on in Jamaica: "He'd swipe golf balls from the rich golfers at that country club and give buckets of them to the Jamaican kids, so they could sell them back to the golfers."

Another area that biographers and Cash's autobiography agree on was his willingness to help unconditionally anyone who was in need. Streissguth notes that despite Cash's problems with the "Old Opry

House" he "spared quite a few who died penniless the indignity of a pauper's grave. In life, I am told, he paid or helped pay for burials and markers all around Nashville.... The cemetery appeared to hold its own biography of Johnny Cash."

Other incidents Streissguth mentions are Cash's willingness

> to harbor [country singer] Patsy Cline in his home when the country star arrived beaten and bruised from a skirmish with a partner. He coughed up 5K in 1965 for Jimmy Rodgers ... [further] he always did this stuff on streets like he handed a guy hitchhiking a thousand dollars to get home and get presents near Christmas time.

What, of course, is somewhat different with Cash—and many others of his time and after, as opposed to, say, Chaplin and Pollock—is the mix of symbols that the class-conscious Cash appeals to and the much more complex influences on Americans of the latter twentieth century. Whereas Chaplin, Wright, Pollock, and Garfield were exposed to the culture of the Left, and most black activists like Malcolm or Hamer were exposed to oppositional movements of civil rights, Cash, born as a white southerner and growing up in postwar America, had very different influences.

Cash's fans themselves are split, and those like Streissguth and John Huss and David Werther (editors of the anthology *The Burning Ring of Truth*, 2008) argue that Cash was clearly a progressive, citing his work for American Indians, his identification with and concerts for prisoners, and his presentation of angry blue-collar workers in songs such as "One Piece at a Time" and "The Wreck of the Old 97." Yet the rebel "man in black" was a deep Christian and was cautious at best in endorsing the civil rights movement, and he waffled on the anti-war movement. He seems more, as Huss and Werther quote Kris Kristofferson in their introduction, "a walking contradiction, a paradox" who went his own way as an individual but, no doubt as most celebrities in the world today, needed to balance his sentiments with his audiences. He needed to keep his fan base among country-and-western fans as well as incorporate (as he did in the 1960s and 1970s) many urban and different audiences.

SUMMARY

Only one of our subjects, Johnny Cash, gives us the reality that class consciousness exists in a sociological sense away from a complete tie with politics, which is somewhat different than a Marxist definition of class consciousness.

Through much of history, class consciousness implied a political meaning, and most of our subjects were conscious of the meaning as a broadly leftist orientation. Because there has been so little research either on the subject of class consciousness or on the issue of poor people and class consciousness, it becomes somewhat difficult to say what a contemporary study would find. I have guessed, based on the later biographies and the political/historical conditions of the post–World War II period, that for most poor Americans, the politically infused class consciousness may be less than it once was.

In this chapter, political activists Flynn, Malcolm, and Hamer were obviously class-conscious figures. Anne Sullivan, Theodore Dreiser, Jack London, Richard Wright, Charlie Chaplin, Edna St. Vincent Millay, Jackson Pollock, and Johnny Cash's histories also suggest a strong degree of class consciousness. One can easily add to this list from our sample John Garfield, Billie Holiday, Marilyn Monroe, and Richard Pryor. Other members of the sample may well fit many of the cultural characteristics of class consciousness but did not necessarily share an oppositional political view (Jack Johnson, Babe Ruth, and Steve McQueen particularly), while Marilyn Monroe and Margaret Sanger show aspects of both cultural and political opposition. Again because of the small size of the sample it is difficult to present this as more than suggestive evidence, but as we shall see in Chapter 7 as we move away from figures born in the nineteenth century or early twentieth century, such class consciousness becomes rarer.

Chapter 5

REBELS AGAINST AUTHORITY

Another strong characteristic uniting the subjects in this book is their often intense battle with authority figures. This characteristic is different from the discussion in the previous chapter of class consciousness because while some forms of authority are political or a part of upper-class power, there are many forms of authority in life that are not directly political or class-based in nature. Anne Sullivan had a tendency to battle with all male authority figures, particularly those who sought to limit her mentee Helen Keller; birth control activist Margaret Sanger also took on gender roles and authority figures, both male and female; Babe Ruth was constantly at war with managers and baseball team owners; and actor John Garfield was in a constant battle with the movie studio system to get the kind of parts he wanted. Many of the people we have discussed were rebels against virtually all rules. Boxer Jack Johnson enraged white America in part (and some of the black leadership) by living by his own rules; artist Jackson Pollock, comedian Richard Pryor, actor Steve McQueen, singer Billie Holiday, and writer William Saroyan are also examples of those who were always getting into trouble, breaking rules, and clashing with all authority.

It is difficult to form a consistent theory about this tendency and whether it can be generalized in a broad way to people born into low-income status. Certainly these figures learned early on that they had to fight for what they got, and often parents and other adult figures were not available to help them. No doubt experience with adult authorities from police to church figures to school officials was often negative (though there were important exceptions). For some, their success may to an extent have reinforced their resistance to authority—a Babe Ruth or a Jackson Pollock, for example, can be allowed many flaws but still be rewarded by society. In this chapter I will distinguish between situational anger at the authorities of employers, publishers, studios, and so on, and those for whom anger kept flowing to any and all targets or to the point of possible dysfunction. The issue of rebellion would be an interesting one to study in a broader population; we know crime and other aggressive behaviors are more widespread among the poor, and particularly among males. What link might growing up without the expected pleasures and protections associated with middle-class childhood have to anger and dislike of authority? Why should low-income or even working-class people like authority anyway? The case is far stronger for middle- and upper-class people to accept and support authority than the poor.

An older literature on many subjects touches on social class and rebelliousness; certainly the work of Robert Merton and his followers Lloyd Ohlin and Richard Cloward on anomie and juvenile delinquency stress rebelliousness as synonymous with lower-class rebellion. Material on social class discussed in the bibliographic essay, for example, Argyle (1994), also supports a broad view of links between social class and crime. Perhaps the 1960s unrest on campuses and the rise of "conscience communities" of middle-class people opposed to various forms of authority (particularly vocal in anti-war and civil rights activity) has changed the perception of social class some. Croteau (1995) provides one of the more intelligent contemporary accounts by noting that the response of one class tends to shape other classes as relational forces. Hence it is an unfortunate truism that many white workers have been more conservative on issues like race than upper-class whites, who have less to lose from the actual surrender of privileges. Perhaps, as important, is that if upper- or middle-class people support a particular policy view it will induce at least suspicion among those in the working and poorer classes. Again, a complete discussion is not possible here; rather, I will review subjects' views about authority in this chapter, and later compare them with more recent subjects.

ANNE SULLIVAN AS "MISS SPITFIRE"

It is interesting that not only her contemporaries (it was Michael Anagnos, the head of the Perkins School for the Blind and her mentor who coined the "Miss Spitfire" label) but biographers of Anne Sullivan have concluded she was very hard to deal with. She comes across in Joseph Lash's *Helen and Teacher* (1980), one of the major biographies of both Sullivan and Helen Keller, as an eagle ready to pounce on anybody who would stand in her and Keller's way. But what was seen as an overprotective stand on behalf of Helen Keller by Lash is in modern terms not only understandable, but would be expected behavior on the part of advocates of the disabled.

Throughout the years between Sullivan's teaching Keller the alphabet and at least World War I, there were many obstacles to the "miracle worker" story, which we now assume to be a success. While there were crowds who did applaud Helen Keller and Anne Sullivan, they also received a hostile response from a variety of people who believed the so-called miracle was a fraud, and Sullivan a puppeteer who was perhaps using Keller as a ventriloquist. Sullivan's anti-authoritarianism (or independence) quickly got her into trouble with officials of the Perkins School when she was interviewed by a newspaper in 1890, and she made clear that Keller was her charge and not the property of the Perkins School. Such insubordination from a former pauper to a widely acclaimed charity (in the press no less!) was seen as a deep affront. Moreover, it was emblematic of a far deeper dispute that was arising between the former friends (and possibly, according to some rumors, lovers) Sullivan and Michael Anagnos about the "credit" for teaching Keller. For Anagnos, director of the Perkins School and the son-in-law of founding director Samuel Gridley Howe and Julia Ward Howe, there was no question that the deceased director remained the hero of the blind and the only one credited with understanding the teaching techniques used with the blind and deaf. Sullivan bristled at this, not only out of her independence but out of her dislike of Julia Ward Howe and family, whom she had known as a teenage student at the Perkins School (see Wagner 2012a).

Another explosion that severely shattered the relationship between Anagnos and the Perkins School and Sullivan and Keller was an allegation of plagiarism made against the twelve-year-old Helen in 1892. After Keller wrote a story called the "Frost King" for Anagnos (as part of her prolific correspondence with him), Anagnos rushed to publish the story. When a newspaper for the blind in West Virginia identified the story as being all too similar to a story by Margaret T. Canby entitled *Birdie and His Fairy Friends*, Anagnos was enraged and began an investigation. Sullivan was furious, as suspicion was cast on her for possibly reading the story to Keller. Lash and others throw suspicion on Sullivan's denials, and also note that the uneducated Sullivan may not have known what plagiarism was any more than the young Keller. Although this may be true, for most of the world, including Mark Twain and deaf advocate Alexander Graham Bell and most of public opinion, the action of placing the twelve-year-old Keller on trial for plagiarism was a shocking spectacle. The "trial" ended in a 4–4 tie as to Keller's guilt but would begin at least a twelve-year battle between Sullivan and Keller, on the one hand, and the Perkins School, on the other, which through older New England transcendentalist Franklin Benjamin Sanborn, would raise a series of charges again in the early twentieth century. While Lash and other biographers see the battles with Anagnos and Sanborn as representing Sullivan's attack on authorities, in fact, to a great extent she was defending herself and Keller against an attempt to totally discredit them. Sanborn and the Howe family wished to write Sullivan out of the historical record and claim that Anagnos had educated Keller. Keller sharply pointed out that Anagnos did not even know sign language or Braille.

In 1897, a major dispute occurred between Anne Sullivan and a male Brahmin figure, Arthur Gilman, the founder of Radcliffe College and the head of the Cambridge School for Young Ladies, which Keller was then attending. Like other disputes, the exact events and nuances differ from the sympathetic Braddy biography (1933) of Sullivan and Keller, and some more recent critical biographies. The crux of the dispute was Gilman's feelings that Keller was "overdoing it" and endangering her health by rushing to get through the Cambridge School. Sullivan rejected his proposal that Keller should spend three more years at the school than did other students when she had already passed Radcliffe's preliminary exams. During the conflict, Gilman decided it was imperative that Keller and Sullivan be split up for good. He wrote to Helen's mother in Alabama to enlist her support, claiming Sullivan was overworking Helen, and that Helen was becoming seriously ill. In December, when Sullivan became aware of the effort to separate her and Keller, she took Helen and went to stay with friends in Wrentham, Massachusetts, while Alexander Graham Bell and other allies caucused on how to fight

Gilman's decision. According to Keller's biography of Sullivan (1955), her teacher was so despondent that she seriously considered throwing herself into the Charles River. In the end, through the refusal of Keller to part with Sullivan, the intervention of their allies against Gilman, and Mrs. Keller's arrival in Boston (at which time she changed her mind and now sided with Sullivan and Keller), all led Gilman to back down. Some, like biographer Joseph Lash, feel Gilman was another victim of Sullivan and Keller:

> Perhaps the poor man [Gilman] (one can only feel sorry for him) had realized that to be an adversary to Helen or Annie was something like taking on motherhood and God; or perhaps he was just being a gentleman, like Anagnos, not wishing to hurt the two women. (Lash 1980, p. 224)

Of course, Keller and Sullivan and their allies saw events quite differently. In her 1955 biography of Sullivan, Keller maintained that Gilman, like others, sought control over her, and was influenced by the prestige that her attendance brought to the school to prolong her attendance there. He strove, Keller charged, to keep her at the prep school for his own self-interest. In any event, unquestionably, as Braddy admitted in her biography of Sullivan, the incident "offended many who stood in positions of authority and dignity," and no doubt people like Michael Anagnos and Franklin Sanborn, who both knew Gilman, may have thought to themselves "there she goes again" about Sullivan, if not about both women. It is not mutually exclusive that Sullivan's mental state and reaction to authority figures may have been a factor as well as the fact that Gilman's motives may have not been so altruistic, and certainly by modern standards Gilman must be seen as acting in a discriminatory way against a disabled individual.

In some ways, the response of biographers is more telling than the contemporary adversaries Sullivan had. No one disputes that Sullivan's extremely difficult childhood led to bouts of anger, depression, and sometimes gloom. Yet a consistent view that the male figures were victimized (a conclusion Lash particularly makes) or that Keller was victimized (a conclusion of writer Dorothy Hermann) seems far-fetched. All of these male figures had their own agenda, and limited sympathy with an Irish pauper as well as the disabled (Sullivan herself was partly blind).

Although the "Miss Spitfire" image is far overdrawn, it is true that Sullivan's experience with authority—both before and after the arrival of Helen Keller in her life—was quite negative. Her political views reinforced a hostile view of authorities such as charity officials, headmasters, and superintendents. Since it was certainly true in late nineteenth-century and early twentieth-century America that officials were hostile to the Irish and other immigrants, to the poor and working class, particularly those who spoke out, and to disabled women, a modern view would certainly have sympathy with Anne Sullivan.

MARGARET SANGER: THE CONTROVERSIAL FEMINIST

If Anne Sullivan has gone from somewhat of a folk hero to a figure criticized by psychologically minded biographers, Margaret Sanger, the birth control activist, has also faced a somewhat negative evaluation from many modern feminists (see Chesler 2007, for example). While Sanger began her famous career as a radical, she spent much of her last several decades not only moderating her views and image but at times seeming to accept the support of eugenicists.

Although Sanger's political views changed somewhat, her anti-authoritarianism remained. She kept to herself many continued radical beliefs, and like other subjects in this study, she remained class conscious and negative toward many of the affluent supporters attracted to the birth control movement in the interwar years.

Few disagree that Sanger's initial fame in the 1910s came from her anti-authoritarian blend of socialism and feminism. In her radical paper "The Woman Rebel," Sanger proclaimed in a large print the IWW banner "No Gods, No Masters!" She trumpeted a radical feminism "because I believe that woman is enslaved by the world machine, by sex conventions, by motherhood and its present necessary childrearing, by wage-slavery, by middle-class morality, by customs, laws, and superstitions" (cited in Chesler 2007, p. 98). Her manifesto trumpeted an anarchist faith and urged women "to look the whole world in the face with a go-to-hell look in the eyes ... to speak and act in defiance of convention" (ibid.). Nor was her indictment as a criminal in the state of New York based only on her illegal use of mail to promote birth control. Less reported was the charge that she violated the law by inciting murder and assassination because of her "Remember Ludlow!" slogan, which was well known as an IWW slogan to avenge the slaughter of dozens of people by Rockefeller interests in a bloody strike in Colorado (Chesler 2007, p. 102).

While in the post–World War I period, Sanger began to move toward a more conventional strategy to fight for birth control, she regarded herself as a socialist (she voted for the Socialist Party her whole life) and most definitely a feminist. Philanthropist Mabel Dodge called Sanger "the first person I ever knew who was openly an ardent propagandist for the joys of the flesh" or "free love" (Chesler 2007, p. 96). According to Ellen Chesler, her commitment to the free-love ideal would endure long after others in the "Village crowd" had retreated in "confusion and unhappiness." While she eventually downplayed this part of her beliefs, she continued to believe in a woman's right to rebel against "established religious, moral and legal codes" (ibid.). Her close friendship and political partnership with British sexologist Havelock Ellis was a reflection of this. Ellis commented in mock horror that anything the two of them could be in favor of could not possibly be acceptable to any church (ibid., p. 319).

The apparent outer conventionality of her life covered up many passionate love affairs and a continued feminism that Chesler (p. 309) remarked would "reveal … feminism so violent as to scare half of her supporters out of their wits if they thought she meant it." Another area where Sanger remained the same radical in her mind was her hostility to many birth control activists from the higher classes. Biographer Elyse Topalian (1984, p. 104) reported that Sanger was greatly distressed by "moves … made to replace prominent members of the 'old guard'—the feminist crusaders who had helped [her] lay the groundwork of the movement by acting in defiance of the law—with socialites and others who were perhaps more educated but who were out of touch with the plight of women in the lower classes." In one of her autobiographies Sanger criticized most charitable organizations and some of the new activists:

> There is doubtless a place for organizations that restrict their scope to the status quo. Most charities are like that—they live on securities … going through the same ritual year after year. Those who disagreed with me believed the emphasis should be on social register membership, and argued that my associations had been (too) radical. (Sanger 2004 [1938 orig.], p. 392)

Sanger even quoted an "indignant old radical who left the birth control movement" saying "This thing has gotten too darned safe for me" (p. 412).

There are those who would criticize Sanger and some of her statements as self-serving. She did marry businessman J. Noah Slee, who kept her in comfort for much of her middle age. The confines of her anti-authoritarianism are also sometimes hard to separate from a strong egotism when it came to the control of the birth control movement. However, I would argue that her discomfort with her own role reflected her upbringing and strong beliefs (even if tempered by middle age), which were critical of much she took part in.

BABE RUTH AND HIS FIGHT WITH BASEBALL

The Great Bambino is another famous person who is easy to criticize. His limited education combined at times with spoken malapropisms and his insatiable love of pleasure at the expense of the rigors of sports to combine to make his comments and actions seem humorous at times. Still, when one considers that no other person did as much to make baseball one of the top businesses in the United States in the post–World War I era, we can get a sense that the Yankees exploited the star and did not give him much in return.

As baseball fans know, major league baseball was a small operation prior to Ruth's day, with the stadiums built for limited-capacity crowds while franchise revenues were modest. The game was played with the hitters poking their hits in the infield and short outfield. The change of Ruth from a pitcher (and he was a very good one) to an outfielder and a hitter in 1919 coincided with a period of affluence in America when large numbers of working-class people lived in cities throughout America, and available public transportation made it possible for baseball to become America's first mass spectator sport. No human ingredient in this match was more important than Babe Ruth, who, it can be said, made the home run. For years before Ruth, the leader of home runs in the major leagues would hit in the single digits or low double digits (the famous hitter "Home Run" Baker never had more than twelve home runs). Suddenly home runs became exciting and could change the game in a flash. Other players began to try to swing for the fences. Ruth's type of play made the baseball owners rich. It was not just Yankee Stadium that was "the house Ruth built" but the rest of the league's stadiums as well.

Still another thing to note about Ruth's war with the baseball owners and managers was how poorly employees were treated by their managements. Today we think of professional sports stars and entertainment figures as princes and princesses, but in the old days before free agency in sports and the breakup of the studio system in Hollywood, even successful sports and movie stars were owned lock-stock-and-barrel by the owners. They had few rights and could be discharged or traded for little cause. They could also be held to their contracts for years by their employers. Conditions in baseball were such that players were stuffed into buses to travel, given few material benefits, and watched over like a hawk by chaperones at night, and punished for minor infractions. Ruth, with his love of food and drink, women, and autos, was an obvious target for discipline.

Even before Ruth came to New York, he clashed with Boston Red Sox manager Edward Barrow. Barrow expected to "rule the Red Sox sternly and firmly," according to Marshall Smelser, and to "use terror as a tool of management" (Smelser 1975, p. 97). When Ruth got off the train the team was taking to go visit his sister, Barrow was enraged and railed against Ruth in front of the whole team. Later their relationship became even more strained. Barrow sat up at night in the hotels occupied by the players, waiting for Ruth. Noting that Ruth never came in before morning, Barrow fined him $500. Ruth threatened to hit him in the nose and quit the team, but he later apologized to Barrow (Creamer 1974, pp. 162–163).

The relationship between Ruth and Barrow seemed like child's play compared to his long and bitter conflicts with the Yankee manager, Miller Huggins. According to Smelser, "the personalities of Miller Huggins and Ruth could not blend." Ruth called him "Little Boy" (Huggins was short) (Smelser 1975, p. 195). Biographer Robert Creamer (1974, p. 279) says Ruth called Huggins "the Flea." To be fair, many of the Yankees treated Huggins very badly. Huggins had an arbitrary and authoritarian style, a very typical managerial style in those days. Not only did Ruth continue his carousing ways, but Huggins hired detectives to find out where he was at any given time. Huggins claimed Ruth's companionship—mostly female—was of a rather dubious nature (Smelser 1975, p. 318). One of the biggest fights broke out in 1925 when after Ruth came in late for practice, Huggins suspended Ruth and fined him $5,000. Ruth poured obscenities at the manager and ended by shouting, "if you were half my size, I'd punch the shit out of you!" (Creamer 1974, p. 293). Ruth told the press that he had disobeyed Huggins's orders on the field twice, and defended his acts. He also said $5,000 was ridiculously high, stating, "Why I know of guys killing people [for that]. And even bootleggers don't get that tough a fine. It ain't right!" (Smelser 1975, p. 320). Ruth appealed to Yankee management, saying he was through, and if Huggins stayed he would quit. Yankee owner Jacob Rupert refused his appeal and backed Huggins, and Ruth stayed.

Chapter 5

Still another well-known battle in these years was Ruth's getting in trouble with baseball commissioner Kennesaw Mountain Landis, who gained fame as a stern judge, and then as the baseball commissioner who threw the 1919 Black Sox team out of baseball. At the time, it was quite common for ballplayers to routinely earn money in the off season by playing exhibition ball, barnstorming around the country (and later overseas). This practice was technically in violation of the players' contracts, but given how little most players made, it was winked at. However, with Landis now in power, things had changed. When Ruth prepared his 1921–1922 season of barnstorming, he received a warning from Landis that such acts would not be tolerated. When Ruth ignored his warnings, Landis snapped that if he went it would be the sorriest thing he ever did, to which Ruth replied, "Aw, tell the old guy to go jump in a lake" (Creamer 1974, pp. 244–246). Ruth was later fined his World Series share ($3,362) and was suspended for the first six weeks of the 1922 baseball season.

As noted earlier, as Ruth's career went on, things calmed down a bit, but Ruth remained a critic of management. When the Yankees demurred on Ruth's becoming a manager, Ruth commented, "Club owners can be awful funny, when they want to. A ballplayer's supposed to be dumb and know nothing. When they get a ballplayer who thinks, they get suspicious" (Smelser 1975, p. 483). Ruth would never forgive the Yankees for letting him go or the club (and professional baseball) for offering him nothing when he got older and was forced into retirement. He was extremely bitter for the remaining years of his life.

While Ruth was perhaps not the poster boy for how to organize a coherent protest against baseball managers, his resistance to them cannot be attributed only to his hedonism and abandon. He resented the managers and owners who lived off the profits he and the players made them, and who gave them little credit for the great success of the Yankees. It is true he was monetarily rewarded, though by today's standards the salary was small and a tiny percentage of owners' profits.

JOHN GARFIELD AND HIS FIGHT WITH HOLLYWOOD

The Hollywood studio system that prevailed for a half century paralleled or exceeded the restraints professional baseball owners held over their players. Actors and actresses were bound to a company by long-term contracts. They had no control over their roles, no ability to play for other companies or act on stage or elsewhere or to obtain more compensation.

In fact, it had taken a figure in this book—Charlie Chaplin (along with D. W. Griffith, Mary Pickford, and Douglas Fairbanks)—to found the United Artists Company as a first blow for independent production from the big studios. John Garfield (born Jules Garfinkle) went from quick stardom in the late 1930s to a nearly decade-long battle with the Warner Brothers studio, which suspended him no less than ten times. Although much of the battle was over the studio's stereotypical parts for Garfield, it took on political overtones as well. Garfield, who was on the executive board of the actors' union, the Screen Actors Guild, made political enemies of the studios and was eventually taken down by the House Un-American Activities Committee (HUAC) and the committee's grip on Hollywood in the late 1940s and early 1950s.

Garfield began his serious acting career with the Group Theater in New York including playing in the famous radical play *Waiting for Lefty*. His first film break came in 1938 when he starred in *Four Daughters*, in which according to the American National Biography Online "he developed the charming, rebellious, hard-luck persona for which he would become famous." Biographer Robert Nott characterizes him as a "Warner Brothers type—dark, brooding, street-smart, and a native New Yorker to boot" (Nott 2004, p. 29). In the aftermath of *Four Daughters'* success (he was nominated for an Academy Award and received a New York Film Critics' nomination for best supporting actor) Garfield did six movies in 1939, but he was unhappy with the parts he was cast in. For example, the movie *Daughters Courageous* (1939) "was an unofficial remake of *Four Daughters*" (Beaver 1978, p. 25). Garfield complained in an interview he did not want to play any more roles like the "snotty fisherman" in the movie. He was quoted, "If an artist does not have a point of view, he does not make a dent. And I mean to make a dent" (ibid., p. 26). This led to Garfield's first suspension. He clashed that year as well with the famous Busby Berkeley, who usually directed musicals, over the movie *They Made Me a Criminal*. According to biographer Robert Sklar (1992, p. 90), the film's unit manager wrote, "I believe this picture has made him [Garfield] a Bolshevik," evidently referring more to Garfield's rebelliousness than his politics. After the 1939 shooting of still another stereotypical prison picture (*Castle on the Hudson*, about Sing-Sing Prison) he refused to report for the next crime picture. He was suspended, reinstated, laid off, and then suspended again, losing four months of work in 1939.

Robert Nott wrote that as an actor, "Garfield resented executives and producers butting in to tell him how he should play a scene ... [and]

he took to the press to voice his discontent." He even critiqued Hollywood itself, saying, "Hollywood, as now constituted, does its utmost to over-develop the actor's ego and so spoil him for the simple business of living, either with others or himself" (Nott 2004, p. 107). Although many actors who were not born poor also clashed with Hollywood, for Garfield, like Charlie Chaplin and Marilyn Monroe, there was a class aspect to his battles. Garfield "hated Hollywood. He hated Errol Flynn. He hated all things that were not New York ... [he considered them] phonies" (Nott 2004, p. 120).

Moreover, Garfield's battle began taking on political dimension. As early as 1938, the Dies Committee (the forerunner of HUAC) cited Garfield as being a communist for joining the Hollywood Anti-Fascist League and the American League for Peace, both later identified as Communist Party fronts (Nott 2004, p. 112). *Time* magazine the next year in its review of *They Made Me a Criminal* described Garfield "as outspoken ... and an amateur left wing politician" (Nott 2004, p. 108). Garfield was never a Communist Party member, though there is some evidence his wife was, and he certainly supported leftist causes. Already referred to on radio as "the bad boy of Burbank," he made clear his desire to do independent films, and with his contract still tied to Warner Brothers, he was suspended six more times. Warner Brothers also warned Garfield against going to a benefit for the radical labor leader Harry Bridges; he took their advice and stayed home (Nott 2004, p. 110). His efforts to avoid conflict failed, though. In the later 1940s when he agreed to do Clifford Odets's play *The Big Knife* on Broadway to expand his acting range, he was criticized for supporting a left-wing attack on Hollywood. The powerful critic Hedda Hopper, who never liked Garfield, said she was happy *The Big Knife* was not a success because Garfield "was not a waif, but a political person" and had failed to succeed in his ideology (Sklar 1992, p. 214). Garfield's participation in leftist director Abraham Polansky's 1948 film *Force of Evil*, one of the most left-wing films of the era, made him even more controversial.

In Polansky's view, Garfield's refusal to step away from his politics, and moreover his friends, by not naming names was his downfall: "He defended his streetboy's honor and they killed him for it" (Sklar 1992, p. 225). Nott sees Garfield's political martyrdom in the McCarthy period as far less conscious, writing, "He was an unlikely candidate for martyrdom." But once he and his lawyer came up with a strategy that appeared to cooperate with HUAC, but really did not do so, his career was over. As Nott explains, "He made the mistake of perjuring himself ... but one thing he would not do was rat on his friends" (Nott 2004, p. 272). By 1951 it was clear that if Garfield was not going to jail, at a minimum he would never work. His death from a heart attack at age thirty-nine that year is linked by many writers to this suffering.

Ironically, Garfield's quiet but rebellious nature came to characterize his life and his own battle with Hollywood as well as his film characters. His motivations as far as we can tell regarding the stage and screen were of a professional acting nature. Critics as well had begun already by 1940 to be noting the repetitious nature of his roles. But no doubt his poor childhood and his class consciousness came together to make him a particular anti-authority figure whose massive funeral in New York City attracted huge crowds.

REBELS AGAINST WHAT? "WHAT HAVE YOU GOT?"

The famous Marlon Brando line from the movie *The Wild Ones* could be applied to almost all of our famous poor. Rebellion (or being a symbol of rebellion) is one of the ways in American society that someone poor can become famous. Those in our sample who seemed to be most known for rebelling are boxer Jack Johnson, author William Saroyan, artist Jackson Pollock, singer Billie Holiday, actor Steve McQueen, and comedian Richard Pryor. But one could make a good case for including authors Theodore Dreiser and Jack London, poet Edna St. Vincent Millay, author Richard Wright, activists Fannie Lou Hamer and Malcolm X, and singer Johnny Cash, as well as Sullivan, Sanger, Ruth, and Garfield. The only partial exceptions in terms of their relations to authority might be Flynn, with her long loyalty to the Communist Party; and Malcolm, with his loyalty to Elijah Mohammed and the Muslims. Marilyn Monroe had a very different style of expression; her anxiety and fears were so great that her anger came out more often in passive-aggressive rebellion against producers, directors, and even colleagues rather than in anger and open rebellion.

Less is known about the childhood of the first African American heavyweight boxing champion, Jack Johnson, than other subjects. He grew up in a poor but apparently unexceptionable family in Galveston, Texas, and at a young age began to tramp away from home and eventually to try boxing. Yet already by his youth, he was proud and self-confident. As biographer Geoffrey Ward commented on Johnson,

> He embodied American individualism—nothing, no law or custom, no person white or black, male or female—could keep him for long from whatever he wanted. All his life, whites and blacks alike would ask him, "Just who do you think you are?" The answer of course was always Jack Johnson. (Ward 2004, p. 4)

Johnson seems to have not only been proud, egotistical, and fond of getting his own way when he was famous but even as a youth to have had the attributes of "independence, restlessness, an ability to improvise, to attract attention, and to get around the rules intended to tie him down" (Ward 2004, p. 11). We do not know if his parents socialized him to be different and reject the constraints of society, particularly white society, or (probably more likely) if his strength and physique combined with his ego to make him believe he could do what he wanted. Even early in his career, Johnson alienated his managers (he had multiple suits with many managers over his life who claimed he had hired them). A potential manager named George Eckhart in California found him "imperious" after he had demanded room and board, and also that someone pick his truck up at the railroad depot (Ward 2004, p. 39). Sometimes his disputes clouded over between racial mixing and other disputes. So, for example, after winning a fight in Bakersfield, California, shopkeepers took out a warrant for his arrest, claiming he had not paid his bills. Ward notes this may well have been true, but that it was additionally true that "he had made himself obnoxious to various persons" and had lived in a "forbidden district" of Bakersfield, seeing no reason he should not move into the white section of town (Ward 2004, p. 53).

What Johnson got in trouble for was his lack of deference. As Ward comments, "It was the lack of deference toward white men and the power they wielded, his refusal ever to remain in his 'place' ... that so inflamed passions" (2004, p. 226). Al-Tony Gilmore notes that Johnson's "personality elevated him to hero status, particularly among the more deprived of his race, because his exploits and life-style gave them, if only for a fleeting moment, the vicarious experience of leaving their inferior position" (Gilmore 1975, p. 19). This symbolic rebellion helps explain why many of our subjects maintained a base of support whether their actions were always rational or strategic.

Johnson's biggest provocation was, as noted earlier, "his conspicuous parad[ing of] all of his white women as if to flout the laws and customs of the nation." As Gilmore says, Johnson "undoubtedly took pleasure in aggravating and annoying whites" (1975, p. 14). To accent his marriage to a white woman, the champion would "grace the bandstand with his bass violin and sing his favorite song 'I Love My Wife'" as she arrived in the house. He also displayed a larger-than-life-size portrait of himself embracing his wife. To further accent his sexuality, he wrapped his penis in gauze bandages, enhancing his size for all onlookers (ibid.). A statement he supposedly made to Lucille Cameron's mother (the so-called victim of his Mann Act prosecution) boasted that "he could get any white woman in Chicago." He later denied making this statement in a meeting with the leaders of the Chicago African American community (ibid., p. 113).

Like many popular figures that develop a large following and an organized retinue, Johnson's coterie often got the boxer and his supporters in trouble. Ward notes that Johnson got into a fight at a vaudeville theater and he and his men threatened to "deck everyone," he smashed the window out of a taxi cab, pulled a gun on a perennial challenger, and piled a chair on a small man and threatened him with his revolver before his friends could calm him (Ward 2004, pp. 177–178). When Johnson was drunk or celebrating or his retinue (or he) was angry at someone, they left all caution to the wind.

Perhaps in simplistic terms fame had gone "to his head," and clearly perceptions turned greatly on Johnson even among the African American community. As we saw with the career of Babe Ruth, there is not much training that a famous athlete (or others) gets that prepares him or her for what to say or do when the world is watching. At times one's comments or actions seem brave. For example, Johnson was unimpressed with President Theodore Roosevelt's dining in the White House with the black collaborationist Booker T. Washington (who disliked Johnson). Johnson thought that if Roosevelt was "sincere from his heart" he would have invited the boxer and his family to dine (Gilmore 1975, p. 16). But at other times, his dramatic actions with women, autos, alcohol, and statements to the press did not always serve him well or help him with posterity.

Whereas Jack Johnson shocked some Americans while smiling his way in the boxing ring and out, William Saroyan was almost from the start a "rebel without a cause." Many biographers attribute his lifelong distrust of authority to both his awful childhood (which has been touched on in earlier chapters) and his Armenian descent—Armenians as a people had suffered unmitigated hardship and had few allies around the world. It was an interesting contradiction that the writer who gave his name

("Saroyanesque") to a sentimental, even maudlin treatment of people actually carried with him a mountain of resentment and anger.

Saroyan's biographers see his resentment as long-seated and starting at an early age, though it would become more seething when his success faded in the mid-1940s. Biographer John Leggett describes Saroyan leaving school early and getting a job at a postal telegraph office. He "could not understand how anyone could put up with the boredom of office work, with the files, the adding machines, and the superintendents with their sharp eyes and self-importance," and quit (Leggett 2002, p. 19). Saroyan did not feel he fit anywhere but as an independent writer. He achieved an astounding success in 1934 when his short story "The Daring Young Man on the Flying Trapeze" was published and won the O. Henry Award. His success continued through the early 1940s when the *Time of Your Life* won the Pulitzer Prize (which he refused to accept). However, even before his success ended, Saroyan refused to "play the game" and fought with editors, publishers, and even had a highly publicized battle with novelist Ernest Hemingway. Leggett describes Saroyan as having "cockiness so apparent in both his writing and his behavior [it] was becoming a trademark, and it was rooted in a newfound self-assertion and dismissal of competitors." Leggett says, "He was convinced of his superiority ... [and] thought most writers, the big shots included, were dabbling, repeating the past in slick and conventional ways" (pp. 25, 29).

Saroyan was, for example, highly resistant to publisher Bennett Cerf of Random House, who had published his first collections of stories. However, Saroyan at one point called Cerf to say he had lost at poker and on the horses (Saroyan was an inveterate gambler all his life) and needed money. When Cerf balked, Saroyan blamed Cerf for his lack of generosity and lack of faith in him (Leggett 2002, p. 49). He also demanded that Cerf publish the book *Little Ones*, which severed his relations with Cerf. Leggett calls his ignoring of Cerf's advice as "baffling," as was his highly public and drawn-out battle with the far more famous Hemingway. Leggett asks, "Why did he feel no deference to those dynamic, influential men?" and concludes that Saroyan "could not bear the short end of the master-apprentice relationship ... in addition, gratitude and deference were alien emotions: they looked to him like weakness" (p. 53).

Of course, all acts are subject to different interpretations. Saroyan refused the Pulitzer Prize because he disliked institutional patronage and did not believe artists should be controlled by outside money. Leggett said his acts "were perfectly in character ... he did resent institutions. He did bridle at the honors and gratitude expected in return. They were transactions in which he seemed to lose some precious independence and to catch an offensive whiff of servility" (Leggett 2002, p. 77). The entry about Saroyan in the American National Biography Online (by Edward Halsey Foster) expresses considerably more skepticism:

> He had much to gain from his refusal [of the Pulitzer], for the rejection surely brought more publicity than acceptance would have. Further complicating the matter, he accepted the New York Drama Critics Circle Award for the same play. Nonetheless, rejecting the Pulitzer gave him the opportunity to make widely reported statements about the need for art to be free of authority.

Saroyan also missed opportunities for allies because he refused to engage in politics, which he deeply distrusted. He was, if anything, an anarchist. Leggett states that Saroyan "resented all governments ... he could see no virtue in a militant patriotism" (p. 40). Because of this and Armenia's subjection to the Soviet Empire, he was also anti-Soviet and was condemned by the *Daily Worker*. His views brought him few friends in the tumultuous 1930s.

When Saroyan had what would be his last success, *The Human Comedy*, published in 1943, he again strongly clashed, this time with MGM. MGM mogul Louis Mayer had pronounced Saroyan simply not experienced enough to direct a film based on the book, and Saroyan walked out of the meeting. The famous screenwriter Budd Schulberg said that in terms of the film industry, Saroyan's acts were like "writing your exit ticket. It wasn't just MGM ... Mayer's power went beyond it" (Lee and Gifford 1984, p. 85). Saroyan's friend, playwright Arthur Shaw, said Saroyan did not understand that the companies "were not dealing in merit, but in making money" and said he "was astounded by Saroyan's reaction, he was so bitter" (ibid., p. 84).

Saroyan tried with all his might to avoid the military in World War II, but he was finally drafted into the US Army. Saroyan felt "absolutely violated by the fact that he was drafted," and according to his wife, Carol, "he was determined to get out ... he did not want to be in any Army or have a regimented life of any kind." His wife ventured that he was never the same after his service (Lee and Gifford 1984, p. 95). His resistance in turn caused the army to put him on months of duty cleaning latrines, and eventually Saroyan was placed in the Section 8 (psychiatric) ward. Later the army decided that he was only "pretending to be crazy" and returned him to the unit. He then refused to wear his private stripes "and for this transgression [he] was again threatened with court-martial" (ibid., p. 110). Carol described Saroyan as in "a constant rage" after the army drafted him. She herself stated, "They just took him because he was well known and because he was very anti-war, completely, and anti-army. He just hated all organization" (ibid., pp. 111, 114). Of course, this orientation during World War II was not popular; Saroyan won "little or no sympathy for his attitude about the war and the army" from the US public.

It is hard to tell if Saroyan would have succeeded any better in the remaining three and a half decades of his life if it had not been for his alienating many of the gatekeepers of Broadway, Hollywood, and publishing. Moreover, his drinking and gambling worsened, and his wife and he split up, yet had constant fights over the children. His personal life deteriorated as did his public fame.

As an individual, it is always a little difficult to derive lessons from lives. Interestingly, while recounting Saroyan's difficult youth, few biographers link fully his attitudes to the suffering he endured. Nor is there a sense that his views may have had validity. It is perhaps as much a reflection on middle- and upper-class values that the failure of some of our subjects to "play by the rules" is used to greatly justify their failures. Though Saroyan did not put his opposition in political terms, there is an alternative reading that could link his views and his work to an anti-authoritarian tradition. He also might be an example of the negative impact of fame in that having tasted the wide success of the decade (approximately 1934–1943) Saroyan no doubt felt some grief and humiliation at having lost such acclaim.

Even compared with Jack Johnson and William Saroyan, more modern rebels like actor Steve McQueen and comedian Richard Pryor have gone further in their consistent visible anti-authority rebellions both in their careers and personal lives. McQueen and Pryor have some similarities too, for while all our subjects were born poor, McQueen's early experience as a street kid and Pryor's growing up in a brothel marked their upbringing as being far more "deviant" or marginal than some other families of our subjects.

As previously noted, McQueen was born in Indiana to a family that was rapidly deserted by his father, and brought up by an alcoholic mother who became a sex worker. As a teen, he escaped to California and roamed the streets. Biographer Marshall Terrill states that "he led the life of a young hobo. Sneaking on freight trains, hitchhiking, and eating around campfires were his way of life now" (Terrill 1993, p. 8). He joined a gang to show he was not a Midwestern hick: "He had to prove he was 'badder' than they, if they would steal ten hubcaps, he'd steal twenty. He mastered two fields of expertise: stealing hubcaps and shooting pool" (ibid.). Eventually sent to a juvenile home, McQueen showed leadership abilities, which may have saved him from a life in prison or a similar fate. But McQueen never lost the "chip on his shoulder," as Terrill quotes McQueen: "I learned early in life not to trust anyone." Terrill himself notes, "He bore that mistrust toward everyone, and it carried into his adult life" (p. 8). He joined the US Marines at age seventeen. During his service, he was busted from his PFC rank a total of seven times. Biographer Darwin Porter said McQueen was "too independent for the Marines" and notes a variety of rebellions including painting a tank pink and driving it into downtown San Diego (Porter 2009, p. 67). Interestingly, a commander of McQueen's opined, "The guy I knew as Steve McQueen—now the actor Steve McQueen—was very similar in real life to the person I saw in his movies" (ibid.).

McQueen next moved to New York City. He had a job repairing shoes for a while, but according to Porter, McQueen got into an argument with a customer and the cobbler fired him. Short of money and desperate, at one point he took to "rolling" sleeping drunks (i.e., stealing money while they were asleep) down in the Bowery (Porter 2009, p. 74). It was also during this period that McQueen began his intrigue with speed racing, which he would later pursue more seriously. He received a lot of traffic tickets as he roared up and down the New York streets, but he would always tear them up. "It's a free country, and I'm a free man. No God-damn cop is going to tell me how fast I can go," Porter quotes McQueen as saying (p. 118).

McQueen almost from the start of his stardom was characterized as "difficult" to work with (Porter 2009, p. 264). Some said he was easier to get along with if you were a stuntman than an executive, which certainly seems consistent with his poor background (ibid., p. 44). Others found him paranoid, a friend telling Terrill, "One day he was your best friend, the next day your enemy, let's just say he was moody" (Terrill 1993, p. 45). His screen character in the movie *The Great Escape* was evidently not that different from the *real* Steve McQueen: a wise-cracking loner, super-brave, cocky and macho, and difficult and overbearing during production (Porter 2009, p. 231). McQueen made many enemies among his fellow actors. He was known as a "screen hog" who was selfish and often pushed others out. McQueen himself denied this, saying, "People call me selfish, a screen hog. I am not being selfish, I'm protecting myself. I learned as a kid that if I don't protect Steve McQueen, no one else in hell is going to do it" (ibid., p. 233). Fellow actor James Coburn, however, remarked, "Why he didn't get banished from motion pictures early in his career before he became a big star is a mystery to me" (ibid.). Producers and directors had consistent troubles with him. Columbia Pictures fought with him to stop his auto racing and the wild chases he went on; they saw only damage to his career as a result. His "bad boy" image continued as he got himself thrown out of hotels and loved to engage in vandalism such as throwing firecrackers out of windows (Frank Sinatra, who befriended McQueen for a while, noted Steve had a way of getting the police to not arrest him). Hollywood knew his background. Coburn said McQueen told him, "I still have nightmares about being poor, of everything just vanishing away" (Terrill 1993, p. 62). Actress Suzanne Pleschette, who liked McQueen, said he had "the psychology of a very, very poor boy who had little to begin with" (ibid., p. 165).

Biographers note some evidence that McQueen's difficult personality and way he related to others in Hollywood may have cost him some status. One of his best performances was in the film *The Sand Pebbles*, for which he was nominated for an Academy Award. Terrill surmises that McQueen's not getting the award may well have been because of his unpopularity. Porter notes that McQueen was so angry to lose the Oscar that he declared he was retiring from the film industry, although he did not (Porter 2009, pp. 279–280). Yet, according to Terrill, when he later won a Golden Globe for his role in the movie *Papillon*, McQueen refused over the phone to go to the ceremony, a condition for the Globe's acceptance in those days; hence, he did not get it (Terrill 1993, p. 165). His friend Philip Parslow says of *Papillon* that not only should McQueen have been nominated, he should have won. He said it was "no secret that Steve was not liked by his fellow actors" (ibid., p. 268).

Like all the rebels and class-conscious subjects we have examined, McQueen was not without his virtues. He always supported the Boy's Brotherhood Republic, where he spent his juvenile term. One anecdote tells of his reading about two Florida teenagers who were caught breaking and entering with intent to commit a misdemeanor. He was incensed, declaring the kids should not be locked up for this offense. He was able by using his renown and persuasion to get Florida authorities to release the young men (Terrill 1993, p. 78). As not only a poor person, but an abused child, McQueen often saw things as "black and white" and reacted strongly one way or the other to situations.

Few people even among those examined so far have combined personal rebellion with political and career rebellion as much as the late comedian Richard Pryor. Biographer Audrey McClusky puts it well:

> Being declared a "crazy" nigger bestowed a reckless freedom upon him, and an abandon he embraced ... someone who defied the dictates of convention ... some might suggest that the perplexity of his early life—its unconventionality and instability—fueled his brilliance and his edgy self-destructive rebellion. (McClusky 2008, p. 1)

Still, despite an array of reasons why Pryor might be rebellious—being born in a "deviant" setting of a brothel, his being born black and poor, his having been sexually abused at a young age, his dropping out of school at a young age and joining something resembling a gang, and his taking part in a racial fight in the military for which he was sent to the brig—like anyone, there was more than one Richard Pryor. There is the young boy who was a favorite of teacher Miss Parker, who had him stand in front of the class and tell jokes (Pryor 1995, p. 47), and there was the adult Pryor who in the first part of his comedy career greatly mimicked Bill Cosby as a funny, but more traditional, mainstream comic (ibid., p. 93). Pryor lived in different worlds always—a political one as well as a comic one, and an often out-of-control personal life even when his career was a great success.

Just as McQueen's movie career seemed to emulate his off-screen persona, it is easy to conflate Pryor's wild personal life with his comedy and his politics. Pryor's own biography *Pryor Convictions* is full of stories of drug use, harshness and violence toward women, and a series of troubles with the law. He notes that after he was arrested for hitting a woman in Pittsburgh he saw himself "as a victim of the system, an outsider for whom justice was out of reach, a dream, and then I saw how closely my situation mirrored the black man's larger struggle for dignity and equality" (Pryor 1995, p. 92). But what would be for most people a dangerous association of one's own personal problems with broader social issues somehow blossomed in Pryor into a unique comedic stance that Mel Watkins sees as bringing to the public a larger history of black comedy that was previously hidden from the outside world (Watkins 1994). By rejecting the world of white-friendly and middle-class comedy of Bill Cosby and other comics of the time, Pryor brought the world "of junkies and winos, pool hustlers and prostitutes" into professional comedy. Film critic Pauline Kael makes the point well by noting Pryor's parallel with Charlie Chaplin: "If [Charlie Chaplin] had found the street language to match his low-life tramp movements, he might have been something like Richard Pryor, who's all of a piece—a master of lyrical obscenity, Pryor is the only great poet satirist among our comics" (Watkins 1994, p. 527).

Pryor was able to bring a lower-class persona to his work and become, depending on your view, either a hero or villain based on that. By becoming the voice of the "crazy nigger" on the street his work became self-consciously political. Pablo Guzman of the *Village Voice* wrote that "the heart of Richard's appeal is that he is a political force. That's right: politics, not mere entertainment ... the politics of being an Everyday African male in America ... after all, Richard's comedy has always been both subversive and revelatory" (McClusky 2008, p. 154).

As McClusky further notes, Pryor's monologue posited whiteness as civility and blackness as savagery. He had the "ethos of his 1970s character" shaped by "the Black Power movement, the black arts movement, and the Black Panthers, as well as the urban riots" (pp. 25, 28).

But it is true that Pryor's personal shortcomings were always stealing headlines from his professional life. He would be married seven times to six women, and be in frequent violent interchanges with them. He had two heart attacks at a young age. His long and extensive drug use came to a dramatic end when in 1980 he almost killed himself freebasing cocaine by setting himself on fire. At forty-six, he was diagnosed as having multiple sclerosis, which would cripple and eventually kill him.

Pryor, like McQueen, was strongly influenced by his times. The 1960s and 1970s were dramatically changing and confusing times, a time in which the public was very open to rebellious characters. At the same time, social norms were dramatically changing, and at least for a while, it was unclear what rules governed personal life. Added to this, of course, have been the residues of lower-class life, particularly being on the society's margins, that were true of the Pryors, McQueens, and for that matter the Saroyans and Ruths of earlier times. The alignment of personal rebellion and artistic innovation and rebellion is a complex one that is dependent on many factors. It is tempting to see people like Pryor and McQueen as naturally occurring together, but many of our subjects, from Chaplin to Elizabeth Gurley Flynn to Fannie Lou Hamer, did not have notably rebellious personal lives.

DISCUSSION

Most people of all social classes and times are not Babe Ruths, John Garfields, or Richard Pryors, and their great skills were what made them famous despite whatever personal deficiencies and problems they lived with. Nevertheless, I am suggesting here that a strong aspect of their rebelliousness against authority came from their lower-class backgrounds, which in turn provided a variety of harsh circumstances to grow up in. Some of our subjects, such as Richard Pryor, Steve McQueen, Malcolm X, and Johnny Cash, would not be famous without aspects of rebellion that colored their lives and careers; while others, such as Anne Sullivan and Babe Ruth, would presumably have accomplished what made them famous even without their rebellious instincts. Few in our sample were not rebellious; it is perhaps the single descriptor that fits almost all of the subjects, more than awful childhoods, pain and suffering, and class consciousness.

As with class consciousness in the previous chapter, testing out how common anti-authority sentiments (or actions) are among contemporary lower-class people would be enormously interesting. Obviously the milieu of the nineteenth century or even growing up in the 1940s and 1950s as a black man (like Pryor) made for conditions somewhat different than today. Still, while the average person lacks some of the skills (and luck) of the subjects in our sample, an analysis of various data might confirm that personal anti-authority actions (for example, arrest records) and personal self-reports (such as drug use) might show higher levels of rebellion among the lower classes. Perhaps one difference (which was noted in Chapter 4) is the depoliticalization of many members of the lower class, at least now as compared to earlier days; this then leaves the aspects of personal rebellion more apparent and unfocused.

CHAPTER 6

FAME AND POVERTY

Despite the many difficulties each of our subjects confronted in their childhoods and the rest of their lives, they all succeeded in accomplishing enough to be famous in their times, and some for a long time into the future. Each person's success against the odds stands as a testimony to skill and luck, both of which are necessary for success. In each case, one can think of numerous chance occurrences that had they occurred might have blocked their discovery by those who help legitimate fame or success, and yet one can also think of qualities that stood out in each figure. Since fame is rare, the success of the twenty subjects we've considered thus far can certainly not be taken as openness to low-income people in general in our social class or social status systems. This chapter will look at the subjects in two ways: First, I will discuss how individual mobility out of poverty was helped by certain factors in the subject's lives, and also stay on the individual level to briefly discuss how they achieved fame at the time they did. In the rest of the chapter, I return to a more sociological question of whether it helped to be poor or not, and how the nature of the mass media and popular culture has changed over time in its treatment of poor people.

INDIVIDUAL MOBILITY

The twenty subjects I have selected as "famous poor" are of course famous for their achievements, not their poverty, and hence some time needs to be spent on how these figures were able to do something extremely hard—move from poverty to fame, if not always to "fortune." Because the subjects were intentionally selected from different time periods, geographies, genders, races, and ethnicities, there is a wide variety in their stories. Scientific answers can't be drawn using this small sample, and we must also separate the subjects' ability to move out from poverty and their ability to achieve fame. With a few exceptions, these movements were different and occurred at different times.

MOBILITY OUT OF POVERTY

A large contemporary literature exists on what is called "exits from poverty" (usually simply a statistical measure of moving out of the poverty line), which emphasizes the much-spoken-of role of "cultural capital" or "social capital" (probably most popularized by Putnam 2000; two other books on the subject are Halpern 2005 and Lin 2001). This is a fancy term for how people can acquire some of what more affluent people have in forms other than money: education, skills and resources, ability to use language and speech, correct dress, large social networks of friends in high places, and so on. Though it is an important concept, the broadness of the term can sometimes obscure the concentration of the vast majority of capital in more affluent hands, and the lack of correspondence in many cases between having cultural capital and achieving affluence. The value of education, both formal and less formal, is the most important form of social capital, but I will also note mentoring as an important factor, as well as travel, marriage, and social movements as playing a role in mobility.

The intellectual or academic side of education needs to be separated from other aspects of education. If we are just looking at learning the skills of speaking and writing well, studying academic subjects and mastering them, and being conversant with the culture's major intellectual questions, at various of the times we are looking at it does not seem as if these skills are unachievable to the self-taught. Charlie Chaplin and Richard Wright, for example, received hardly any formal education yet both were enormously literate, with the latter becoming a well-known literary figure himself. Malcolm X noted many people were amazed at his speech and references, which came primarily from the reading he did while in prison, rather than during his eighth-grade education (Malcolm X 1965, p. 171). But education, particularly at the college level, also provides a place where connections are passed on, both from teachers and mentors and from contact with other students. Edna St. Vincent Millay, whose poetry came to the attention of Caroline B. Dow, the dean of New York's YMCA Training School, gained admission into Vassar College with Dow's help. Millay was the only one of our subjects who earned a four-year college degree. More typically, our subjects had only brief stays in college: Theodore Dreiser completed a year at the University of Indiana–Bloomington supported by a sympathetic teacher, and Jack London finished a semester at the University of California–Berkeley and passed the written exams, but could not afford to go back.

Still, education provides different types of advantages, and in the days we are looking at, even good contacts and mentors at less than a college level can be critical to people's lives. Anne Sullivan's transfer from a poorhouse to the Perkins School, one of the best schools for the blind in the United States, was fortuitous. She obviously was able to take great advantage of this as she rose to be the school's valedictorian. Despite her and Helen Keller's later criticisms of the school, she was exposed to the rudiments of a humanist, classical education. Her contact with the director, Michael Anagnos, led to her being assigned as a teacher to Helen Keller in Alabama. Later, she was able to use her education augmented by her own studies to attend Radcliffe with Keller, even if she got no formal credit for all her hand signing of difficult college work to her mentee. Margaret Sanger was also lucky that despite her poor background, her sisters were able to put money enough together for her to attend Clavarack College (not a four-year college) in the Catskills of New York, and later to train at nursing school, which even if she had not become a leader of the birth control movement would have at least moved her out of poverty.

Education—even relatively limited amounts—can serve as encouragement in career endeavors. Although Elizabeth Gurley Flynn never went beyond junior high school, she won English and debating medals while in school, which certainly would have encouraged her in embarking on a speaking and organizing career (Camp 1995, p. 9). Babe Ruth spoke his whole life of Brother Matthias, his mentor during his many years at the Industrial School. Matthias clearly encouraged Ruth's budding baseball prowess though another brother ventured that he would also "have made a good tailor." Actors and artists gain from mentorship as much as any formal university or high school classes. John Garfield was extremely lucky his high school principal saw his acting potential and sent him to special classes. Garfield later applied to the American Laboratory Theater, where he met some of the most famous "method actors" of the day. Marilyn Monroe gained from her time in 1947 studying with the Actors Lab in California, and Steve McQueen was taken into acting classes by Steven Meisner in New York. Jackson Pollock had a mentor in the Manual Arts High School in Los Angeles, a public school specializing in industrial arts, where he studied art under Frederick St. Vrain Schwankovsky. When he went to New York City and studied at the Art Students League, he was taken under the wing of Thomas Hart Benton, a well-known American realistic artist whose work Pollock's own later paintings would have nothing in common with.

The large numbers of mentors and course work in or out of universities suggest that individuals do not become "overnight successes" without training, and that for this group activities like acting, painting, and music were somewhat accessible—and so a university education was less necessary.

Travel or the ability to travel to gain work is an important component of advancing. In a mobile economy, being in the right place at the right time can be critical. Theodore Dreiser's move from Indiana to Chicago and then to New York was important to both his reporting career and his writing career. Jack London's geographical mobility uniquely helped his writing career—particularly his trip to the Klondike in Alaska, which provided him the environment of some of his famous stories. Jack Johnson began his travels as a young teenager and was able to test his boxing skills across the East and gain training from some established boxers. Charlie Chaplin took a great and successful risk in moving to the United States with the Karno Company, which paid off handsomely. Richard Wright's move from the South to Chicago was key in the shaping of both his writing and activism in the Communist Party. Jackson Pollock, Steve McQueen, and Richard Pryor made the frequent decision of artists and actors to move to New York City, where all eventually found success.

Several subjects' marriages are worth mentioning. Margaret Sanger and Edna St. Vincent Millay gained some financial stability by "marrying up," Sanger prior to her fame, but Millay afterward. At least two men—Jackson Pollock and Johnny Cash—gained considerable stability through marriage. Pollock's marriage to artist Lee Krasner particularly gave him a stalwart advocate for his work (to the exclusion of her own success). Cash's greatest accomplishments were while June Carter was his partner. I have mentioned as well Babe Ruth's second marriage as a major stabilizing force in curtailing his many habits that could have taken him out of professional baseball sooner.

Finally, social movements were critical to some of our subjects' success—most obviously, Elizabeth Gurley Flynn and Fannie Lou Hamer, whose notoriety came from movements. But others in our sample saw movements play an important role in their lives. Margaret Sanger began her birth control movement as a member of the Socialist Party, and later used her notoriety to branch off independently. Edna St. Vincent Millay benefited both intellectually and in terms of her reputation by association with the radical Village crowd of the 1910s. Richard Pryor also benefited when he took time off from his comedy career in the late 1960s and made his home in Berkeley, California, where he associated with political radical Angela Davis, novelists Ishmael Reed and Claude Brown, and Black Panther leader Huey Newton, among others (Pryor 1995, pp. 115–120). Pryor's change to a more radical comic and voice of the black lower classes came out of this experience.

The roles of all these elements—education and less formal mentoring and course work, travel, marriage, and social movements—in our subjects' success are all clearer than in most cases. To answer why they became famous, though, much of it boils down to luck and skill.

BECOMING FAMOUS

As I will stress in this chapter, fame as a commodity is limited, even if its contours are hard to know and quantify. Later in the chapter I will show how being poor was more of a barrier to fame in the earlier years of our study than in later years, when a mass market and a popular culture was open in some cases to accepting poor people. The role of segmented markets in the later twentieth century (and twenty-first century) is important as well, as it is now possible for entertainment and communication industries to target groups by race and ethnicity, age, geography, and even make money from relatively small groups if they are well targeted (e.g., it is not necessary for national majorities to like a "hip-hop" singer as long as he or she earns the company enough money).

Even so, there are figures where chance still looms large in their fame. We can spell out the type of society that the "miracle worker" gained her acclaim in, better than why it was Anne Sullivan or why it specifically happened in 1887. Clearly, when Sullivan was sent to Alabama no one could know—Sullivan or Keller or Sullivan's mentor Anagnos—what would result. Marilyn Monroe's career in the scope of her success also relied a lot on chance as well as talent. There had been sex goddesses before, and some—Clara Bow and Lana Turner come to mind—were from the lower classes. Monroe's posing for nude pictures could not have been predicted to have such a key effect on her worldwide fame as an image of sexuality. In retrospect, the fame of Monroe had to be predicated on the decline of American Puritanism, which we will touch on below in relation particularly to the lower classes and the legal display of sexuality, which affected Theodore Dreiser and Margaret Sanger in very different ways than Monroe. The post–World War II culture of prosperity and rising image of the male breadwinner and housewife may have made a fitting, if paradoxical, environment for Monroe's fame.

Those who wrote, painted, sang, or acted had to have great abilities and skills, but they also had to be appropriate for their times. Dreiser's work, which remains powerful today, was accepted with difficulty for reasons of censorship and the dominant culture's hesitancy to accept his naturalist style. By the 1920s when he wrote *The American Tragedy*, America seemed more ready than it had been when his first book, *Sister Carrie*, was published. Jack London did not suffer these problems with his male youth–oriented stories and books, but he could not have been successful only a few years earlier, before there was enough of a literate market. This resulted in large part from the era's mandatory public schooling for children. Edna St. Vincent Millay's poetry also crosses time, but the new freedom for women in the 1920s and the radical changes of the 1910s–1930s structured most of her writing. William Saroyan's brief success occurred during the Great Depression, when his sentimental paeans to the average "Joe and Jane" gained a high degree of recognition. Richard Wright could probably not have expected an audience for a novel by a black man, particularly books as grim as *Black Boy* and *Native Son*, before the Great Depression and early 1940s. Yet, of course, afterward other great African American writers would arise, such as James Baldwin and Ralph Ellison.

It is hard to predict except by retrospective history when people will succeed. Jackson Pollock spent much of his life not as an abstract painter and was not well known. His ability to break into a new paradigm of totally abstract painting with his famous drip method made him famous, but he had help from critic Clem Greenberg, who was very much a figure of 1940s America. Billie Holiday's singing gained acceptance during the opening up of black music, blues, jazz, and later rock in the early and mid-twentieth century. Her success in many ways was (like Pollock's) more posthumous as people got a lasting chance to listen to her recordings after her death. Both Pollock and Holiday's severe personal problems also limited their ability to enjoy the fruits of what they accomplished while living. Johnny Cash had a couple of careers, the first coming in the 1950s when he broke into a nascent musical genre (along with Elvis Presley and Roy Orbison) that combined country, black music, and rock. Starting in the late 1960s, his persona of the "man in black" and his association with prisons and American folk music made him famous to a broader audience of Americans.

Actors and sports stars are both time bound and *sui generis*. Charlie Chaplin, as we shall explore below, was part of a revolution in popular culture that with film, and later other popular media like radio and television, democratized taste. He may well have paved the way for others of the lower class by the acceptance of the antics of the "tramp" throughout the culture despite initial highbrow opposition to his character and the medium of film in general. Being British, whereby the tramp and similar characters had a history in vaudeville, also made his American presence more unique. Steve McQueen, who in many ways played himself, was a product of the post–World War II anti-Puritanical, "cool" American persona that Hollywood and other cultural carriers would take to other parts of the world. Jack Johnson and Babe Ruth, both great sports stars, were also creatures of their times. Eventually being a black heavyweight boxing champion would be less newsworthy, but it also was true that the lesson of Jack Johnson made many African American sports figures (and other stars) watch their personal behavior carefully. As we will discuss, Babe Ruth came at an important time in baseball history and his home-run hitting helped make professional baseball a huge success. The failure of others who have made or neared his record suggests how socially constructed fame is to a particular time.

Margaret Sanger struggled in the aftermath of Puritanism's grip to make birth control legal. Malcolm X came to fame at the time of the beginning of the civil rights movement, and while not originally intended, his voice eventually became a lower-class counter to the more restrained mainstream civil rights movement of Martin Luther King Jr. He is probably more famous in his afterlife as a symbol that many African Americans and others cling to, though the symbol is a bit emptied of meaning.

POVERTY AND FAME AT DIFFERENT TIMES

What part did being poor or coming from a poor background play in our subjects' success, and to what degree was it a hindrance? I suggest that at least early on, being poor served as a barrier to fame as gatekeepers were reluctant to convey established laurels on them. Anne Sullivan was an example. While the popular press hailed the "miracle worker" and Helen Keller, those involved with the blind and with "charities," as the nonprofits were then called, found it incredulous that a pauper could rise to high status. There was a fight over Sullivan's status, with class and ethnicity being an issue. Writer Theodore Dreiser and Margaret Sanger had to challenge the power of established censorship and notions of decorum and morality to become successful, and their work was blocked for intertwined reasons of politics, religion, and proper taste. Although his fame may have been pivotal to broader change, Charlie Chaplin also confronted some "blow back" from established church and other voluntary groups who saw the "tramp" as promoting bad values and behavior.

The development of a mass market and a new popular culture appears to have changed the rules considerably about what type of character was desirable for fame. While it is true that "the log cabin myth" had long been around in politics as a populist symbol, in actuality, such symbolism often did not reflect real poverty as much as a "self-made man" of the middle class (most "log cabin" presidents did not come from poor backgrounds), nor did this populism extend into many other realms of fame besides politics. Rather, the Charlie Chaplins, Babe Ruths, John Garfields, Billie Holidays, and others in our sample served as important markers in a new era of the common man or woman who might even be crude or unruly but still "make it" with the public.

A word of caution is in order about the achievement of fame as a type of social status. Fame brings a certain legitimacy to people among a large audience, but it does not necessarily imply acceptance into high-class or high-status venues, and it does not lead necessarily to high social class. While like social class, status is a desired state, it is more particular by its nature to the arena in which it is achieved. That is, while money no matter how made (even criminal enterprises or disapproved occupations) will eventually buy a certain amount of class, status as a symbolic order of privilege is much more dependent on the nature of how it was achieved. So, for example, fields such as boxing have long been dominated by lower-class people. Being a political organizer like

Malcolm X or Elizabeth Gurley Flynn may give you status from some people but hatred from many other people. High-status people, at least until recently, did not much recognize these types of status. We might say that fame and status became more complex in the twentieth century; some people won over the mass market with a combination of achievement and symbolic appeal, yet their social life was often limited, such as was the case with Babe Ruth and Billie Holiday. Despite humble origins, others might win prizes or awards that convey higher status, such as some of our later-born figures like Johnny Cash and Richard Pryor. Finally, fame does not ensure high social class. Among others, Edna St. Vincent Millay, William Saroyan, Richard Wright, Jackson Pollock, Billie Holliday, and Richard Pryor ended up without much money, as of course did those famous for political organizing such as Elizabeth Gurley Flynn, Fannie Lou Hamer, and Malcolm X.

Despite this caution, the democratization of status and fame did parallel changes in the twentieth century that led to hard-fought new forms of equality, such as the civil rights movement, the struggle for women's equality, and the gradual acceptance of different ethnic and religious cultures in the United States. So, for example, while the acceptance of Richard Wright as a great writer and Billie Holiday as a great singer did not immediately signal a shift in African American rights, their accomplishments are certainly milestones along the way. The large number of ethnic movie heroes (Jewish, Irish, Italian) similarly were both causes and effects of the acceptance (and assimilation) of white ethnic groups. Not every woman added to an image of women's equality, but certainly Edna St. Vincent Millay, Billie Holiday, and Fannie Lou Hamer did. Marilyn Monroe struggled against the sexualization she herself helped create, but she was blocked from ever completely leaving this image.

NINETEENTH-CENTURY CLASS AND STATUS SYSTEMS

Despite the widespread myth of democracy in America, and the more fluid economic system of preindustrial America, if anything, social status played an even larger role in stratifying society in this period of American history. The elite classes of the major cities in the East and later the South and Midwest lived in a different world from not only the lower classes but different ethnic groups and all those who were not white property owners of Protestant descent. The nation was also deeply stratified by region and place of living. Western settlers and rural folk who were not large landowners were in a different world. Many of the movements of the nineteenth century—the Bible Tract Societies, the temperance movement against alcohol, the YMCAs and later Salvation Army, the first women's movement, the Sunday School movement, and the movement for poorhouses, mental asylums, prisons, and orphanages, for example—were grounded in white Protestantism, a segment of US society that was fearful of the large numbers of immigrants and poor and working people, whom Charles Loring Brace called the "dangerous classes" (Brace 1872). Nineteenth-century historians describe these movements as being part of the "status anxiety" of white Protestants (see, for example, Gusfield 1963; Rothman 1971).

Religion, language and accent, behavioral norms, a person's family background, their residence—all these and other characteristics had to be assessed by those who shaped opinion. Moreover, gatekeepers were not in a position to allow different norms or opinions to be propagated if they could help it. Hence while some praise the nineteenth century as a populist republic more open to people, in fact, for women, African Americans, Native Americans, paupers, and also immigrant groups like the Irish and even Germans, this was not quite the case. Nor was it the case for those who favored opinions different from the norm.

It is for these reasons that a number of our early subjects found it difficult to achieve success and a degree of status even in the late part of the nineteenth century and into the twentieth century (although things were beginning to change, as we shall see). Anne Sullivan's teaching of Helen Keller would make her suddenly famous, but both were subject to attack, particularly Sullivan, because as an Irish pauper she was not believed by many people to be a creditable or as worthy a successor to the more Brahmin Samuel Gridley Howe. Both Theodore Dreiser and Margaret Sanger were met by hostility to their messages but also the mediums they used, and both confronted one of the most powerful men in Victorian-era America: Anthony Comstock, America's chief censor. Still, the success of Jack London (1876–1916) despite his radical views is illustrative of how the opening of new markets—in his case for young people's books—helped provide an arena where someone could achieve success despite his or her modest beginnings.

DIFFICULTIES FOR POOR PEOPLE IN ACHIEVING FAME: SULLIVAN, DREISER, AND SANGER

Status as well as social class prejudices did make it hard to achieve fame for our subjects, at least through the end of the nineteenth century. As

I have said earlier, it would remain hard for poor people to gain fame in the twentieth and twenty-first centuries; however, the opening of a mass market and more inclusive popular culture made some areas such as entertainment and sports more accessible.

Anne Sullivan's well-known teaching of Helen Keller in 1887 quickly made her (and Helen Keller) famous through the day's newspapers and other sources. The teaching of a deaf-mute appealed to the sense of the times; that people regarded as "dumb" and "mute" could be reached seemed to reflect the optimistic nature of the Victorian era's belief in the power of the supernatural at work. Still, there were large parts of the public who insisted that the story was "too good to be true," and that Sullivan was either making up what Keller said or force-feeding Keller lines that she interpreted. Although some of the skepticism was due to Keller's unbelievable intellect and keen memory for such a young child, the discovery that Sullivan was an Irish woman who was for years a poorhouse inmate was a major discrediting theme for their opponents. In Boston, then still a seat of the elite Brahmins, the power of the Howe family (Julia Ward Howe, the widow of Samuel Gridley Howe, her children, and her son-in-law Michael Anagnos, the director of the Perkins School, perhaps the most prestigious school for the blind) as well as hero worshippers of Howe disputed Sullivan's credentials as Keller's teacher. This battle ensued for much of the 1890s and the first decade of the 1900s. Not only did the prestigious Perkins School for the Blind drive out Sullivan and Keller with a trial charging the twelve-year-old Keller with plagiarism (although the "trial" ended in a tie vote, it was clearly meant to embarrass them) but later those connected to Perkins published an anonymous 158-page booklet called "Miss Sullivan's Methods," which implied that Sullivan helped Keller plagiarize and that the words in Keller's first book, *The Story of My Life*, were actually the words of Sullivan (Wagner 2012a, chapter 5). In a formal motion, longtime abolitionist and transcendentalist Franklin Benjamin Sanborn asked the trustees of Perkins to endorse a resolution claiming Sullivan had no real role in Keller's teaching and censoring her for being a "bad influence" on Keller (Wagner 2012a).

Although the long battle did not succeed in eliminating Sullivan as a famous person, it did cause her to take a "back seat" and vow never to talk to the media again. She was as an interpreter extremely careful to provide Keller's opinions, not her own, as time went by. When Keller became a socialist in the 1910s, Sullivan and her husband, John Macy, received hostile press coverage, charging them with being "Marxist propagandists" because of Keller's views (Wagner 2012a, chapter 6). The venture into radical politics by Keller and the Sullivan-Macys brought intense hostility, and since most of their funding came from speeches and events, the attack caused their income to dry up. By 1918, Keller and Sullivan were reduced to doing vaudeville. Nevertheless, the strength of popular culture in the mid- to late twentieth century kept alive the "miracle worker's" fame. The American Federation of the Blind traces some of the history of the myth-making, including a Wonder Woman cartoon from 1945 glorifying Sullivan Macy (see AFB website). By the 1950s there was a play called *The Miracle Worker* based on Sullivan and Keller, and, in the 1960s, the famous movie of the same name starring Anne Bancroft and Patty Duke. Still, it should be noted that like some others of our subjects, Sullivan's posthumous fame did not gain her status or money during her life. Sullivan was never accepted by the public in the way Keller would eventually be, and she had very little money when she died in 1936.

Writer Theodore Dreiser and activist Margaret Sanger found themselves on the wrong side of the strong line in Victorian times between respectability and obscenity. It is striking in a nation if anything now obsessed with talk of sex, that for many generations, not only was the mention of sex forbidden but a dominant script was that the respectable must triumph and those without virtue had to be defeated. The latter norms were enforced as late as the 1930s, when the Hays Code for movies demanded that movies show criminals being defeated by police or the FBI (only in the 1960s was this code relaxed). In the years before a mass popular culture, codes of conduct and even the telling of stories were enforced by publishers, newspapers, politicians, and officials of churches and voluntary organizations.

Dreiser, whom biographer Jerome Loving calls "the first great American novelist from the wrong side of town" (Loving 2005, p. 92), was educated by his hardscrabble life and felt a kinship for all those who feared failure in American society. When he moved from doing menial work to being a reporter, he naturally gravitated to and covered what he saw, which included the underside of life. He sympathized with the laboring man and the unemployed. It is not surprising that in his dreams of wanting to be a writer he brought his passion for describing what he saw, and he would be one of America's first writers in the "naturalist school," who would present "sordid conditions" including drunks, domestic violence, illicit sex, and the "flotsam and jetsam" of society (Loving 2005, pp. 50, 51).

Yet Dreiser's first novel, *Sister Carrie*, which would become the first great novel of the twentieth century, almost did not make it to publication, and when it did, as Richard Lingeman notes, it went "through a minefield of censorship, prejudice, and snobbery, clearing a path for the generation that went over the top after him" (Lingeman 1986, p. 13). *Sister Carrie* was one of the most explicit books about social class in America and how in Darwinian terms people were competing to climb the rungs of success and many were falling. Not only did the book include illicit sex, but its script defied the Victorian conventions. Carrie, a prostitute, not only survives the story but is not punished, while other characters such as arrivists Hurstwood and Drouet fall and fail. Virtue does not win out. As Lingeman notes, Dreiser's attitude is not at all moral, it is scientific, creating what he calls "the most realistic gallery of urbanites yet to appear in an American novel" up to that time (pp. 247, 255).

The publisher Harper rejected *Sister Carrie* and doubted that any publisher "would touch it because of the reigning standards of decency." Dreiser was crushed, says Loving, "believing he had written a novel in the tradition of Balzac and Hardy" (Loving 2005, pp. 153–154). But Doubleday had expressed interest and Dreiser gained two positive reviews. Suddenly then, the company balked. One persistent historical rumor (but evidently not true) was that Doubleday's wife had read the book manuscript and strongly advised her husband not to publish it. Evidently it was a third reviewer who would tell the publisher that this book was not the kind of book that would interest ladies and gentlemen or the great majority of Doubleday's readers (Loving 2005, p. 155). Doubleday felt forced by previous letters to publish the book but did so in a way that did little or nothing to publicize the book. As Lingeman notes, the "book was outfitted in the drabbest possible cover, [and] the title was not even listed in the [Doubleday] catalogue" (1986, p. 294). Dreiser made a dismal $68.40 in royalties for a book that later would be one of the American classics, but at the time was denounced by the few critics who read it as "godless." Lingeman points out that "censorship was used by the dominant class" at this time "to banish truth by branding it as obscenity" (p. 333). Dreiser was so distraught he would suffer a nervous breakdown, fearing that he had become "a literary pariah, shunned by editors, friends, and relatives alike" (Lingeman 1986, p. 306).

Interestingly, as Dreiser went to a sanitarium, the book was much better reviewed in England, where a tradition of literary independence and freedom from censorship was more established. Still, it would take a full seven years from *Sister Carrie*'s first publication in 1900 for Dreiser, then working as a women's magazine publisher, to accumulate enough money to buy the plates to his own book. With the plates, he was able to convince a British publisher, B. W. Dodge, to republish it. Dodge used the American censorship as a tease to help its publication, and it sold its initial run in ten days. By 1908 *Sister Carrie* had sold 10,000 copies.

It is difficult to describe what a marker this was in the literary world. For here was an author who was willing to tell "it as it is" and bring the situation of America's cities, its poor, its prostitutes, beggars, and its ruthless competing businessmen into the open with no moral precept to favor the status quo and capitalist system. Something like this had been seen, of course, in political pamphlets and underground alternative presses, but not in the major literary world. Dreiser would never forget this experience despite his success; he distrusted publishers and all the people at the top of society, and he moved more and more into an open socialist position as the years went on.

Like Dreiser, Margaret Sanger's passion stemmed directly from her poor upbringing. She was the sixth of what would be eleven children born to her mother, Annie Higgins. Sanger was convinced her mother's early death at age forty-eight from tuberculosis came from her weakened condition of constant pregnancies and the burden of caring for her house and so many children. When Sanger became a nurse, she heard over and over from poor women, "how do we control our childbirths?" or "please tell us the secrets of not having more children" (Topalian 1984; Chesler 2007). But birth control was an utterly taboo subject. Its mention in print was a federal offense. Only Emma Goldman of the radical left had dared talk of this before Sanger. In fact some on the Left were angry that Sanger never attributed her inspiration to the radical anarchist. Ben Reitman claimed Sanger simply stole her ideas and that their intense rivalry made Sanger never mention Goldman's name. Reitman claimed Goldman did more than any other person to popularize birth control (Chesler 2007, p. 75). In any event, after Sanger joined the socialist movement she wasted no time and championed birth control. She could find no publisher but the socialist *Call*, but when the US Postal Service saw her column "What Every Woman Should Know," it stopped the run, and the *Call* ran a blank page with a headline "What Every Girl Should Know! Nothing! By Order of the Post Office Department" (Topalian 1984, p. 34).

Since everyone in America knew that the censor-in-chief would stop any information on birth control or for that matter anything with explicit or implicit reference to sex from being mailed, Sanger actually was intentionally provocative. Her paper the *Woman Rebel* held the radical slogan of the IWW, "No Gods, No Masters!" Printer after printer refused to print it, terming it a "Sing Sing job"—that is, that they would end up in jail. Her father and the rest of her family of origin were shocked; thinking Margaret had had a nervous breakdown, they asked her to go to a sanitarium (Topalian 1984, p. 51). In 1914 she was indicted on nine counts by the US government, but she had already left the country. Her husband, however, was arrested in her stead, and upon her return she was reindicted. Later found not guilty, she was indicted on charges of handing out birth control literature and sent to a New York City workhouse.

It seems amazing that less than a century ago in the United States social policy relating to sexual information was based on total censorship. Did people support this? Policy makers drawn mostly from white Protestant small towns, particularly in certain parts of the nation, certainly did support this. Like behavior ranging from drinking to boxing to playing cards to viewing pornography, open talk about sex was seen as godless, immoral, and lower class to boot! There were, however, professionals and intellectuals who thought such censorship ludicrous, and many ethnic groups who were less represented in the halls of power did not necessarily agree with such policies.

Sanger would spend most of her life locked in combat, but a major change was on the horizon. By the late 1910s, *Harper's Weekly* offered its readers a long series on family limitation. The magazine defined the issue in scientific terms, not moral terms (Chesler 2007, p. 129). A key victory was the gradual persuasion of many physicians that if they did not take over the task of counseling women about birth control, radicals or nonprofessionals would do so (after all, the American Medical Association had fought bitterly against providers of abortion and against midwives, both from a competitive vantage point). Eventually, though it took until the 1930s, the medical community legitimized the use of birth control under the care of a doctor. Sanger would never convince the Roman Catholic Church to support birth control, and she changed her public persona by allying with medical authorities and promoting clinics where birth control information could be dispensed. Eventually she was not seen as a radical, but a reform lobbyist.

Although of course there would be many for whom Sanger continued to arouse anger and contempt (including those that remembered her as a socialist), the change in Sanger's fortune suggests the early twentieth century was a time when norms and mores were changing. Women, who were struggling for the suffrage, were no longer content with the status quo, and modern medicalization of personal issues of many sorts was starting. For many people the idea of discussion of family limitation gradually became legitimate. And, of course, as has been pointed out, there became nothing left-wing about this issue as the promoters of eugenics were at their heyday in the 1920s and early 1930s, and were suggesting family limitation might be useful in eliminating unproductive citizens, an idea later picked up by Nazi Germany.

CHARLIE CHAPLIN AS A BREAKTHROUGH STAR

Although the battle to represent the poor, the working class, immigrants, and the many nondominant American cultures would go on for many decades in American popular culture, the immediate and total success of Charlie Chaplin and his character of the tramp is an important milestone in the decline of the old norms of the Victorian status society and the rise of new mass culture in twentieth-century America.

First, the fact that Chaplin came out of British vaudeville, which was intensely class conscious, was an important factor. Tramps as well as inebriates had a longer comic history in the music halls of England, and, in fact, Chaplin did among the best impressions of the latter before taking on his tramp character. While Chaplin described the process whereby he came to the tramp in his autobiography as a contradiction "with baggy pants, big shoes, a cane and a derby hat … the coat tight, the hat small, and the shoes large" (Chaplin 1964, p. 145) there was no question that the tramp by his looks was and acted as a poor person and was extremely anti-authority to boot. Second, the fact that Chaplin, unlike most actors or directors, would retain complete control over his work did not make him easily susceptible to the kind of pressure other entertainers then felt from the studio system and from critics. Steven Ross calls Chaplin "the first political movie star" in that he

> was at the vanguard of a new form of political communication that bypassed traditional authority figures and spoke directly to millions of immigrants and working-class people who felt as though no one cared

about them ... [while] his silent films did not promote communism ... they did mock the power and legitimacy of those who gave ordinary Americans a hard time; employers, foremen, police, judges, the idle rich, and even world leaders. (Ross 2011, p. 12)

Chaplin explained his comedy not in political terms at the time, but in terms of getting the most laughs:

Did you ever see what happens when a policeman in uniform slips on a greasy street and takes a tumble? The policeman's uniform and his club are symbols of authority. He is a power in the land. When he slips and gets mussed up the crowd shrieks with laughter. Why? Well, even good people have a sneaking dislike for a "cop." They like to see him get a tumble. Visualize a bloated capitalist with Dundreary whiskers, light trousers, spats, frock coat, silk hat—all the insignia of a million dollars ... even the most inoffensive among us has some time or other considered the idea of pulling those whiskers.... (quoted in Louvish 2009, pp. 112–113)

Chaplin's anti-authoritarian tramp hit the United States in 1914 and within one year made him a millionaire. Already in 1914, his name was so well-known that *The Knockout* was advertised as a "Charlie Chaplin film" (Robinson 1994, p. 124). In 1915 there was, as David Robinson puts it, "the great Chaplin explosion": "every newspaper carried cartoons and poems about him. He became a character in cartoon strips ... there were Chaplin dolls, toys, books ... Ida Lupino sang 'that Charlie Chaplin Walk'" (p. 152).

What is fascinating is, not unlike previous low-income heroes or symbols, Chaplin was attacked. Robinson notes, "his fame was at its zenith here in America when suddenly the critics made a dead set at him ... they roasted his work wholesale; called it crude, ungentlemanly and risqué, even indecent" (1994, p. 146). Some examples that are quoted in different sources include a speaker at the Woman's Alliance at a Unitarian Church who called him "a moral menace. His is a low type of humor that appeals only to the lowest type of intellect. I cannot understand how any resident of Flatbush can go see [the films]" (cited in Robinson 1994, p. 213). In the *Minneapolis Tribune*, Chaplin's character, particularly "when the tramp was drunk," was cited as disturbing Minneapolis teachers and ministers along with film thrillers' vice, uncensored Wild West films, and actresses "sans clothing" (cited in

Louvish 2009, p. 120). A pastor in a Detroit church was quoted in the *Detroit News* as saying, "Low Grade Persons Only Like Charlie Chaplin and Mary Pickford" (Ross 2011, p. 15), and the paper noted that "the fact that Charlie Chaplin now receives the largest salary paid to any man in the United States ... is clear evidence of the enormous numbers of the low-grade, unintelligent, shallow-minded men and women in the United States" (Louvish 2009, p. 121).

What is interesting about these attacks—as well as a general attack on the movies as being "coarse," "vulgar," and "crude"—was how little the critical attack mattered to the American people. Films were enormously popular, particularly with immigrants and working people; as Steven Ross notes, to "many of whom could neither read nor understand English, movies provided an important visual language that allowed them to see what was happening in the nation" (2011, pp. 16–17). Gwendolyn Foster, quoting cultural critic Andrew Ross, noted more than that,

> film broke down isolation of different immigrant groups from culture and from one another. Charlie Chaplin and Buster Keaton were role models as much of the humor in these films comes from being able to identify with the on-screen plight of the hero. Many could identify with his unemployment, his hope for a better future, and his quest for the American Dream. (Foster 2005, p. 9)

In his book about the clash of popular culture and high culture, Herbert Gans noted how the poor quality of popular culture would become a major theme for "highbrow" culture, the "fear being that with increasing leisure time, the more intensified use of mass culture would lead to boredom, discontent, and possibly even social chaos." Originally upper-status people aimed their criticism at the music hall, the tavern, and the brothel, but "from about the 1920s to the 1950s, [they] focused on movies, comic books, radio, and spectator sports" (Gans 1975, p. 4).

As many experts would be correct to argue, popular culture is hardly without its controls. In many ways, it is extremely hard today to become a Charlie Chaplin, particularly with his brand of politics and anti-authoritarianism. Nevertheless, once someone becomes highly popular he or she is far more immune to the forces of religion, highbrow criticism, or the censorship that prevailed in the old status-bound society. They are more subject perhaps to informal screening out and to the desires of publishers, movie companies, and music producers and other major corporate centers of culture, for example, to be noncontroversial. Still, Americans have grown to enjoy their heroes, and at least a percentage of them can now be from humbler origins, particularly if the person fits other needs of the market (targeting specific minority groups, women, youth, or other market segments). In this sense, many of our later figures can thank Chaplin for preceding them, as it proved that the market surpassed status concerns in twentieth-century America.

NEW SPACE FOR PEOPLE FROM THE BOTTOM

The new mass culture market now began to thrive on images of the "everyman," including some people from the lower classes. The needs of new mass consumer capitalism to appeal to wide interests made it become more comfortable with styles that earlier were called "crude" or "vulgar." Babe Ruth certainly could be this, both on the field—when he literally chased yelling fans up the stadium steps with a bat—or outside of work, where his prodigious eating and drinking caused wild scenes. Yet Babe Ruth was not only the most popular baseball player of all time but the one man who made baseball enormously popular. Often popularity started in Bohemia, a demimonde now associated with higher class but initially just the opposite, a part of the city with cheap rents that allowed artists to mingle with the poor. It was this environment that the 1920s' most popular woman, Edna St. Vincent Millay, came out of. She combined a background in poverty with the new hipness and radicalism of Greenwich Village (which included the likes of Floyd Dell, Max Eastman, Eugene O'Neill, John Reed, and others). Similarly, Billie Holiday was one of a group of African American entertainers who combined a ghetto background with an appeal to white "hipsters" who went out of their way to hear jazz and blues. No doubt some found these people "vulgar" as they would the new movie heroes from John Garfield and Jimmy Cagney to Steve McQueen. Yet again the opinion of the "highbrow" sorts of critics or the church or civic groups mattered little to the entertainment industry, and the same can be said for country music stars (Johnny Cash is an example, despite his official rejection by country music officials) and, for the great comedian of African American lower-class society, Richard Pryor.

It is always hard to look at history through a retrospective lens and analyze what aspects of people made them popular, and what the results would be had they not lived or accomplished what they did. Clearly, though, professional baseball owed much to Babe Ruth, gangster movies owed much to John Garfield, African American (and particularly ghetto) culture to Malcolm X, Hollywood to Steve McQueen, the music industry to Johnny Cash, and the modern comedy business to Richard Pryor. A variety of entertainment industries owe much to Marilyn Monroe, who following in the footsteps of other women born poor (like Lana Turner and Jean Harlow) made open sexuality a major American cultural trait and export.

BABE RUTH, JOHN GARFIELD, MALCOLM X, MARILYN MONROE, AND POPULAR CULTURE

As noted, professional baseball in the pre-Ruth era was hardly the "national pastime" or a big business. As biographer Marshall Smelser notes, "Babe Ruth and the conditions of profitable baseball arrived on the American scene at the same time, the crowds could be in the park because of the rise of the city, the trolley line to the park, [and] the free time of working people" (Smelser 1975, p. 59). No doubt someone or some number of players might arise had Ruth not lived. But Ruth was so valuable to baseball for what he provided both on the field and off. First, on the field was the home run. Ruth was a fantastic pitcher, but he would never have made history that way. Rather, his transformation to a batter allowed him to discover that fans loved home runs. Ruth himself in 1919 commented in surprise that "the fans would rather see me hit one homer to right than three doubles to left" (Creamer 1974, p. 115). The American National Biography Online gives Ruth credit for "home-run hitting [that] transformed baseball's style of play from [a] low-scoring, 'scientific' game, with its emphasis on pitching and defense, to the explosive, 'big bang' style that continues in part to this day."

But heroes, particularly those who change a sport or an industry, need more than physical prowess. After all, Lou Gehrig, who also was from a poor background, achieved many records before his untimely death in a similar time period. Smelser remarks that "folklore demands that the muscle hero live riotously and leave tales of revelry and sprees" and that Ruth gave people this (1975, p. 142). Babe Ruth

> became the idol of everybody who would like to flout every rule of conduct and still be a champion ... he took up vices that most poor Baltimore waterfront slobs would have liked to follow if they became rich ... he was a plain-spoken, unpolished provincial general suddenly raised

by his men to be Emperor, he was the most conspicuous high liver, said to have trained on scotch. (Smelser 1975, pp. 142–143)

Of course, Ruth's lifestyle would probably be frowned upon now, but we must recall that the 1920s and 1930s were an age of exuberant rebellion by working-class and poor people (and by nonrural Protestants) against the regime of Prohibition, which symbolized the rich and Protestant control over average people's pleasures. Moreover, as Edna St. Vincent Millay played a role in, this was the era of the "flapper" and a rebellion by women against the staid dress and behavior of middle-class Puritanism.

But unlike more remote sports stars, Ruth "seemed totally dependent on the appreciation and admiration of others, he had the common touch that politicians needed, his honest indifference to social standing may not have pleased people of status but it delighted the crowd" (Smelser 1975, p. 148). Ruth was a universal hero, always mentioned in the daily press including his bodily measurements, his alleged diet, and his daily record. When he visited the George M. Cohan Theater to publicize a police widow's benefit, he drew a crowd of 15,000 and stopped traffic for nearly forty-five minutes. Ruth's childlike pleasure in his success and his loyalty to his fans helped make him a hero as well as benefited the storied New York Yankees and baseball. His ability to attract thousands of children rested on his sincere ability to get along with them, and his constant visitation to orphanages and other institutions for children.

Although comparisons across time are always speculative, the failure of recent home-run hitters who challenged Ruth's record can be contrasted to Ruth. Roger Maris, the virtually colorless New York hitter, who got an asterisk next to his name, excited more anger in chasing Ruth than support. Although the competition between hitters Mark McGwire and Sammy Sosa did gain more attention and media coverage, neither in this day of relatively "cool" television coverage (where displays of emotion are extremely risky) did either fully flesh out a unique personality; nor did Barry Bonds receive much support at all. Of course, nostalgia may account for some of this, but there is also a sense that Ruth "earned" his records in a way more recent hitters did not (this has been compounded by the revelation of many modern ball players' use of steroids).

The great actor of the 1930s and 1940s John Garfield today has nowhere near the fame of a Charlie Chaplin or Babe Ruth. Nevertheless, his career marked part of an important milestone in Hollywood's representation of folk heroes who came from the ranks of the poor.

According to Robert Sklar, who analyzed actors James Cagney, John Garfield, and Humphrey Bogart, by 1929 the gangster had surpassed the cowboy as a folk hero, and initially Garfield was seen as another Cagney (Sklar 1992, pp. 8, 88). But Garfield actually would be, as biographer John Nott noted, "the first 'rebel' actor in film history: the one who opened the door to all other cinematic anti-heroes to step through—Brando, Clift, McQueen, Newman and De Niro" (Nott 2004, p. xi). Although the America of the Great Depression found gangsters heroic, the film code and its enforcers opposed the making of heroes out of criminals as immoral, and Garfield (like the Brandos and Clifts of the future) was more ambiguous. As Sklar writes, "He transmitted an uncanny rapport with the young, rootless, working-class city boys ... more victim than rebel, more social case than social phenomenon, more a pouter than a fighter, the Garfield screen persona was a reactive, a product of environment and chance" (1992, p. 88). The studios also found his New York City streets and Jewish immigrant background a plus. Warner Brothers, known as "the gangster studio," was interested in representing the underdog and had a special relationship with New York crowds because of the important income the market provided (Nott 2004, p. 76; Sklar 1992, p. 88).

A poor street boy who earlier had swept floors and cleaned toilets at the American Laboratory Theater, Garfield was eventually given roles as American theater became more "intimate, communal and political" (Nott 2004, p. 53). In the theater, Garfield began to reverse the shame he felt about his poverty and came to view it as "a badge of honor" (p. 66). His looks made him a Warner Brothers fit, "dark, brooding, street-smart and a native New Yorker to boot." As Nott describes it, these early rebels like Garfield, unlike some of the future heroes, had a cause, one that Depression-era America would empathize with. "They wanted a piece of the American pie, a place to live, a shot at life" (p. 88), or, as James Beaver puts it, "He epitomized the ideology of the common man for Depression and post-Depression America ... [he] was a loser who, in the final understanding, won out after all" (Beaver 1978, p. 43).

Unfortunately, in what would be a similar experience for other actors, Marilyn Monroe among them, Garfield was so successful he was typecast. Despite his protests, his roles again and again seemed a repeat of previous ones. His opposition to Hollywood studios led to repeated suspensions when he refused these roles. No doubt some of Garfield's drop from the historical canon came because of his untimely death (at age thirty-nine in 1952) and his ostracism as a result of the McCarthy period. Actors such as Humphrey Bogart, who actually shared much of Garfield's politics, made some better films and avoided career death at the hands of the House Un-American Activities Committee. (Interestingly, Bogart was from a more affluent background.)

Although entertainment and sports remain the most frequent vehicles for people of low-income status to rise, social movements have often helped move some charismatic leaders to fame. The labor movement, for example, had its heroes in the IWW's Elizabeth Gurley Flynn and Joe Hill, the Congress of Industrial Organization's John L. Lewis, and more recently the United Farmworkers Union's Cesar Chavez. Of course, not all movements arise from particularly poor people, and the movement leaders of some 1960s movements—such as the New Left and the women's movement—were more likely to come from the middle class. The African American civil rights movement, not surprisingly, gave rise to a number of leaders from the ranks of the poor such as Malcolm X and Fannie Lou Hamer, along with the Black Panther Party's Huey Newton and Eldridge Cleaver, among others. However, the role of more middle-class African Americans, such as Martin Luther King Jr., came to dominate the history books.

It is not surprising that for millions of African Americans, a poor black man who lived for years in the ghetto and then in prison and rehabilitated himself would become a hero. Malcolm's own writings and quotations in fact equate both his low social status and militant posture as necessary for black liberation:

> The only person who can organize the man in the street is the one who is unacceptable to the white community. (Quoted in Dyson 1995, p. 175)

> I believe that it would be almost impossible to find anywhere in America a black man who has lived further down in the mud of human society than I have; or a black man who has been any more ignorant than I have been; or a black man who has suffered more anguish during his life than I have. But it is only after the deepest darkness that the greatest joy can come. (Malcolm X 1965, p. 379)

Many commentators on Malcolm X see one of his assets with the black masses during his short time of fame as being his distrust for the middle-class African American leadership (see Dyson 1995; Wood 1992). Despite the growing success of the civil rights movement, even in 1963, Malcolm made fun of the lack of militancy of the civil rights march on Washington:

> Talk about "integrated!" It was like salt and pepper. And, by now, there wasn't a single logistics aspect uncontrolled. The marchers had been instructed to bring no signs—signs would be provided. They had been told to sing one song: "We Shall Overcome." They had been told how to arrive, when, where to arrive, where to assemble, when to start marching, and the route to march. First-aid stations were strategically located—even where to faint! Yes, I was there. I observed that circus. Who ever heard of angry revolutionists all harmonizing "We Shall Overcome ... Suum Day ..." while tripping and swaying along arm-in-arm with the very people they were supposed to be angrily revolting against. (Malcolm X 1965, pp. 280–281)

As Michael Dyson notes, "Few resources [were] available to blacks before Malcolm's oversized and defiant rhetoric rallied black rage and anger to their defense ... Malcolm's ... 'life was itself an accusation—a passage to the ninth circle of that black man's hell and back'" (1995, p. 47).

Of course, one could argue that the extremism of Malcolm and the Muslims in the late 1950s and early 1960s did much to enhance his and their fame among scared whites. The 1959 CBS documentary *The Hate That Hate Produced* brought millions of viewers to a heat of fear and fury after it presented the Black Muslims as white-hating revolutionaries. By 1963, Malcolm X was the second most requested speaker on the college circuit (with Barry Goldwater being first), and it would be naïve to believe at this time that the great majority of inviters were his supporters (Wood 1992, p. 10).

Malcolm X, then, was historic in his open expression of rage against white America, Christianity, and the dominant civilization of the West. But along with his militancy, the ambiguity of Malcolm's message also aided his fame. Killed while still a young man, Malcolm's ideas were changing rapidly in 1964–1965, and many writings have speculated on the many ways to characterize his thinking before his death. But this ambiguity, as with other young fallen leaders (one thinks of the Kennedy brothers also, for example), may well have helped make Malcolm retrospectively more of a hero than when he lived. Noting that the "paradox of Malcolm X ... [is] marketed in countless business endeavors and is stylishly branded on baseball hats and T-shirts by every age, race, and gender," Dyson believes "his moral perspective … most likely would have disdained rap's materialistic impulses to get paid, spurned its hedonistic joie de vivre, its celebration of vulgar expression" (1995, pp. xiii–ix).

Whether Dyson is right or not, one of the new features of fame in the late twentieth century and early twenty-first century is the increased role of symbolic fame emptied of content. To wear a hat with an X or a T-shirt with Malcolm's picture can convey many things, but the things are not specific any longer; their original reference to the Muslims or even the man are gradually being lost. They represent black pride and militancy, but when worn by non–African Americans they can convey broad sympathy with the movement or perhaps a kind of hipness. It is interesting that only in the 1990s, when leadership among African Americans was far more vague and contested than earlier, did the symbolism of Malcolm X take off. But there need not be any specific reason for this fame, either: Che Guevara, once a province of a small group of radicals, has become a popular poster, hat, and T-shirt as well, and who can even count the representations of nonpolitical icons such as Marilyn Monroe?

Interestingly, many of the poor women I have discussed are not spoken of in most biographies as representing in any way their social class background. That is, while biographers certainly review their subjects' childhood poverty, they tend (unlike Babe Ruth, Malcolm X, or Richard Pryor) to leave any adult connection to their subjects' background aside. While I will focus here on Marilyn Monroe, women like Edna St. Vincent Millay and Billie Holiday carried much social class symbolism as well as personal influences of social class with them. The fame of Millay was integrally connected with her symbolism of the "new woman" of the 1920s: the freer, cigarette-smoking and presumed sexuality of this new woman found its symbolism in Millay, who perhaps reflected some of the "best of both worlds" in her poor background and rebellious Vassar student persona. But it is important to remember that circa 1919–1920 both tobacco use and nonprocreative female sexuality were coded as the marks of poor women. All of the symbols of Millay's fame, even her clothes, were drawn as presenting a contrast of the new radical "poetess" with earlier female artists. Billie Holiday's music and lyrics were, of course, part of the underworld of African American life, and later, the Bohemian rebellion in the 1930s–1940s, which existed in the fringe America, also coded then as lower class. The visitation of some white middle-class people—as the Harlem Renaissance attracted visitors as well—does not detract from the point that this world was different, and marked ethnically and in social class ways as different from the mainstream.

Marilyn Monroe's rise to fame and her iconic sexuality were also coded as much by social class as gender (and unseen racial norms as well—it is difficult to imagine the rise of a nonwhite sexual idol at that time). Norma Jean's gradual rise from poverty and a miserable childhood was always partly a function of using sex to achieve mobility. Most biographies note the likelihood that she spent part of her early Hollywood days as a prostitute and provide large hints of her sleeping with her early producers. When it came to be public knowledge that she had posed nude for the famous calendar shots, Monroe appealed to the public based on her poverty; she only posed because she was out of work and without any way of support. As Spoto notes,

> She turned potential personal and professional disaster into conquest, gaining with this single deed unprecedented access to the press and a favorable publicity stage ... [because] of her candor and apparent purity of heart ... she ... appeared as innocent as a cherub in a Rembrandt painting. For weeks she humbly met the press, a grown-up ragamuffin straight from the pages of Dickens. (Spoto 1995, p. 212)

While, of course, it is speculative as to why Monroe was so quickly forgiven—both by her biographers and by other potential detractors about her sexual dalliances before her stardom and by the public and press about her nude appearances—it stands to reason that her social class was part of the reason, along with her beauty and seeming innocence, that she was so quickly forgiven. Monroe also skillfully played to an "all-American" blue-collar audience, not seeking out elite or even upper-middle-class support. Her well-advertised fondness for military men and her insistence that the American public, not her producers or directors or Hollywood in general, made her, were consistent. As Spoto notes, "She chose pictures of [her]self, she wanted a certain blue-collar appeal ... the presentation of a woman for the average working man, not the aristocrat" (1995, p. 477).

Monroe's "campness," which led to so much (and continued) posthumous fame and continued iconic presentations on seemingly a thousand objects, is in part about both her social class appeal and her ability to seem exaggeratedly sexy in an ironic sense. Monroe's poses and famous appearances were never subtle, they often appear "over the top" now because they seem "so 1950s" or so obvious. Yet it is hard to remember (for the culture) that famous blowing up of a skirt by the engineered wind had not been done before then, and that it was considered prurient enough for her then-husband Joe DiMaggio to beat her after its filming. Similarly, as Spoto notes, her songs such as "Diamonds Are a Girl's Best Friend" in *Gentlemen Prefer Blondes* were performed as a bit of satire by an "exaggeratedly, dishily seductive blonde" in a stereotypical role (1995, p. 231). A postmodern reading of her performances by cultural critics is easily made, and it is sometimes hard to tell if Monroe is serious or the culture is just more sophisticated in what it now sees as less subtle uses of sexuality.

SUMMARY

This chapter has explored the process of achieving fame in America from several vantage points using the subjects of our sample. Fame, of course, represents a type of high social status, and I discussed the aspects of our subjects' lives that appeared to help them achieve fame as individuals. However, importantly, fame changes greatly as American and other societies adopt different codes of social status and fame. I have shown how earlier in American history, being of the lower class made potential well-known people suspect in the eyes of those gatekeepers who help Americans achieve fame. Gradually the development of a mass market for products and a consumer culture based on popularity overcame earlier limits on fame. Charlie Chaplin and the rise of film itself was one turning point in America where the popularity of consumer items overcame more Puritanical and upper-class status systems. Although critics, scholars, and church leaders may continue to attack popular culture, it is clear that popular culture has kept its dominant role. In terms of our subjects, the popular mass market is open to new entrants even of the poor if they can increase sales (and possibly even to increase legitimacy of a product). There has certainly been no mad rush to embrace poor entrants (see Chapter 7), but they are less notable than in the past.

CHAPTER 7

CONTEMPORARY FAME AND POVERTY

Throughout the research for this book, quite a few friends, and several people knowledgeable about research and writing books, asked the obvious question of why I had not included subjects who are still alive. There are, as I shall discuss, some problems in writing an intelligent analysis about people who are currently *famous but still alive*, which went into my original thinking about excluding them from the book. Nevertheless, with the help here of Jenna Nunziato, I have accepted the challenge of making at least a few tentative assessments of fame and poverty in recent times with a number of caveats associated with a small sample.

One difficulty is that there is no academic or scholarly source for a list of "famous" people who are still alive. For example, the American National Biography Online profiles only deceased individuals. We had to roam through Internet sites such as Wikipedia and Biography.com to develop a list of those born in the past five decades, and identify those we could consider famous, which usually was far fewer people than Wikipedia or other sites list (i.e., there were many people that we had not heard of).

A more major difficulty is how to assess whether current prominence will continue into the future. It is extremely hard to predict who in the current array of Hollywood stars, sports figures, and music heroes, for example, will be remembered thirty, forty, or fifty years from now. It is not just a problem that always existed, but is one that has been exacerbated by the impermanence of fame in our Western culture, as Andy Warhol's proverbial "fifteen minutes of fame" sometimes seems like far less in the twenty-first century's technological universe. In choosing the subjects for this chapter, it became even more difficult for the two of us to agree, as our generational placement clearly had a relation to whom we considered famous. I am not familiar with many of the younger popular figures that Jenna knows, and she doesn't know many of the older figures known to me. Another important point is that fame is measured differently for different types of success: though we criticize our presidents and Supreme Court justices, they are likely once elected or appointed to remain somewhere on the list of famous people. Though we provide far more cheering and bravado for our sports, music, and entertainment heroes, their fame is often more ephemeral. For example, actresses like Demi Moore (1962–) or Hillary Swank (1975–) who appear to be from poorer backgrounds did not make our subject list because we were not sure that they would be remembered as stars thirty or forty years from now. More current singing stars like Britney Spears or Carrie Underwood prove to be even more problematic, as do sports figures (a decade and a half after they competed with Babe Ruth's home-run record, Sammy Sosa and Mark McGwire may be on the path to being forgotten by the public at large).

The third issue is the lack of secondary sources on many current or recent stars. Ordinarily the first books to appear about a celebrity are those that are approved (if not sponsored) by the subject ("the official biography"). There are also fan books with material that cannot necessarily be trusted as accurate. This too was a reason why some of the current stars who might have made our subject list did not. For example, on Hillary Swank, there was a complete lack of impartial sources about her life.

Still, there are some generalizations about fame and poverty we can make. First, people from actual poor backgrounds continue to be declining on the list of the famous. The use of Wikipedia.com and Biography.com websites produces a potential list of famous people, and as with the ANB, the majority continue to be of nonpoor backgrounds. In fact, while nineteen people appear from lower-class backgrounds in the years of birth 1936–1945, the years 1946–1976 (or three full decades) are needed to find nineteen people, a hint that if anything, fewer people are emerging from poverty (these are from biographies of many hundreds if not thousands of people). Of course, an intervening variable is that the period at least until the early 1970s was a more prosperous one in America, so there were fewer poor people than before this time and after the late 1970s. We may need to see more fully how the generations coming of age since 1980 fare in the future. Also, many people do claim they grew up in poverty, but a closer examination finds that the subject was not exactly poor. For example, there is much talk on some websites and biographies about former president William Clinton being poor, but on examination he appears to have grown up in the lower middle class, to a mother who studied nursing and whose grandparents (who raised him for a while) owned a grocery store. After returning home, his mother married a man who owned an automobile dealership. His boyhood was certainly troubled, but not poverty-ridden (see Wikipedia.com, William Clinton).

If poor people are not very common among those who are famous, their association with entertainment and sports areas has continued unabated from the earlier period. In 1936–1945 only four out of nineteen people, and in 1946–1975, just three out of nineteen people were *not* in entertainment or sports. This again bespeaks the difficulty low-income people have in obtaining access to areas such as politics or government appointments, academic or scientific accomplishment, or even high-culture areas such as serious literature and the arts.

Finally, consistent with the civil rights movements and the concentration of poverty among African Americans and Latinos in recent years, more famous poor people are people of color. In politics, among the few people born in poverty was prominent office holder Barbara Jordan (a US senator and representative who was particularly known in the Watergate scandal), born in 1936; Russell Means, a Native American activist, born in 1939; Huey Newton, the Black Panther Party leader, born in 1942; Supreme Court Justice Clarence Thomas, born in 1948; and governor of Massachusetts Deval Patrick, born in 1956. Similarly, many of the poor people in entertainment are nonwhite: singer Buffy St. Marie (1941–), musician Curtis Mayfield (1942–1999), musician Isaac Hayes (1942–2008), musician Jimi Hendrix (1942–1970), singer Barry White (1943–2003), singer Mary Wilson (1944–), entertainment star Oprah Winfrey (1954–), comedian and actor George Lopez (1961–), basketball player and personality Dennis Rodman (1961–), rap star MC Hammer (1962–), singer Tracy Chapman (1964–), hip-hop star and entertainment mogul Jay-Z (1969–), and boxer Mike Tyson (1966–).

As with the first part of the book, those we chose had to meet the criteria of being born into poverty and having achieved a large degree of fame. With an effort to vary the subjects by gender and race and at least somewhat by profession or field, we chose singer and entertainment star Dolly Parton (1946–), writer Stephen King (1947–), entertainer and personality Mr. T (1952–), former talk show host and entertainment mogul Oprah Winfrey (1954–), basketball player Larry Bird (1956–), comedian and entertainer George Lopez (1961–), and musician-entrepreneur Jay-Z (1969–).

GROWING UP IN POVERTY: NOT MUCH DIFFERENCE IN RECENT TIMES

Singer-songwriter (and occasional actress) Dolly Parton was born in 1946 in a one-room cabin in rural Tennessee, the fourth of twelve children. Her father initially worked as a sharecropper, growing corn and tobacco. He lacked the finances to pay the doctor for Dolly's delivery and instead bartered him a sack of cornmeal. The family moved frequently in search of somewhere they could afford. By the time Dolly was five, however, her father had saved enough to buy his own land, paying $5,000 for several hundred acres of land to farm and a house that desperately needed his hard work to fix up to a livable condition. She reports that they wallpapered the home with newspapers to seal cracks in the wall and insulate the house. The home was far from anywhere and only accessible through dangerous roads and paths. Dolly walked several miles down the mountain in treacherous conditions to get to school, sometimes arriving with frozen feet. The Parton children would get a reprieve from this walk when their father needed them to stay home to help him bring in the crops. After three years at Locust Ridge, the family moved several more times. In one move, they experienced a wagon wreck that destroyed all of their furniture.

Parton comes from a poor family in a poor area of the country, and she recognizes the struggles of those around her. She says that people in the mountains are "trying every day, literally every minute, to make things a little bit better" (Parton 1994, p. 24). To this end, her father began to take on multiple jobs outside the home to support his ever-growing brood, including ditch digging, pipe laying, and concrete laying.

Parton's classmates constantly made her aware of her poverty and how it made her different. She recalls how her father would tell her not to participate in classroom events like Secret Santa, but she wanted to avoid embarrassment from being the only one not participating.

It was a traumatic thing, though. Even if I could explain away not being able to buy someone a gift or worse yet, give the person a really cheap or homemade gift, there was always the possibility that somebody would give me something really nice. This made me feel terrible—guilty, poor, and terrible. The worst thing about poverty is not the actual living of it, but the shame of it. (Parton 1994, p. 51)

Parton experienced further mockery from her classmates in an event she documented in her song "Coat of Many Colors." Her mother made her a new coat for winter by piecing together many different rags and scraps, and used lots of colors because of Dolly's vibrant personality. Her mother told her the story of Joseph and the coat of many colors as a sign he was loved and special and so Dolly felt the same way about hers. Lots of individual time with mom in a family of twelve kids was rare, and her siblings were jealous of Dolly's individual attention. She would strut around in her coat all the time, making everyone tell her how pretty it was. When she wore it to school for picture day, she expected the same, but instead was mocked all day by the kids and even locked in a cloakroom, but wouldn't take off the coat because of her pride.

Parton's rise out of poverty and into stardom started at age eight, when she attended a theater show with her mom and siblings and asked to sing a religious number. The crowd responded positively to her and she was smitten with the limelight. Her uncle Bill Owens took an interest in Parton's talent and drive, taught her to play piano, and helped her get appearances on radio shows. For two years, Parton made regular appearances on the Cas Walker show, a radio program run by a local self-made multimillionaire. She so impressed Walker that he then made her a regular part of the program, starting her salary at $20 a week, and by the time she turned eighteen, she was making $30 a week plus $25 a night for live shows out of town. For her appearances on the show, Parton would travel 40 miles from the family's home in Sevierville, Tennessee. Parton would appear three times a day, three days a week. As if this didn't show enough dedication, any time Parton was out of school for at least a few days, she would go to Knoxville to stay with her aunt and uncle so she could take buses to radio and TV appearances more easily. Her ultimate goal was to appear on the Grand Ole Opry, a goal fulfilled in 1959 when Jimmy C. Newman gave up his slot to her. Parton's star continued to climb from there, and she was briefly associated with Mercury Records, but when that did not have much of a result, she opted to return to and finish high school, the first of her family to do so. Upon graduation, Parton immediately moved to Nashville to seek her big break. She reports that when she said this was her plan, the crowd at her graduation laughed uproariously at her, which she says "instilled in me an even greater determination to realize my dream in a kind of 'I'll show them' way" (p. 139).

Writer Stephen King's (1947–) books and their film adaptations are known the world over, making him a household name and unequivocally linking him with the horror genre. What is less well-known about him is the dire poverty he not only grew up in but continued to experience until his book sales miraculously took off.

King was born in Portland, Maine, but he didn't stay put for long. His father was a merchant marine and the family settled in New York, but upon his retirement he became a traveling salesman. King describes him as "the only man on the sales force who regularly demonstrated vacuum cleaners to pretty young widows at two o'clock in the morning" (Underwood and Miller 1989, p. 35). When King was two years old, his father left for a pack of cigarettes and never came back. Faced with the care for two young boys and the shame of being left (her kids were instructed to say their father was away "in the navy"), King's mother had to find any job she could and any place to stay that would take them. This led to frequent cross-country journeys for the family, who could be in Wisconsin one month and Massachusetts the next. In 1958 they settled in the town of West Durham, Maine, to take care of King's mother's ailing parents. As a result of the constant moving and poverty, King not only had the stress of continually being the new kid in school, but always being ill. He spent most of first grade in bed with measles, ear infections, and strep throat. King recalls, "Those were very unhappy years for my mother. She had no money, and she was always on duty" (Singer 1998). Her hands would bleed from repeatedly washing her incontinent mother's linens. The Kings had to live by bartering and on charity from relatives. When their well would dry up, they would have to walk a half mile for water. When a new school opened in Durham in 1960, Stephen King was excited to finally have access to running water and a flush toilet.

King's childhood poverty continued into his adult life as he tried to establish himself as a writer. Although he received a full scholarship to the University of Maine, he had to work long and grueling hours in a factory to pay for his books and other needs. For $40 a month he moved with friends into an apartment with floors that iced over. He was unfazed by the quality of his new home, having grown up in similar conditions. As a backup plan for if writing didn't pan out, he got a teaching certificate that led to a job in the tiny town of Hampden, near Bangor, Maine. He lived in a trailer with his wife and baby daughter, and made a mere $6,400 a year. King discusses how he felt his dreams leaving him: "Teaching school is like having jumper cables hooked to your ears, draining all the juice out of you. You come home, you have papers to correct, and you don't feel like writing. We were planning to have a car, we were supposed to have a real life, and we were worse off than when I was in the laundry" (Rogak 2008, p. 62).

The book *Carrie* (and its subsequent movie success) in the mid-1970s launched Stephen King's career, and he remains one of the country's foremost authors.

Actor Lawrence Tureaud (later Tero), better known as Mr. T, was born on the South Side of Chicago in 1952, the tenth of twelve kids and the eighth son. He began going by "Mr. T" in 1972, as he felt that being addressed as "Mister" was the only way he could get respect as an African American man. He explains, "Sure that name doesn't appear on my birth certificate; more importantly, 'nigger' doesn't appear on my birth certificate either, but I have been called nigger plenty of times" (Mr. T 1984, p. 96).

In his autobiography, Mr. T reports that his father worked primarily as a minister, as well as holding down several odd jobs to make ends meet. While largely unemployed, his father once had to tear down his own fence for heat (p. 19). To make do, he became what Mr. T called a "junkman"—rummaging through the trash in white neighborhoods to find clothes, toys, and even food. He would take his boys with him to garner more sympathy from whites.

> My father came around so much, with that smile and big "thank you" on his lips that those rich whites really started liking him. I mean they would buy extra food and give it to him. They would invite my brothers to play with their sons. Sometimes they would even invite my father and brothers to stay for dinner—yes, dinner over at the rich white folks' house! ... I guess they considered us to be "good niggers," and therefore we were all right. They would even take us on trips with them and to their family reunions to meet more of their relatives. (Mr. T 1984, p. 13)

With fourteen mouths and very little income, there often wasn't enough food to go around. As a child at school Mr. T hid his lunches

Chapter 7

so no one could see how meager they were or that he could not afford a one-cent bottle of milk. He was made fun of by other kids for wearing ripped and stained hand-me-downs, and says, "I would always be ready to fight them, because the truth hurts" (p. 35).

Mr. T's parents, like many poor people still today, realized that being married prevented them from receiving benefits. According to Mr. T, his father "figured out how it was and that he had to beat the Man at his own game, because if you don't play the game, you starve to death" (p. 16). Unbeknownst to Mr. T and his siblings, his father continued to send money to the family, but stayed away because of concerns that if a social worker asked the kids about the whereabouts of their father, they may accidentally spill the secret. As Mr. T grew and saw other families doing the same thing, he began to understand the importance of fighting "the system" through whatever means necessary.

In 1962, all fourteen members of the Tero family moved into a four-bedroom apartment in the Taylor Homes Projects. As with all subsidized housing in 1960s Chicago, it was dangerous, chaotic, and full of crime. Mr. T describes it as "almost like a prison" (p. 38). He describes how life in the projects takes away one's sense of social responsibility and replaces it with a criminal element in what he terms "Project Paralysis." As people moved in, a part of them seemed to die among the boarded-up buildings, dangerous schools, and constant gang violence, and he watched those he knew get sucked into the lifestyle. Staying focused on bettering himself and moving out, Mr. T told himself, "I live here in the projects but I refuse to let the projects live within me. I am not going to be filthy, nasty, ignorant, low-life, and most importantly, I will give due respect to all. With that affirmation, I became a winner, I became proud of myself, proud of being black" (p. 66).

He used that drive to excel in school and subsequently received offers from thirty-six colleges. He opted to leave college following an incident in which he was falsely blamed for a riot, and soon turned to work as a bodyguard, pouring himself into the passion by working in security and studying police tactics. In a return to his roots, he performed freelance bodyguard work for residents of the ghetto, keeping mothers safe as they cashed their welfare checks. Mr. T made his biggest splash as a bodyguard when he was offered the opportunity to appear on an NBC game show, *America's Toughest Boxer*, in 1980. He claims to have trained by going to abandoned buildings and running through walls. This led to his being offered his breakout role as Clubber Lang in *Rocky 3*.

Oprah (originally "Orpah") Winfrey was born in the small town of Kosciusko, Mississippi, in 1954. Like many things about Oprah's almost magical achievement of fame, there is some controversy surrounding her various statements about her life, some of which have also been contradictory, depending on when and where she said them. No doubt Winfrey grew up in poverty, though many critics, including her family, dispute the level of poverty. Born to a teenage mother, Vernita Lee, she was brought up by her grandparents, who had a small farm. Winfrey has claimed she never had a store-bought dress or a pair of shoes until she was six years old, "and the only toy I had was a corn cob doll with toothpicks," and since her family could not afford a pet, she made a cockroach her pet (Kelley 2011, p. 19). However, her sisters noted that "we sure weren't rich. But [she] exaggerated how bad we had it … she never had cockroaches as pets, she always had a dog, and she also had a white cat, an eel in the aquarium and a parakeet" (ibid., p. 20). Her cousin, the family historian, said, "Yes we were poor—but Aunt Hattie owned her own home, plus two acres of land and a few chickens, which made her better off than most folks in [that] community" (ibid., p. 22). There is some dispute too about her grandparents' care. They were definitely traditional, very religious, and "old school," but whether her mother "used tree branches as 'switches'" and would "whip [her] for days and never get tired" (Westen 2005, pp. 17, 18) is disputed. Unquestionably, they brought Oprah up extremely religiously—so much so that children called her "Preacher" and "Miss Jesus," mocking her pious zeal (Garson 2004, p. 14).

When Vernita moved to Milwaukee, she asked to have the six-year-old Oprah come back to live with her. Oprah has particularly criticized the poverty and emptiness of being raised by a mother on welfare (she also worked periodically as a maid). No doubt conditions were very challenging, although family members, including Vernita, dispute Oprah's story that she was asked to sleep on the porch because she was more dark-skinned than Vernita and family. Others say actually she slept there due to the fact that Vernita rented only one room where she kept her newborn baby, and the only option was to sleep in the back of the rooming house (Kelley 2011, pp. 26–27). To ease the strain on Vernita, Oprah moved in with Vernon, her putative father (his paternity has also been disputed, although he did play a major role in raising Oprah), but she soon went back to Milwaukee. At around age nine Oprah was sexually molested by a cousin, and abuse continued with other family

Chapter 7

members until she was fourteen. Winfrey made headlines when she first announced her sexual abuse on *The Oprah Winfrey Show* in 1986.

Whatever all the facts were about the first years of her life, by age fourteen Winfrey was an angry and troubled child who began acting out. With Oprah staying out late, running away, and being sexually promiscuous, Vernita considered sending her to a halfway house for troubled teens (Westen 2005, p. 29). Luckily, she decided instead to send her back to Vernon in Nashville. Oprah arrived seven months pregnant, but the baby died shortly after she gave birth. Vernon, also a very religious man who was a church deacon and ran a respectable barber shop, "put his foot down" with Oprah and demanded that she live by his rules or leave. Most accounts suggest Oprah began "straightening out" and taking her school classes more seriously. Although Oprah would by age seventeen win the Miss Tennessee beauty pageant and attract the attention of local media, she was also "for her age naïve and somewhat unworldly" (Garson 2004, p. 31), and not surprisingly, she had not dealt with the years of abuse and other issues such as anger at her family. It would take many years, if ever, before Oprah would lick all her personal demons from her childhood years.

Basketball star Larry Bird's (1956–) early years are subject to less controversy. He was born in rural Indiana to a large family barely supported by his blue-collar father and a mother who waitressed and cooked to help support the family. Bird's background gained him the nickname "the Hick from French Lick," and indeed Bird said he was rarely ever out of the area until after high school and was isolated from the outside world, not even watching much television (Bird and Ryan 1990, p. 35). Bird's poverty is evident from the fact that the family's food would usually run out by Thursday of the week, and that the house was so crowded Bird often stayed at his grandmother Lizzie Kearns's house (she lived nearby). Bird moved a total of fifteen times during his youth (Popporich 2009, p. 3) either because of eviction threats or the family's seeking cheaper rents. Bird's father worked hard but had spells of unemployment, and with six children to support "we were lucky if he made $120 a week." Bird tells stories of keeping a basketball for two years that had melted because it was too close to the stove, even though it had bumps all over it, because he could not afford another (Bird and Ryan 1990, p. 22). A big baseball player as a youth, Bird accidently broke many of the house's windows. Because his family could not afford to replace them, the windows were covered with cardboard (ibid., p. 7).

As Bird grew older, his father, who was prone to drinking, began drinking more heavily and his relationship with Bird's mother worsened. He would spend a lot of money on drinking and also spending generously on his friends, but not his family. Although not noted in Bird's own account, some write-ups offer the opinion that Joe Bird (his father) had post-traumatic stress disorder from service in the Korean War (Wikipedia.com, Larry Bird). Eventually Bird's parents divorced, and after Joe fell behind in his monthly support payments he said his good-byes to his family and friends and killed himself with a shotgun (Larry was eighteen at that time). Larry Bird believes his father was deeply convinced the family would be better off without him, and would be eligible to collect from insurance and other benefits:

> I think he started to feel as if he was beating his head against a wall because things just weren't changing ... by Christmas time I could tell that Dad had lost the desire to go on. He was deeply depressed. He told [us] "I am not going to be around much longer. No use me living this way. You kids would be better off if I was gone." But like I said dad really thought he was helping us by doing this. (Bird and Ryan 1990, pp. 15–16)

Although Bird had a tough time as a young adult as a result of his father's death (including a very short stay at college and a short-term troubled marriage), he seems to have managed his way through adult life, if not without any problems, certainly relatively easier than some others.

Like Oprah, Latino comedian George Lopez (1961–) was raised by his grandparents after his twenty-year-old mother, Frieda, left him with them to raise. Frieda had her own deep troubles, having fallen out of a moving car at thirteen because of her epilepsy. Lopez describes her as "a deeply troubled woman, going so far as to slash her wrists at one point. She ended up at Camarillo State Hospital (a state psychiatric hospital) at that time" (Lopez 2004, pp. 18–19). But his grandmother Benito and grandfather Refugio (known as "Cuco") were hardly a respite and became the model for Lopez's dysfunctional family on the *George Lopez Show*, which aired from 2002 to 2007 and still thrives in syndication (his mother Benita, played by Belita Moreno, is based on Lopez's real grandmother, and constantly puts Lopez down as well as displays an "over the top" stereotype of a drunken and sometimes out of control middle-age woman). In his book *Why You Crying?*, Lopez centers his theme on his grandmother's asking him "why he was crying" after she hit him. Lopez explains, "I am crying because [I] am thinking about the father [I] never had and the mother [I] never had. I wake up thinking about how long I lived on the defensive—never smiling, never comfortable with myself or my body.... I cry over my deeply dysfunctional family" (p. 1).

Both his grandparents had hard lives. Benito was born in El Centro, a farming community in the Imperial Valley, 90 miles outside San Diego. She did not know her mother, who was sent back to Mexico, and was raised by her aunt. She too was very unhappy as a child, and ended up running away from home when she was sixteen. Her first husband beat her up and warned her he was going to shoot her dead with a gun. Lopez said after living with him for nineteen years, she wore "her abuse as a badge of honor, somehow proud she [had] stuck it out" (p. 22). His grandfather Cuco was a day laborer who "worked as a mule, dug ditches for a living, often doing the job of two or three men" (p. 25). His grandfather was an alcoholic and sometimes beat his wife, and sometimes the word went out from his grandmother to "hide" as Cuco went after George.

Beyond the physical abuse, however, Lopez recalls, "I don't think there was ever a moment in my childhood when I felt it was great to be part of the family" (Dougherty 2011, p. 18). His birthdays and other occasions often went uncelebrated by his family. Living alone with them (an unusual upbringing for a Mexican child) on an isolated cul-de-sac in San Fernando, "we called the street Without Hope." He felt isolated but eventually had one other friend, and together they felt like misfits (the character of Ernie in the Lopez show reminisces about their unhappy and isolated childhoods). His family offered no encouragement about his schooling because they regarded "educated people as snobby or arrogant" (Lopez 2004, p. 18). Lopez's biggest complaint was psychological abuse, his "family ruthlessly making fun of him" (ibid., p. 16). His poor self-image was not helped by his dark complexion; some of his school cohorts' parents called him a "nigger" (ibid., p. 9). Because of the negative self-image imposed on him, he became angry and alone, feeling teased and tormented. Despite many years of psychotherapy and the ability to play out part of his past life in a prime-time comedy, Lopez has not forgiven his grandmother:

> Today, as millions of you know, my show explores the twisted, tortured relationship I share with my mother, standing in for my real-life

grandmother.... She did not have positive emotion, expected the worst from everyone. To this day she never has said she is proud of me. Never. [She has] not once expressed happiness for my success in life. (Lopez 2004, p. 21)

Indeed, Lopez's former wife Anne Serrano noted on meeting his real-life grandmother, "I did not know a Latino woman could be so negative" (ibid., p. 35). Nevertheless, Lopez has said that years of therapy have made him realize his grandmother provided him a home he probably would not have had at all with his actual mother (p. 23).

Rapper and entrepreneur Jay-Z (originally Shawn Carter) was born in 1969 in the Marcy Housing Projects in Brooklyn, a run-down ghetto largely ignored by authorities. He describes the projects as "a great metaphor for the government's relationship to poor folks: these huge islands mostly in the middle of nowhere, designed to warehouse lives" (Jay-Z 2011, p. 155). His net worth is now estimated at half a billion dollars (Greenburg 2012). He became aware of rap music at a young age by listening to boys in his neighborhood freestyling. Believing he could do better, he would use any spare moment or any burst of inspiration to start writing his rhymes. He says he would "spend free time reading the dictionary, building [his] vocabulary for battles" (Jay-Z 2011, p. 7).

Jay-Z showed great potential for academic achievement, testing at a twelfth-grade level in sixth grade, but shortly thereafter his father left home to track down a man who had stabbed his brother, and subsequently left the home permanently after becoming addicted to alcohol and crack cocaine. He did not reconnect with his son for another twenty years. At age twelve, when his brother admitted to stealing a ring from him for drug money, Jay-Z pulled out a gun and shot him in the shoulder. His grades declined and he did not graduate. He had been attending Westinghouse High School, a dangerous school in poor condition, and discovered he could do better for himself selling drugs. He would travel to Trenton, New Jersey, on weekends with a friend at age fifteen to sell drugs, and before long they went into business full time and he left home. Crack took over quickly in his neighborhood and he reports that everyone was either using it or selling it, and he saw an opportunity for self-advancement. Jay-Z wasn't the only drug-dealing teen in the neighborhood by a long shot, as many saw it as their ticket to basic survival. "Guys my age, fed up with watching their moms struggle on a single income, were paying utility bills with money from hustling" (p. 13). He admits to drug dealers becoming his role models and taking on the missing father role in his life. Fortunately, he also connected with local rappers who looked after him and helped to give him a start in a more legitimate career.

Although Jay-Z was able to talk his way onto other rappers' tours or tracks as a young man, he found that he wasn't making nearly as much money as he was used to, and went back to selling drugs. Utilizing business skills that served him well later in life with his own record label, he targeted "undeveloped markets" where crack had not taken hold as strongly as his home neighborhood, such as Maryland and Virginia. Many of his raps allude to the anxiety of transporting kilos of cocaine across state lines and the thrill of going undetected by the police. Still, he struggled to find fulfillment in this lifestyle, feeling shame over selling drugs "to addicts who were killing themselves" (p. 19).

Jay-Z had earned enough money to get himself out of the ghetto, but by choosing to sell drugs he still faced danger every day of his life. He was once shot at three times when attacked by rival drug dealers, and was saved only by the gun jamming. He discusses his turning point for choosing to leave the drug scene: "It was more so out of fear. You can't run the streets forever. What are you going to be doing when you're 30 years old, or 35 or 40? I had a fear of being nothing—that pretty much drove me" (Greenburg 2012, p. 30).

At this time, Jay-Z connected with Russell Simmons, and admired how he had acquired wealth and independence legitimately through rap. Jay-Z had tried to make his own name through the record labels but hadn't been promoted. They formed their own label, Roc-A-Fella, and eventually a clothing company, and worked hard to promote themselves, selling records everywhere from clubs to barbershops. As they continued to promote themselves and build alliances with powerful people, their stars continued to rise and the money began to come in. It wasn't long before Jay-Z was playing sold-out shows and getting heavy radio airplay.

As with the other subjects, Jay-Z emphasizes the shame of poverty and the reluctance to identify oneself with it no matter the circumstances.

> Poor people don't like to talk about poverty because even though they might live in the projects surrounded by other poor people and have, like, ten dollars in the bank, they don't like to think of themselves as poor. It's embarrassing. When you're a kid, even in the projects, one kid will mercilessly snap on another kid over minor material differences, even though by the American standard, they're both broke as shit.... The burden of poverty isn't just that you don't always have the things

you need, it's the feeling of being embarrassed every day of your life, and you'd do anything to lift that burden. (Jay-Z 2011, p. 218)

Many rappers discuss their impoverished roots in their lyrics, so frequently that it almost seems to be necessary for their credibility. As with Dolly Parton being ashamed of her poverty as a child and making light of it when famous, Jay-Z was able to take the indignity of food stamps and public housing and turn it into an angle to get himself listened to; he spoke to people who were never spoken to by pop or rock music and united their struggles with his. He learned how to turn his poverty around to make himself idolized and admired for getting away from it, which in turn has served to keep him wealthy.

PAIN AND SUFFERING IN ADULT LIFE

Although not every person born into poverty suffers pain in adulthood, it is not surprising that those whose poverty is combined with abuse during childhood, deprivation in emotions or education, and feelings of hurt, loneliness, and sorrow that stem from childhood do suffer. We can see that Stephen King, Oprah Winfrey, George Lopez, and Jay-Z spent most of their young adult lives aching from their childhood.

Although King found money and success beginning with the book and movie *Carrie*, he found that money could not heal deep wounds. When his son Joe was three, he "wanted to write like Daddy" and colored all over King's manuscripts. King was completely enraged at his son, and hoped if he wrote out his negative feelings he wouldn't act on them—an exercise which later turned into the mystery *The Shining*. Still, he found that he still lived with the shame of his father's absence and his own hostile feelings from childhood, although this is a subject he generally avoids discussing. When asked if he longed for the relationship they never had, King says, "My father was just an absence. And you don't miss what's not there. Maybe in some sort of imaginative way I'm searching for him or maybe that's just a lot of horseshit, I don't know. There does seem to be a target that this stuff pours out toward. I am always interested in the idea that a lot of fiction writers write for their fathers because their fathers are gone" (Rogak 2008, p. 123). Indeed, many of the fathers in King's stories are either absent or abusive, the most obvious example being Jack Torrance of *The Shining*. King expressed reservations about ever finding his father, concerned that there may be things about him he didn't want to know.

Chapter 7

When King was in high school a teacher accused him of wasting his talent by writing horror, despite the fact that his classmates loved it. King says about the incident, "I have spent a good many years since—too many, I think—being ashamed about what I write" (King 2000, p. 213). Though he is one of the most prolific and popular writers of the modern era, critics still view his work as lesser because it is considered horror, not literature. Even when King branches out into other genres, as with *The Green Mile* and *Dolores Claiborne*, he is never given the credit he is due. King started drinking in high school, and it remained a major part of his life from there as he used it to mute his demons and fears of failure. As an adult, King drank only to get drunk, and justified this by feeling that alcoholism and depression were central to being a writer and "sensitive fellow," as well as to prove masculinity (p. 94). King's increased wealth provided increased access to substances, and he states, "There was never a time for me when the goal wasn't to get as hammered as I could possibly afford to" (Rogak 2008, p. 69). He drank constantly, showing up intoxicated to book signings. He developed a habit of pouring any unconsumed beers down the sink at the end of the night, because "if I didn't, they'd talk to me as I lay in bed until I got up and had another. And another. And another" (King 2000, p. 96). His drinking continued unabated, and in 1985, drugs were added to the mix. Although others raised concern about his substance use, King wasn't interested in hearing it, as his ego began to get the better of him. He says, "My kind of success does not lead you humbly to say 'Yeah, I guess you're right. I'm an asshole.' Rather, it leads you to say, 'Who the fuck are you to tell me to settle down? Don't you know I'm the king of the fucking universe?'" (Rogak 2008, p. 155). Indeed, King's career was able to give him not only the financial advantage to be able to spend huge amounts of money on intoxicants without destroying the family finances, but also the ability to stay up all night drinking without missing work the next day. It was therefore easy for him to be an addict, especially with his family too concerned about his mental health should he be unable to write when sobering up. His wife was worried that if he stopped using, he'd stop writing, because she'd seen when he wasn't writing and it was somehow even worse than when he was using. She felt that would be more difficult for them than the addiction, so she cut him a lot of slack and made excuses for him. King also believed if he stopped snorting coke and drinking he would stop writing so prolifically. He had the same concern about therapy—he feared that talking about deep-seated demons would get rid of the things that create his stories.

His substance abuse worsened as the 1980s went on, with his blackouts becoming increasingly long, and his drug and alcohol use now happened around the clock. King's wife would sleep alone at night then come downstairs to find him passed out in his own vomit in his office. His work began to deteriorate and he admits to having no memory of writing his novel *Cujo*. In 1987, King published *The Tommyknockers*, a book almost universally panned even by die-hard fans. He admits that its poor quality is due to his cocaine and alcohol use resulting in his only being sober about three hours a day. He attempted to moderate his use when his wife staged an intervention, gathering up all of the beer cans and drug paraphernalia, including Listerine bottles, which King had thought he had hidden and dumping the huge trash bag out in front of him. After two years of failing to cut back, however, he stopped "cold turkey" in 1989. King was concerned he couldn't write sober, as he'd been drinking as long as he'd been writing, and had been "high most of the 80s" on cocaine, but with time, he found his natural abilities were unaffected (Rogak 2008, p. 160). Although of course there are many reasons that people use substances, there is no doubt that a mixture of bitterness about his childhood and residual anxiety about making it in life played a big part.

Few people had as quick a path to fame and fortune as Oprah Winfrey, who became the first black woman billionaire and one of the best-known American figures in every poll in the past two decades. Starting out in Nashville in the 1970s as the youngest news anchor and the first black female one, she moved to Baltimore in 1976 to co-anchor the six o'clock news. By 1978, she was co-hosting *People Are Talking*, her first talk show. Her show was a surprising success, even outdrawing *Phil Donahue* in the local market. In 1983 she moved to Chicago, where she did a half-hour morning talk show, *AM Chicago*, which also overtook the *Donahue* show. The key move in her rise was her decision to go into syndication, and by 1986 she went national in the *Oprah Winfrey Show*. Winfrey's genius was in hitting the large untapped market of women who watched daytime television but wanted alternatives to soap operas. She also made a wonderful fit between her personal style with the increasing therapeutic and self-help culture of the 1980s and 1990s (Kelley 2011, pp. 96–97).

Part of Oprah's appeal in her immensely popular show was a therapeutic confession of her many difficulties as well as revealing guests' and the audience's deepest problems. Although less critical of Winfrey, most biographers agree with biographer Kitty Kelley that Oprah's shows revealed her "adolescent promiscuity, an unwanted pregnancy, abysmal relationships with men ... drug abuse, an obsessive need to control, and the compulsive eating that drove her weight up and down the scale for decades" (Kelley 2011, p. 16). Kelley goes further than others in seeing Oprah's "excessive need for control, plus the immense gratification she derived from being the center of attention, applause, and approval had its roots in her adolescent sexual abuse" (p. 18).

To Kelley, Winfrey never revealed anything by chance, and her own revelations constantly came only one step ahead of someone else revealing them. Both her admission of her teen pregnancy (just ahead of her sister's making contact with the tabloids) and her sudden admission in 1994 about having used crack (coming ahead of more tabloid stories) were intentional rather than spontaneous admissions. Kelley also reported that a torrid but unrequited love affair Oprah had with a married man earlier in her life was covered up by a $50,000 cash payment (p. 105).

There is no doubt that despite success Oprah had many troubled periods. She apparently considered suicide in 1981 when a love affair went bad and professional success did not appear in sight. Winfrey denied that her suicide threat was real, but according to Kelley her friends responded with a suicide watch and suggested she go into psychotherapy (Kelley 2011, p. 109; Westen 2005, p. 51). Winfrey has attributed most of the pain to self-hatred:

> The reason I gained so much weight in the first place and the reason I had such a sorry history of abusive relationships with men was I just needed approval so much. I needed everyone to like me, because I didn't like myself much. So I'd end up with these cruel self-absorbed guys who'd tell me how selfish I was, and I'd say "Oh thank you, you're so right" and be grateful to them. Because I had no sense that I deserved anything else. Which is also why I gained so much weight later on. It was the perfect way of cushioning myself against the world's disapproval. (Wikipedia.com, Oprah Winfrey)

Despite some factual differences in biographies and a cloud of secrecy that Winfrey clamped on her employees years ago for fear of leaks about her personal life, Oprah's own show and writings about her life suggest she went through a great deal of pain from her childhood in her adult life. She has been rather consistently hostile to family members. For example, she has said, "If my mother hadn't given me up, I would be in deep trouble now. I would have been barefoot and pregnant, [have] had at least three kids by the time I was 20. No doubt about it. I would have been part of that whole ghetto mentality that's waiting for somebody to do something for them" (quoted in Kelley 2011, p. 152). Oprah has had a great deal of controversy in the years of her talk show for her deeply personal attacks on welfare mothers and others she claims lack personal responsibility. As we shall see, she is a good example of someone famous embracing success while distancing themselves as much as possible from their poverty roots.

Like Oprah, comedian George Lopez's troubled childhood turned into a troubled young adulthood, though he had some early success as a comedian. Originally combining improv shows and small gigs with factory work, he found comedy "when the audience did like him to be the first time in his life that he felt loved and accepted" (Dougherty 2011, p. 26), but Lopez "got angry when his career did not take off quickly." He felt "self-pity, anger and depression" (ibid., p. 9). Lopez quit comedy altogether for a while. While working at a defense plant, he was convinced by a co-worker to buy some pills, only to find the worker was an undercover cop. Fired from his job, his grandparents, with whom he was still living, threw him out of the house. Lopez describes in his autobiography how humiliated he was at being thrown out: "Holy shit! I don't know about you, but in a Mexican family that's like excommunication. You can't watch TV. You can't eat the food. You can't use the backyard weights. You can't bring home a woman ... no money. [I had to] sleep ... on my friend Arnold's couch" (Lopez 2004, p. 72).

In the late 1980s, things began to break a little better for Lopez. With new comedy agents and a chance meeting with the then red-hot Arsenio Hall, Lopez began getting some exposure, and even became the "novelty" of a Chicano comic. He also met his wife (now ex-) Anne Serrano, who would have a big effect in stabilizing his life. However, despite some success in California and the Southwest, including fifteen appearances on *The Arsenio Hall Show*, he considers the early 1990s as the "I Hate Me Years when I was the Angriest Most Depressed Man Alive" (p. 83). Part of it was Lopez's depression about not "going anywhere" even though now he was making more than a thousand dollars a week, the lifestyle was hard, and he spent much of the week on the road, hardly seeing his wife. He used pills and alcohol to dampen his depression and anger. He admits, "my set offered essentially no originality ... a critic ... called my show 'mundane' and [he] was right" (p. 85). His wife said in retrospect she had made a "lot of excuses for him" because of his awful childhood, but finally when she found out the extent of his drinking, she threw Lopez out of the house. Lopez described in his autobiography how depressed he was sitting in a lonely condo away from his wife and daughter, Mayan (p. 88). Finally Lopez turned to psychotherapy to try to get his life in order. Lopez sees many reasons now for his problems:

> Love and intimacy were foreign words to me ... I had no idea what it meant to be close with a woman, to share.... I've finally learned that for so long I cried over all the wrong things: the absent father and the distant mother; the heaping pile of thoughtless insults and abuse; the horrible self-image. (Lopez 2004, pp. 83, 185)

Lopez got a couple of breaks late in the 1990s and early 2000s that changed his life. One was the offer by film director Ken Loach for him to appear as a mean boss in the film *Bread and Roses* (2001). While not exactly a hit film, his decent acting job put him more on a national plane than before this. Then in 2002, actress Sandra Bullock in an effort to get more ethnic minorities on TV finally convinced ABC, which had been criticized by Hispanic groups for its lack of Latinos on the station (Wikipedia.com, George Lopez), to air *The George Lopez Show*. The situation comedy, which in part re-created the struggles of Lopez's life, was on from 2002 to 2007, but was a surprise greater hit when it went into syndication in the late 2000s. As we will see, Lopez certainly carries aspects of a poor Latino who continues to at times voice his critique of the networks and even other actors and TV figures, but he no doubt has become a star, and one of the best-known Latino figures in the United States.

Like the other subjects detailed in this chapter, rapper and music entrepreneur Jay-Z was able to make a dramatic success of himself. But his move from his impoverished background and illegal subculture to the mainstream was hardly accomplished without ambivalence and a residue of the impact of his earlier life. In 1999 he got involved in a music bootlegging dispute with record executive Lance Rivera at a nightclub, and he stabbed Rivera. Jay-Z in his autobiography notes he went into a state of shock. "Before I realized what I was doing, I headed back over to him, but this time I was blacking out with anger. The next thing I knew, all hell had broken loose in the club" (Jay-Z 2011, p. 110). Although never exactly admitting to the stabbing, he opted for a guilty plea to third-degree assault and avoided jail time, being given just three years' probation.

Jay-Z remarks that "I think it was a wake-up call, and the calling card for me that—to let me know, like, it could just all go down the drain; like, it could all be taken away from you" (*60 Minutes II*, 2002). Growing up in a violent community seriously influenced Jay-Z's reactions and proclivity toward violence as a response to being wronged.

> The streets can start to make you see the logic in violence. If a thing surrounds you and is targeted at you, it can start to seem regular. What may have once seemed like an extreme or unacceptable measure starts to seem like just another tool in your kit. Even after I left the streets, I was still under the kind of pressure that made me sometimes act without thinking. (Jay-Z 2011, p. 111)

Jay-Z also confronted painful feelings in relation to his family. His father abandoned him when he was only eleven. Jay-Z was quite open about his hurt:

> I changed a lot. I became more guarded. I never wanted to be attached to something and get that taken away again. I never wanted to feel that feeling again [of being left]. I never wanted to be too happy or gung ho about something or too mad about something. I just wanted to be cool about it. And it [affects] my relationships with women. 'Cause even when I was with women I wasn't really with them. In the back of my mind I'd always feel like, when this shit breaks up, you know, whatever. So I never really just let myself go. I was always guarded, always guarded. And always suspicious. I never let myself just go. (*Rolling Stone* 2005)

At his mother's urging, Jay-Z agreed to meet his father, but his father did not show up for the meeting, reinforcing many of the feelings of abandonment. But ultimately they did connect, and Jay-Z expressed a lot of his strong feelings toward him. He later rented an apartment for his father, who died shortly afterward (*Rolling Stone* 2005).

Jay-Z also reconnected with a nephew, Coleek Luckie, whom he became close to. He was later devastated by the news that Luckie had been killed in a car accident when he was a passenger in a car that Jay-Z had given him as a graduation present. When asked about the loss in 2005, Jay-Z was visibly shaken and replied, "it was the toughest shit. Nothing close to it. Numbingly. Like I'm numb. I'm numb" (*Rolling Stone* 2005). The loss of Luckie was additionally devastating as it took away Jay-Z's opportunity to build the paternal relationship he himself was unable to have. Jay-Z's statements about his painful reunions and attempts to regain human feelings evoke similar insights that George Lopez had about not feeling and not showing emotion, which is so paramount in tough environments, particularly for males.

DECLINE IN CLASS CONSCIOUSNESS AND ANTI-AUTHORITY FEELINGS

The subjects studied in this chapter had many different levels of consciousness and orientations toward power and authority. Still, it is a good generalization—being cautious because of the small size of the group—that those who grew up in more recent decades (the late 1950s through the 1980s at least) are as a group less class conscious and less anti-authoritarian than the twenty subjects profiled earlier.

While one person—author Stephen King was heavily involved in Students for a Democratic Society (SDS) at the University of Maine—had contact with a political left, most of the subjects were either in places geographically distant from any protests or concentrations of activity (Larry Bird, Dolly Parton, and Oprah Winfrey, for example) or missed out on the period of civil rights and minority protest (for example, Jay-Z and George Lopez fit this characterization). But probably more significant was the decline in general social class activism compared to the days of both the nineteenth century and the first four decades of the twentieth century. To the extent some subjects displayed class and anti-authority views, they often were filtered through statements about race and ethnicity (certainly true of George Lopez and Jay-Z, and at least earlier in Mr. T's career).

Stephen King is an example of a baby boomer who has maintained a class consciousness as a working-class person. Cautious his money would not last, King held to a very modest style of life in his generally working-class city of Bangor, Maine. When asked about this, as he so often is, King's reply to professor Anthony Magistrale "took me in with a look that suggested he had just swallowed some particularly offensive species of bug—indeed, that perhaps I myself was a member of that insect species. His response was a sardonic, 'Now, just where would you have me live—Monaco?'" (Magistrale 2010, p. 25). Later when Magistrale asked King for recommendations for the best food in town, King named three local diners. Though King's prosperity has placed him in a financially very comfortable position, he does not identify with upper levels of society and instead views life from the perspective of his blue-collar beginnings.

King is eager to share his wealth with the less fortunate, and he established a charitable foundation with his wife. He provides four scholarships a year for graduates of the school at which he used to teach, and in 2012 donated $120,000 to help residents of Maine pay for heating oil (moreover, he often gives money without the fanfare that other philanthropists gain). The heroes of his stories are, unsurprisingly, tough and practical working-class people; King certainly doesn't celebrate the wealthy businessman or young socialite. In 1999 King was offered $15,000 for spending three days lecturing at the University of Vermont. When Professor Anthony Magistrale gave him the check and apologized for not having more to give, King handed it back to him and told him it wasn't necessary. Recognizing his providence for having established his name so quickly, he opted to lend his star power to help developing novelists and filmmakers, writing blurbs and selling film rights for his short stories for a dollar, provided the films aren't shown for profit and he gets a copy of the final product. Regarding wealth accumulation, King says, "The idea is to take care of your family and have enough left over to buy books and go to the movies once a week. As a goal in life, 'getting rich' strikes me as fairly ludicrous. The goal is to do what God made you for and not hurt anyone if you can help it" (*New York Times* 2000).

King also falls within an anti-authoritarian tradition. King is well aware of the experience of being marginalized by poverty.

> I have a sense of injustice that came from my mother. We were the little people dragged from pillar to post. We were latchkey kids before there were latchkey kids, and she worked when women basically cleaned up other people's messes. She never complained about it much, but I wasn't dumb and I wasn't blind, and I got a sense of who was being taken advantage of and who was lording it over the other people. A lot of that injustice has stuck with me, and it's still in the books today. (Rogak 2008, p. 147)

This sense of injustice fueled his anti-authoritarian views, as he began to see that things were unfair not only for his mother but for many around him. King's resistance to authority developed when he was in college. He states that his political views were "extremely radical, largely due to the fact that nobody seems to listen to you unless you threaten to shut them down, turn them off, or make some kind of trouble" (Magistrale 2010, p. 7), which quickly became part of his character and campus persona. Although he entered school as a staunch conservative, this quickly changed with the onset of the Vietnam War. King joined Students for a Democratic Society and became a radical member of counterculture and opponent of the war. He was well known throughout the campus for his sometimes-incendiary opinions in his college newspaper column, *The Garbage Truck*. He took his propensity for leadership and change to the English department, where no acknowledgment was given to any literature beyond "the classics." King not only fought for a class on popular fiction, he became the teacher.

King's views on authority and social institutions are well documented in the themes of his novels. In the book *The Mist*, town residents barricade themselves into a supermarket for protection from an unseen menace. There are a few attempts to escape but the decision is quickly made that this is the only way to guarantee safety, and those who do later attempt to form a different plan are subjected to the religious zeal of Mrs. Carmody, who preys upon the fears of the trapped to convince them that the monsters outside are God's retribution for their sins, using Christianity as justification for striking down any who challenge her and the fervor she has stirred up, even to the point of murder. This is paralleled with the blind devotion of the military who unleashed the monsters. Both establish power from fear and use it as means for intimidation and control (Magistrale 2010, p. 55).

Conformity and punishment for failure to adhere to the wants of dominant others are a major theme in King's works, also noted in *Carrie* by the title character's punishment for refusal to conform to either of the two worlds she is caught between—her mother's religious fundamentalism and the world of high school girls. In both cases, women are punished for individuality and deviation from expected behavioral standards. *Carrie* was in fact written as a result of a $10 bet that King couldn't write a story from a female point of view.

Although King is no longer a radical, but a liberal activist, he and his wife, Tabitha, are well known as important contributors to a multitude of causes without the usual fanfare that the affluent seek when giving.

In her style of exemplifying wealth as well as in her many career-long statements on race and class, Oprah Winfrey stands at an opposite end from Stephen King. As early as her late teenage years, when she won the Miss Fire Prevention award in Nashville, she marked herself as different from the contenders who when asked what they would do with a million dollars, said "give to charity." Winfrey remarked, "If I had a million dollars, I would be a spendin' fool. I'm not quite sure what I would spend it on, but I would spend, spend, just to be a spending fool" (Kelley 2011, p. 56). She continued throughout her adult life to uncategorically express her desire to be the richest black woman in America and buy everything she needs. Biographer Helen Garson said her emphasis on individual achievement has at various times led to attacks on Oprah as "conservative" and "capitalistic" and that indeed she is a "luxury queen [who] enjoys spending on anything and everything that catches her eye" (Garson 2004, pp. 28, 37). Winfrey has even defended a rather classist view of people. When asked about her boyfriend Stedman Graham, an affluent man, she stated it did matter how much money he had: "I do care about whether or not he is a ditch digger. I know that sounds elitist but I have such great aspirations for myself in life … that I do not understand people who don't aspire to do or be anything" (quoted in Kelley 2011, p. 170).

Redbook magazine at one point did an exposé of the way of life on Oprah's show. Revelations of "wretched excess" and "unimaginable extravagance," mostly in terms of gifts to employees and parties and trips for everyone, shocked readers (Kelley 2011, p. 282). Winfrey has given away much money to charity as well, but some critics find her efforts self-serving or out of step with what people need. One of the biggest backlashes came after her show's famous giveaways of cars to audience members. So many members later complained about their inability to afford the taxes on the cars and other expenses that the show later agreed to take all the cars back from people who could not afford them.

Winfrey did succeed (according to *Forbes* magazine) in not only being the richest black woman, but the richest black person, and with eBay CEO Meg Whitman, the richest self-made woman in America, at $2.7 billion in assets (Wikipedia.com). Her annual income as of 2008 was $275 million, and she had homes in Montecito, California (her 42-acre estate), and Lavallette, New Jersey; an apartment in Chicago; an estate on Fisher Island, Florida; a house in Douglasville, Georgia; a ski house in Telluride, Colorado; and property on Maui and Antigua (Wikipedia.com).

In addition to representing the joys of being wealthy rather than the ambivalence of many earlier subjects, Winfrey spent most of her career distancing herself from black activism or any other potentially radical or militant movements. As far back as college she indicated little patience with her fellow African American students. Biographer R. Westen says

Oprah "did not feel as though she had experienced discrimination. This set her apart from many of the other students. She said her college classmates resented her [and] 'I refused to conform to their militant way of thinking'" (Westen 2005, p. 41).

She said earlier in her career when asked why she did not champion civil rights or other efforts, "Whenever I hear the words 'community organization' or 'task force' I know I am in deep trouble. People feel you have to lead a civil rights movement every day of your life, that you have to be a spokesperson.... Blackness is something I just am. I am a woman, I am a size ten shoe" (cited in Kelley 2011, p. 124).

She has consistently avoided calls by other African Americans to weigh in against discrimination. For example, when in 2004 Jesse Jackson criticized the Academy Awards' record on ethnic minorities winning awards, she and several other high-profile African Americans criticized Jackson.

With her high-profile early endorsement of Barack Obama for president in 2006, she did openly intervene politically for the first time. It is hard to judge the entirety of her political views, which are certainly socially liberal (for example, her long support of gay rights) but may or may not be liberal in other areas. Critics in the years of her talk shows still believe Winfrey's self-help and New Age messages were conservative. Kitty Kelley says her message that "you can be born poor and black and female and make it to the top" was "a fraudulent sop to her white audience" (Kelley 2011, p. 145). Although Kelley perhaps reads too much intentionality in her statement, many cultural critics do see the highly individualistic ethic of Winfrey's talk show as one of the many cultural factors in promoting this ideology in America of the 1980s, 1990s, and 2000s.

As a generalization, it appears comedian George Lopez and entertainer Dolly Parton have some features of class consciousness and anti-authority views while former basketball star Larry Bird would seem closer to the viewpoint of Oprah Winfrey. Of course, compared to open radicals of the past we have profiled like Anne Sullivan, Jack London, Margaret Sanger, Elizabeth Gurley Flynn, Fannie Lou Hamer, and Malcolm X, all of the contemporary famous people are quite different. But given the need to sustain a mass-media image of their professions (writing, music, acting, sports, etc.), symbolism and nuances of individual biographies must be read more carefully to discern a view, as noted earlier in the discussion of Johnny Cash.

While both Dolly Parton and George Lopez are certainly comfortable with success and live a far less spartan lifestyle than Stephen King, both express aspects of resistance, and consciousness, if not always exactly about class, of their group (gender, ethnicity) in terms of whom they may be leaving behind in their success. Parton has felt a strong loyalty to her local region (she created the Dollywood Foundation, which assists school children in her poverty-ridden area, and later also formed the Imagination Library, a program to aid low-income children). Parton has fought hard on a personal level and made many statements about the difficulty of being a female entertainer in a man's world. As a cultural icon, she can be read as a feminist (her song "9 to 5" and appearance in the eponymous film were not only a feminist statement but dovetailed an effort by the same name to organize women workers in the 1980s) or by some as not so much of one (according to Wikipedia she did appear on the cover of *Playboy* in 1978 in a bunny suit and admitted to Oprah Winfrey in 2003 that she had quite a bit of "body work"). Like Johnny Cash and other country singers, her image can be read from different political, social, and cultural perspectives. One interchange she reports with actor Sylvester Stallone sparks some interest:

> While filming the movie *Rhinestone* with Sylvester Stallone, they encountered a homeless man shivering in the cold. Parton took her shawl off and put it around him, and Stallone walked up and jerked it away, yelling, "Don't you put that good shawl over that scum! He could've made something of himself! We did." Parton was mortified and put the shawl back on the man and told Stallone, "Hey, look! That could've been you, you ungrateful son of a bitch! Except by the grace of God." The film's crew stood by in amazement, having never before seen anyone stand up to Stallone. Stallone himself was so taken aback, he later went back and gave the man a blanket and some money. (Parton 1994, p. 252)

Lopez has waged a considerable war of words with the networks and studios about the lack of Latinos on TV and movies as well as the stereotypical acting parts for Latinos. He has refused to take quite a few parts because of their ethnic stereotypes (in Lopez 2004, p. 79, he stated he refused auditions to play Latino gun dealers, pimps, and gang leaders, among others). He has further sometimes stirred controversy in his act, telling people that immigrant labor runs the country (Guzman 2009, p. 94), and that whites had better get used to cleaning their own homes (a remark that was booed by the audience) (Dougherty 2011, p. 66). On the other hand, Lopez seems to have a temper that muddies the waters a bit. According to Wikipedia, Lopez has a number of running feuds with people including Jay Leno, Carlos Mencia, Erik Estrada, and Kirstie Alley as well as ABC Entertainment (Wikipedia.com, George Lopez). It is difficult to get at a common theme here, although having been a poor kid who was humiliated and abused, Lopez's anger may be linked to aspects of his background. Though he has said he may run for mayor of Los Angeles, his exact politics remain a bit unclear although likely on the liberal side (in 2008 Lopez narrated a video on labor activist Cesar Chavez, for example).

Larry Bird presents the image of a rather conservative background from his Midwestern poverty roots. There were no doubt issues that existed for Bird because of his low-income roots, such as his difficulty for a long time in learning how to deal with the media, often not feeling like there was anything to talk about besides his performance on the court. It took him a long time to "play the game" of a sports star. But whatever the many adjustments in his life, Bird, while affirming that he never forgets his poverty and home area, makes few references to difficulty with his status as first a star player, head coach, and then president of the Indiana Pacers. He remarks early in his biography (Bird and Ryan 1990, p. 8) that many people expect too much from their employers and he does not understand this. He notes you should expect to work hard, but the implication is you have no right to expect much more than a minimum for your labor.

In sum, while most of the small number of poor people we were able to track in recent times have some vestiges of class consciousness, because of both the times and the need for cross-class appeal at least some of their comments have to be muted. There is some sense, as no doubt there always was, among some successful poor people (like Oprah, Mr. T, and Larry Bird) that others could make it if they took more responsibility and made more effort. Since this ideology is so appealing to Americans of all stripes, this is not a surprise.

SUMMARY

Our effort in this chapter was to update the study of the earlier poor subjects in American history with some contemporary biographies of now-famous people from poor backgrounds. Given the limitations of the size of the group (itself drawn from a very small number of people), they must be seen as exploratory in nature.

It appears, as one would expect, that growing up in poverty has not changed in its negative experience on subjects, and, in general, the tendency of those who grew up this way to experience pain and suffering throughout their lives. However, in other aspects of their lives, such as the discussion of class consciousness and anti-authoritarian views, generally the subjects stand out less in their views or commitments than the earlier subjects. Of course, as noted, the need to maintain a mass-market popularity with a broad audience of many different views makes modern celebrities like Jay-Z or George Lopez have a different environment than, say, Theodore Dreiser or Anne Sullivan. Or the lesser consciousness may reflect the changed circumstances of American life and ideology in more recent decades.

APPENDIX
BIBLIOGRAPHIC ESSAY FOR CHAPTER 1

The Culture of Poverty was a major debate that dominated the 1960s and related to critiques of Oscar Lewis's "culture of poverty" and the Moynihan Report on the Negro Family (1965). As William Julius Wilson notes in his 1987 *The Truly Disadvantaged* (University of Chicago Press), the disputes led to several decades of silence about poverty's effects on cultural life, the family, behavior, and other controversial issues (see particularly his chapter 1). The unfortunate result was that any inkling that poorer people or any such subgroup was in any sense "different" from middle- and upper-class people was almost banished from discussion.

In *Poverty and Psychology: From Global Perspective to Local Practice* (Kluwer Academic, 2003), editors Stuart Carr and Tod Sloan examine the psychological and social impacts of living in poverty, including topics such as the culture of poverty, related powerlessness, and psychopathology. Michael Argyle offers an in-depth look at the differences in values and moral attitudes between poor and middle classes in *The Psychology of Social Class* (Routledge, 1994), covering a variety of issues including values surrounding family relationships, sex, achievement, self-esteem, crime, education, and mental health.

Defining and Measuring Poverty. Two good sources about the US poverty rate and other ways to measure poverty are John Iceland, *Poverty* *in America: A Handbook* (University of California Press, 2009), and his first edition, 2006, chapter 3. Another series of discussions about the poverty rate appeared in the many editions of Sar Levitan, Garth Mangum, and Stephen L. Mangum, *Programs in Aid of the Poor* (Johns Hopkins University Press, 1998, 2003), and previous editions by Levitan (1976, 1985, 1990).

Life Expectancy and Physical Health. The Louisville study is well-documented in the film *Unnatural Causes: Is Inequality Making Us Sick?* (California Newsreel 2008). Both the Washington, DC, to Montgomery County ride and The Fifth Avenue study are cited in Michael Marmot, *The Status Syndrome* (Henry Holt, 2005, pp. 2, 183). Citations on pp. 16 and 39 concern the four-times risk of death among low-income people. The tuberculosis reference is from Marmot; on cardiovascular, stroke, and other diseases see also Lipina and Colombo, *Poverty and Brain Development during Childhood* (American Psychological Association, 2009); Catherine Magnuson and Elizabeth Votruba-Drzal, "Enduring Influences of Childhood Poverty," in M. Cancian and S. Danzinger, eds., *Changing Poverty, Changing Policies* (Russell Sage, 2009); and also California Newsreel, above. Obesity and smoking tobacco references are from the film *Unnatural Causes*. Poor people are shorter than rich people comes from Argyle, *Psychology*, 1994; and Marmot, *Status Syndrome*, 2005. On chronic stress see B. and B. Dohrenwood, *Social Status and Psychological Disorder: A Casual Inquiry* (Wiley, 1969); G. Duncan and J. Brooks-Gunn, eds., *Consequences of Growing Up Poor* (Russell Sage Foundation, 1997); Lipina and Colombo, *Poverty*, 2009; Magnuson and Votruba-Drzal, "Enduring Influences," 2009; K. Mossakowski, "Is the Duration of Poverty and Unemployment a Risk Factor for Heavy Drinking?," *Social Science and Medicine* 67: 6 (September 2008), pp. 947–955; N. Mulia et al., "Stress, Social Support, and Problem Drinking among Women in Poverty," *Addiction* 103: 8 (August 2008), pp. 1283–1293; as well as Argyle, *Psychology*, 1994; and Marmot, *Status Syndrome*, 2005. On more bad cholesterol see Marmot, *Status Syndrome*, 2005; on more depression see A. Albers, "Poverty, Social Context, and Children's Mental Health across the Early Life Course," PhD dissertation, University of Virginia, August 2001; Argyle, *Psychology*, 1994, p. 273; Carr and Sloan, *Poverty*, 2003, p. 77; A. Hollingshead and F. Redlich, *Social Class and Mental Illness* (John Wiley, 1958), pp. 224–225; P. Klebanov, J. Brooks-Gunn, and G. Duncan, "Does Neighborhood and Family Poverty Affect Mothers' Parenting, Mental

Health, and Social Support?," *Journal of Marriage and the Family* 56: 2 (May 1994), pp. 441–455; Lipina and Colombo, *Poverty*, 2009, pp. 68, 70; Magnuson and Votruba-Drzal, "Enduring Influences," 2009, pp. 155, 165, 166; Marmot, *Status Syndrome*, 2005, pp. 124, 126, 152; J. McLeod and M. Shanahan, "Trajectories of Poverty and Children's Mental Health," *Journal of Health and Social Behavior* 37: 3 (September 1996), pp. 207–220; J. Moren-Cross, "The Effects of Life Course Poverty on Depression," *Gerontologist* 44: 1 (2004), pp. 650–651; C. Muntaner et al., "Social Class, Assets, Organizational Control, and the Prevalence of Common Groups of Psychiatric Disorders," *Social Science and Medicine* 47: 12 (December 1998), pp. 2043–2053; and D. Stauffer and R. Jayakody, "Prevalence of Mental Health Problems among Welfare Recipients: Implications for Welfare Reform?," Paper, American Sociological Association, 1998. On low birth weight and thinness in infancy see Brooks-Gunn and also Koorman and Miller in Duncan and Brooks-Gunn, *Consequences*, 1997; Lipina and Colombo, *Poverty*, 2009; and Marmot, *Status Syndrome*, 2005, p. 234. On having lower IQs see Argyle, *Psychology*, 1994; Duncan and Brooks-Gunn, *Consequences*, 1997; Lipina and Colombo, *Poverty*, 2009, pp. 13, 59, 68; and Marmot, *Status Syndrome*, 2005, p. 225. On being more likely to be without teeth see Argyle, *Psychology*, 1994, p. 264; Lipina and Colombo, *Poverty*, 2009, p. 58; and L. Peck and E. Segal, "The Latent and Sequential Costs of Being Poor: Exploration of a Potential Paradigm Shift," *Journal of Poverty* 10: 1 (2006), pp. 1–24. On suffering from deafness and other hearing problems see Argyle, *Psychology*, 1994, p. 264; Magnuson and Votruba-Drzal, "Enduring Influences," 2009, p. 167. On speech and vision problems see Magnuson and Votruba-Drzal, "Enduring Influences," 2009, p. 167; Peck and Segal, "The Latent," 2006. On having high blood pressure see Argyle, *Psychology*, 1994, p. 264; Lipina and Colombo, *Poverty*, 2009, p. 69; and Marmot, *Status Syndrome*, 2005, pp. 234–235. Experts say that low-income people have poorer development of nervous systems; see Lipina and Colombo, *Poverty*, 2009, p. xi. Children in poverty have higher incidence of lead, methyl mercury, polychlorinated biphenyls, dioxins, and pesticides in their systems; see Lipina and Colombo, *Poverty*, 2009, p. 65.

Concentration of Poverty ("neighborhood poverty"). William Julius Wilson and his associates have done much work on the difference between concentrated poverty and poor people who live in other areas. See, for example, Wilson, *When Work Disappears: The World of the New Urban*

Poor (Knopf, 1996); N. Smelser, W. J. Wilson, and F. Mitchell, eds., *America Becoming: Racial Trends and Their Consequences*, Commission on Behavioral and Social Sciences and Education, National Research Council (National Academy Press, 2001); W. J. Wilson, *More Than Just Race: Being Black and Poor in the Inner City* (Norton, 2004); Wilson and Taub, *There Goes the Neighborhood: Racial, Ethnic, and Class Tensions in Four Chicago Neighborhoods and Their Meaning for America* (Knopf, 2006); and F. H. Wilson, *Race, Class, and the Postindustrial City: William Julius Wilson and the Promise of Sociology* (State University of New York Press, 2009). In relation to mental health and alcoholism and other impacts of concentrated poverty, see Albers, "Poverty, Social Context," 2001; Aneshensel and Sucoff, "The Neighborhood Context of Adolescent Mental Health," *Journal of Health and Social Behavior* 37: 4 (1996), pp. 293–310; R. Jones-Webb et al., "Alcohol Related Problems among Black, Hispanic, and White Men: The Contribution of Neighborhood Poverty," *Journal of Studies on Alcohol* 58: 5 (September 1997), pp. 539–545; Klebanov, Link, and Dohrenwood, "Formulation of Hypotheses about the True Prevalence of Demoralization in the US," *Mental Illness in the US: Epidemiological Evidence*, ed. B. P. Dohrenwood et al., pp. 114–132 (Praeger, 1980); Marmot, *The Status Syndrome*, p. 189; Tiggs, Browne, and Green, "Social Isolation of the Urban Poor: Race, Class, and Neighborhood Effects of Social Resources," *Sociological Quarterly* 39: 1 (1998), pp. 53–77; A. Valdez, C. Kaplan, and R. Curtis, "Aggressive Crime, Alcohol, and Drug Use, and Concentrated Poverty in 24 US Urban Areas," *American Journal of Drug and Alcohol Abuse* 33: 4 (July 2007), pp. 595–603.

Mental Health. The classic work about the relationship between poverty and mental illness is Hollingshead and Redlich, *Social Class and Mental Illness*. Another older study is Dohrenwood and Dohrenwood, *Social Status and Psychological Disorder*, which is a meta-study of studies on class and mental health looking back as far as the 1850s. For recent publications, see Horwitz, *Creating Mental Illness* (University of Chicago Press, 2002): p. 158 cites several recent studies that still find high levels of all mental distress in poorer areas. Children's mental health, especially the diagnoses of attention deficit disorder, conduct and other behavioral disorders, anxiety, and depression, are discussed in Albers, "Poverty, Social Context," 2001; Duncan and Brooks-Gunn, *Consequences*, 1997; Lipina and Colombo, *Poverty*, 2009; Magnuson and Votruba-Drzal, "Enduring Influences," 2009; and McLeod and Shanahan, "Trajectories," 1996.

Schizophrenia and Personality Disorders. The Dohrenwoods, *Social Status*, 1969, found the strongest class correlations with these disorders; see also Argyle, *Psychology*, 1994, p. 272.

Alcoholism and Drug Addiction. See below.

High Rate of Depression among Poor Women. See, for example, Argyle, *Psychology*, p. 273; and Staufer and Jayakody, "Prevalence," 1998.

In earlier periods of American history. From the beginning of US history, the "insane" or "lunatic" and "distracted people" were part of the Poor Laws and mingled with other paupers. When mental asylums were established they filled with poor immigrants, and before deinstitutionalization they remained a repository of poor people. The small following that Freudianism had among the intellectual class did not become a more popular movement until the various therapeutic movements of the 1960s. For two useful histories of mental health, see Albert Deutsch, *The Mentally Ill in America* (Columbia University Press, 1949); and Gerald Grob, *From Asylum to Community: Mental Health Policy in America* (Princeton University Press, 1991). Horwitz, 2002, does an excellent job in explaining the twentieth-century change in the popularity of psychiatry, chapters 2–4.

Education. The most detailed book on most of the aspects listed is Duncan and Brooks-Gunn, *Consequences*, 1997. See also Lipina and Colombo, *Poverty*, 2009, on cognitive problems, IQ, and school dropouts. See Argyle, *Psychology*, 1994, pp. 250, 252, on low school achievement; Magnuson and Votruba-Drzal, "Enduring Influences," 2009, on cognitive and behavioral problems; and McLeod and Shanahan, "Trajectories," 1996, on low test scores.

Social Problems: Alcohol, Drugs and Crime. During the 1980s and 1990s teen pregnancy emerged as a consensual "moral panic" among conservatives and liberals; see my book *The New Temperance: The American Obsession with Sin and Vice* (Westview Press, 1997); and my article "The Universalization of Social Problems: Some Radical Explanations" in *Critical Sociology* (1997).

On boys living in poverty, see Duncan, Magnuson, Kalil, and Ziol-Guest, 2012, which found that boys living in poverty during the first five years of life were more than twice as likely to be arrested as boys who had family incomes over twice the poverty threshold (28 versus 13 percent), cited in Magnuson and Votruba-Drzal, "Enduring Influences," p. 166.

The issue of alcohol was historically a major social class and ethnic divide in America, at least between the 1840s and the 1930s, in which Protestant rural and middle-class leaders blamed alcohol for all the troubles that befell the lower classes, and also racial minorities and immigrant whites; see, for example, Joseph Gusfield, *Symbolic Crusade: Status Politics and the American Temperance Movement* (University of Illinois Press, 1963); and Wagner, *The New Temperance*, 1997. Although the twentieth and twenty-first centuries have brought more of a classlessness about alcohol use per se, experts agree that substance abuse has consequences out of proportion for those in lower social classes. As Callahan and Room show in *Problem Drinking among American Men* (Rutgers Center of Alcohol Studies, 1974), many studies indicate problem drinking is more prevalent among the poor and working classes: they are more likely to suffer work problems, arrest, family problems and divorce, organic brain problems, and from domestic violence issues. Also see Room's 2005 publication in *Drug and Alcohol Review*, "Stigma, Social Inequality, and Alcohol and Drug Use," for more on the disproportional harm, marginalization, and stigma of substance abuse in poorer classes. There is a similar phenomenon in the use of almost all illicit drugs from marijuana to cocaine and heroin to psychedelics or oxytocin. Of course, the differences are to some extent due to the different enforcement of laws by class, but also the professional and white-collar workplace is more conducive to allowing different behavior from its workers, alcohol and drug rehabilitation is more available, and (certainly in the case of movie stars) far less stigmatized than among the poor and working classes.

For a sample of some interesting recent work, see M. Eisner, "Crime, Problem Drinking, and Drug Use: Patterns of Problem Behavior in Cross-National Perspective," *Annals of the American Academy of Political and Social Science* 580 (March 2002), pp. 201–225, which shows national correlations between inequality levels and poverty and problem behaviors with alcohol and drugs. R. Jones-Webb et al., "Alcohol Related Problems," 1997, shows that neighborhood poverty exerts a powerful influence on blacks and males in particular. P. Marzuk et al. show poverty status accounted for 69 percent of the variance in drug overdoses in a sample: "Poverty and Fatal Accidental Drug Overdoses of Cocaine and Opiates in New York City: An Ecological Study," *American Journal of Drug and Alcohol Abuse* 23: 2 (May 1997), pp. 221–228. In Mossakowski (2008), a strong association is shown between heavy drinking and poverty and periods of unemployment. Mulia et al. (2008) show the high presence of alcohol problems among a sample of welfare mothers and women in poverty. Muntaner et al. (1998) also show a link between social class and alcohol and drug use. M. C. Snead and W. Cockerham, "Health Lifestyles and Social Class in the Deep South," *Research in the Sociology of Health Care* 20 (2002), pp. 107–122, correlates social class and drinking, smoking tobacco, and unhealthy food eating. Valdez, Kaplan, and Curtis (2007) also show how criminal activity correlates with the structural conditions in urban environments. J. Woodward, "The Examination of the Effects of Race and Socioeconomic Status on Health Behaviors," PhD dissertation, Arizona State University, January 2001, also shows the strong influence both race and socioeconomic status exert on drinking, smoking cigarettes, and obesity.

Child Abuse and Neglect and Domestic Violence. See my article "The Universalization," 1997. Also see the work of Leroy Pelton, for example, "Child Abuse and Neglect: The Myth of Classlessness," pp. 23–28, in L. Pelton, ed., *The Social Context of Child Abuse and Neglect* (Human Sciences Press, 1981); Gelles and Straus, *Intimate Violence: The Definitive Study of the Causes and Consequences of Abuse in the American Family* (Simon and Schuster, 1988); Kruttschnitt, McLeod, and Dornfeld, "The Economic Environment of Child Abuse," *Social Problems* 41 (1991), pp. 299–313; D. Kurz, "Corporal Punishment and Adult Use of Violence: A Critique of Discipline and Deviance," *Social Problems* 38 (1991), pp. 155–161; D. Loseke, "'Violence Is Violence' or Is It? The Social Construction of 'Wife Abuse' and 'Public Policy,'" pp. 189–206 in J. Best, ed., *Images of Issues: Typifying Contemporary Social Problems*, first edition (Aldine de Gruyter, 1989); and B. McNeil, "Poverty Causes Child Abuse," pp. 91–95 in K. Koster and K. Swisher, eds., *Child Abuse: Opposing Viewpoints* (Greenhaven Press, 1994).

Historians of Drug Use. See H. Becker, *Outsiders: Studies in the Sociology of Deviance* (Free Press, 1963); H. Morgan, *Drugs in America: A Social History 1800–1980* (Syracuse University Press, 1981); D. Musto, *The American Disease: The Origins of Narcotics Control* (Yale University Press, 1988); and Rainerman and Levine, *Crack in America: Demon Drugs and Social Justice* (University of California Press, 1997), for example.

BIBLIOGRAPHY

Albers, A. "Poverty, Social Context, and Children's Mental Health across the Early Life Course." PhD dissertation, University of Virginia, August 2001.

Amell, J. "An Examination of Mental Health and Mental Health Trajectories among African American and White Men: The Effects of Poverty and Perceived Social Supports on Psychological Distress, Self-Esteem, and Life Satisfaction." PhD dissertation, University of Wisconsin, March 2007.

American Federation of the Blind. Letters between Helen Keller and Anne Sullivan Macy, 1916–1917. Available at www.afb.org/asm/.

American National Biography Online (ANB). Oxford University Press, 2010. Available at www.anb.org.

Aneshensel, C., and Sucoff, C. "The Neighborhood Context of Adolescent Mental Health." *Journal of Health and Social Behavior* 37(4): 293–310, 1996.

Argyle, M. *The Psychology of Social Class.* London: Routledge, 1994.

Baxandall, R., ed. *Words on Fire: The Life and Writings of Elizabeth Gurley Flynn.* New Brunswick, NJ: Rutgers University Press, 1987.

Beaver, J. M. *John Garfield: His Life and Films.* London: Thomas Yoseloff, 1978.

Becker, H. *Outsiders: Studies in the Sociology of Deviance.* New York: Free Press, 1963.

Bird, L., with Ryan, B. *Drive: The Story of My Life.* New York: Bantam, 1990.

Blackburn, J. *With Billie.* New York: Vintage Books, 2003.

Blau, D. "The Effect of Income on Child Development." *Review of Economics and Statistics* 81(2): 261–276, 1999.

Brace, C. L. *The Dangerous Classes of New York and Twenty Years' Work among Them.* New York: Wynkoop and Hallenbeck, 1872.

Braddy, N. *Anne Sullivan Macy: The Story behind Helen Keller.* Garden City, NJ: Doubleday, 1933a.

Bibliography

———. Notes for manuscript above. Perkins School for the Blind, Watertown, Mass., 1933b.

Braithwaite, J. *Inequality, Crime, and Public Policy*. London: Routledge, 1979.

Brody, G. H., Stoneman, Z., and Flor, D., et al. "Financial Resources, Parent Psychological Functioning, Parent Co-Caregiving, and Early Adolescent Competence in Rural Two-Parent African-American Families." *Child Development* 65(2): 590–605, 1994.

Brooks-Gunn, J., Duncan, G., and Mariato, N., in Duncan, G., and Brooks-Gunn, J., eds., *Consequences of Growing Up Poor*. New York: Russell Sage Foundation, 1997.

Brown, K. *Malcolm X: His Life and Legacy*. Brookfield, CT: Millbrook Press, 1995.

Calhoun, A., ed. *A Social History of the American Family from Colonial Times to the Present*. New York: Barnes and Noble, [1919] 1945.

California Newsreel. *Unnatural Causes: Is Inequality Making Us Sick?* Film, 2008.

Callahan, D. *Problem Drinkers*. San Francisco: Jossey-Bass, 1970.

Callahan, D., and Room, R. *Problem Drinking among American Men*. New Brunswick, NJ: Rutgers Center of Alcohol Studies, 1974.

Camp, H. C. *Iron in Her Soul: Elizabeth Gurley Flynn and the American Left*. Pullman, WA: Washington State University Press, 1995.

Carr, S., and Sloan, T., eds. *Poverty and Psychology: From Global Perspective to Local Practice*. New York: Kluwer Academic, 2003.

Cash, J., with Patrick Carr. *Cash: The Autobiography*. New York: HarperCollins, 2003.

Chaplin, C. *My Autobiography*. New York: Simon and Schuster, 1964.

Chesler, E. *Woman of Valor: Margaret Sanger*. New York: Simon and Schuster, 2007.

Chiricos, T. "Rates of Crime and Unemployment: An Analysis of Aggregate Research Evidence." *Social Problems* 34: 187–212, 1987.

Clarke, D. *Billie Holiday: Wishing on the Moon*. Cambridge, MA: Da Capo Press, 2009.

Conger, R., and Elder, G. *Families in Troubled Times: Adapting to Change in Rural America*. New York: Aldine de Gruyter, 1994.

Conger, R., and McLoyd, V. C., Wallace, L. B., Surt, Y., Simons, R. L., and Brody, G. H. "Economic Pressure in African American Families: A Replication and Extension of the Family Stress Model." *Developmental Psychology* 38(2): 179–193, 2002.

Coontz, S. *The Way We Never Were*. New York: Basic Books, 2000.

Costello, E., et al. "Relationships between Poverty and Psychopathology: A Natural Experiment." *Journal of the American Medical Association* 290(15): 2023–2029, 2003.

Cowen, T. *What Price Fame?* Cambridge, MA: Harvard University Press, 2000.

Cox, V. *Margaret Sanger: Rebel for Women's Rights*. Philadelphia: Chelsea House, 2005.

Creamer, R. *The Babe: The Legend Comes to Life*. New York: Simon and Schuster, 1974.

Croteau, D. *Politics and the Class Divide: Working People and the Middle Class Left*. Philadelphia: Temple University Press, 1995.

Crum, R., Helzer, J., and Anthony, J. "Level of Education and Alcohol Abuse and Dependence in Adulthood: A Further Inquiry." *American Journal of Public Health* 83: 830–836, 1993.

Currie, J., and Wanchuan, L. "Chipping Away at Health: More on the Relationship between Income and Child Health." *Health Affairs* 26(2): 331–344, 2007.

Dash, L. "When Children Want Children." *Society* 27: 17–20, 1990.
Deutsch, A. *The Mentally Ill in America*. New York: Columbia University Press, 1949.
Dohrenwood, B., and Dohrenwood, B. *Social Status and Psychological Disorder: A Casual Inquiry*. New York: John Wiley, 1969.
Dougherty, T. *George Lopez*. Farmington Hills, MI: Lucent Books, 2011.
Dubner, Stephen J. "What Is Stephen King Trying to Prove?" *New York Times*, August 13, 2000.
Duncan, G., and Brooks-Gunn, J., eds. *Consequences of Growing Up Poor*. New York: Russell Sage Foundation, 1997.
Duncan, G., Magnuson, K., Kalil, A., and Ziol-Guest, K. "The Importance of Early Childhood Poverty." *Social Indicators Research* 108(1): 87–98, August 2012.
Dyson, M., ed. *Making Malcolm*. New York: Oxford University Press, 1995.
Edelman, M. "Reducing Teen Pregnancy Would Decrease Childhood Poverty." In Wekesser, C., ed., *America's Children: Opposing Viewpoints*, pp. 149–156. San Diego: Greenhaven Press, 1991.
Edwards, L. *Johnny Cash and the Paradox of American Identity*. Bloomington: Indiana University Press, 2009.
Eisner, M. "Crime, Problem Drinking, and Drug Use: Patterns of Problem Behavior in Cross-National Perspective." *Annals of the American Academy of Political and Social Science* 580: 201–225, 2002.
Evans, G. "The Environment of Childhood Poverty." *American Psychologist* 59(2): 77–92, 2004.
Evans, G., Saltzman, H., and Cooperman, J. "Housing Quality and Children's Socioeconomic Health." *Environment and Science* 33(3): 389–399, 2001.
Fantasia, R., McNall, S., and Levine, R., eds. *Bringing Class Back In: Contemporary and Historical Perspectives*. Boulder, CO: Westview Press, 1991.
Farber, N. "The Significance of Race and Class in Marital Decisions among Unmarried Adolescent Mothers." *Social Problems* 37: 51–63, 1990.
Flynn, E. G. *The Rebel Girl, an Autobiography: My First Life (1906–1926)*. New York: Masses and Mainstream, 1955.
Foster, G. *Class-Passing: Social Mobility in Film and Popular Culture*. Carbondale: Southern Illinois University Press, 2005.
Friedman, B. H. *Jackson Pollock: Energy Made Visible*. New York: Da Capo Press, 1995.
Gans, H. *Popular Culture and High Culture*. New York: Basic Books, 1975.
Garson, H. *Oprah Winfrey: A Biography*. Westport, CT: Greenwood Press, 2004.
Gelles, R., and Straus, M. *Intimate Violence: The Definitive Study of the Causes and Consequences of Abuse in the American Family*. New York: Simon and Schuster, 1988.
Gilmore, A. *Bad Nigger! The National Impact of Jack Johnson*. Port Washington, NY: National University Publications, 1975.
Gordon, L. *Heroes of Their Own Lives*. Champaign: University of Illinois Press, 1988.
Gould, J. *The Poet and Her Book: A Biography of Edna St. Vincent Millay*. New York: Dodd, Mead, 1969.
Greenburg, Z. *Empire State of Mind: How Jay-Z Went from Street Corner to Corner Office*. New York: Portfolio Trade, 2012.
Grob, G. *From Asylum to Community: Mental Health Policy in America*. Princeton, NJ: Princeton University Press, 1991.

Gusfield, J. *Symbolic Crusade: Status Politics and the American Temperance Movement.* Champaign: University of Illinois Press, 1963.

Guzman, L. and R. *George Lopez: Latino King of Comedy.* Berkeley Heights, NJ: Enslow, 2009.

Haley, J. L. *Wolf: The Lives of Jack London.* New York: Basic Books, 2010.

Hall, T. "Smoking of Cigarettes Seems to Be Becoming a Lower-Class Habit." *Wall Street Journal*, June 25: 1, 17, 1985.

Halpern, D. *Social Capital.* Cambridge: Polity Press, 2005.

Halpern, J. *Fame Junkies: The Hidden Truths behind America's Favorite Addiction.* Boston: Houghton-Mifflin, 2007.

Hampton, W. *Babe Ruth: A Twentieth-Century Life.* New York: Viking, 2009.

Hartz, L. *The Liberal Tradition in America: An Interpretation of American Political Thought.* New York: Harcourt, Brace, 1955.

Herman, D. *Helen Keller: A Life.* New York: Alfred A. Knopf, 1998.

Hochschild, J. *What's Fair? American Beliefs about Distributive Justice.* Cambridge, MA: Harvard University Press, 1981.

Hollingshead, A., and Redlich, F. *Social Class and Mental Illness.* New York: John Wiley and Sons, 1958.

Horwitz, A. V. *Creating Mental Illness.* Chicago: University of Chicago Press, 2002.

Huss, J., and Werther, D., eds. *Johnny Cash and Philosophy: The Burning Ring of Truth.* Chicago: Open Court, 2008.

Iceland, J. *Poverty in America: A Handbook.* Second edition. Berkeley: University of California Press, 2009. First edition, 2006.

Inciardi, J. *The War on Drugs: Heroin, Cocaine, Crime and Public Policy.* Palo Alto, CA: Mayfield Press, 1986.

Jackman, M., and Jackman, R. *Class Awareness in the United States.* Berkeley: University of California Press, 1983.

Jay-Z. *Decoded.* New York: Spiegal and Grau, 2011.

Johnson, J. *My Life and Battles.* Edited and translated by Christopher Rivers. Washington, DC: Potomac Books, [1915] 2009.

Jones-Webb, R., Snowden, L., Herd, D., Short, B., and Hannan, P. "Alcohol Related Problems among Black, Hispanic, and White Men: The Contribution of Neighborhood Poverty." *Journal of Studies on Alcohol* 58(5): 539–545, 1997.

Keller, H. *Teacher.* Garden City, NY: Doubleday, 1955.

Kelley, K. *Oprah: A Biography.* New York: Three Rivers Press, 2011.

Kershaw, A. *Jack London: A Life.* New York: St. Martin's Griffin, 1997.

Kessler, R., and Cleary, P. "Social Class and Psychological Distress." *American Sociological Review* 45(3): 463–478, 1980.

King, S. *On Writing: A Memoir of the Craft.* New York: Scribner, 2000.

Klebanov, P., Brooks-Gunn, J., and Duncan, G. "Does Neighborhood and Family Poverty Affect Mother's Parenting, Mental Health, and Social Support?" *Journal of Marriage and the Family* 56(2): 441–455, 1994.

Klebanov, P., Link, B., and Dohrenwood, B. P. "Formulation of Hypotheses about the True Prevalence of Demoralization in the US." In B. P. Dohrenwood et al., eds., *Mental Illness in the US: Epidemiological Evidence*, pp. 114–132. New York: Praeger, 1980.

Korrman, S., and Miller, J. "Effects of Long-Term Poverty on Physical Health of Children in the National Longitudinal Survey of Youth." In Duncan, G., and Brooks-Gunn, J., eds., *Consequences of Growing Up Poor*, chapter 5. New York: Russell Sage Foundation, 1997.

Kruttschnitt, C., McLeod, J., and Dornfeld, M. "The Economic Environment of Child Abuse." *Social Problems* 41: 299–313, 1991.

Kurz, D. "Corporal Punishment and Adult Use of Violence: A Critique of Discipline and Deviance." *Social Problems* 38: 155–161, 1991.

Lareau, A. *Unequal Childhoods: Class, Race, and Family Life*. Berkeley: University of California Press, 2003.

Lash, J. P. *Helen and Teacher*. Reading, MA: Addison-Wesley, 1980.

Leaming, B. *Marilyn Monroe*. New York: Three Rivers Press, 1998.

Lee, C. K. *For Freedom's Sake: The Life of Fannie Lou Hamer*. Urbana: University of Illinois Press, 1999.

Lee, L., and Gifford, B. *Saroyan: A Biography*. Berkeley: University of California Press, 1984.

Leggett, J. *A Daring Young Man: A Biography of William Saroyan*. New York: Alfred Knopf, 2002.

Levitan, S., Mangum, G., and Mangum, S. *Programs in Aid of the Poor*. Baltimore: Johns Hopkins University Press, 1998, 2003.

Levy, D. *Richard Wright: A Biography*. Minneapolis: 21st Century Books, 2008.

Lin, N. *Social Capital: A Theory of Social Structure and Action*. Cambridge: Cambridge University Press, 2001.

Lingeman, R. *Theodore Dreiser: At the Gates of the City*. New York: G. P. Putnam and Sons, 1986.

Lipina, S., and Colombo, J. *Poverty and Brain Development during Childhood*. Washington, DC: American Psychological Association, 2009.

Lipset, S. M. *The First New Nation: The United States in Historical and Comparative Perspective*. New York: Basic Books, 1963.

Lopez, G., with Armen Keteyian. *George Lopez: Why You Crying?* New York: Touchstone, 2004.

Loseke, D. "'Violence Is Violence' or Is It? The Social Construction of 'Wife Abuse' and 'Public Policy.'" In Best, J., ed., *Images of Issues: Typifying Contemporary Social Problems*, first edition, pp. 189–206. New York: Aldine de Gruyter, 1989.

Louvish, S. *Chaplin: The Tramp's Odyssey*. New York: Thomas Dunne Books, 2009.

Loving, J. *The Last Titan: A Life of Theodore Dreiser*. Berkeley: University of California Press, 2005.

Lupien, S., King, S., Meaney, M., and McEwen, B. "Can Poverty Get under Your Skin? Basal Cortisol Levels and Cognitive Function in Children from Low and High Socioeconomic Status." *Development and Psychopathology* 13(3): 653–676, 2001.

Magistrale, T. *Stephen King: America's Storyteller*. Denver: ABC-CLIO, 2010.

Magnuson, C., and Votruba-Drzal, E. "Enduring Influences of Childhood Poverty." In Maria Cancian and Sheldon Danziger, eds., *Changing Poverty, Changing Policies*. New York: Russell Sage, 2009.

Malcolm X. *The Autobiography of Malcolm X, with the Assistance of Alex Haley*. New York: Grove Press, 1965.

Bibliography

Males, M. "School Age Pregnancy: Why Hasn't Prevention Worked?" *Journal of School Health* 63: 10, 1993.

Marmot, M. *The Status Syndrome.* New York: Henry Holt, 2005.

Marzuk, P., Tardiff, K. L., Hirsch, C., Stajic, M., Potera, L., and Hartwell, N. "Poverty and Fatal Accidental Drug Overdoses of Cocaine and Opiates in New York City: An Ecological Study." *American Journal of Drug and Alcohol Abuse* 23(2): 221–228, 1997.

Maseie-Taylor, C., and Nicholas, G. *Biosocial Aspects of Social Class.* Oxford: Oxford University Press, 1990.

McClusky, A. T., ed. *Richard Pryor: The Life and Legacy of a "Crazy" Black Man.* Bloomington: Indiana University Press, 2008.

McLanahan, S. "Parent Absence or Poverty: Which Matters More?" In Duncan, G., and Brooks-Gunn, J., eds., *Consequences of Growing Up Poor*, chapter 3. New York: Russell Sage Foundation, 1997.

McLeod, J., and Kessler, R. "Socioeconomic Status Differences in Vulnerability to Undesirable Life Events." *Journal of Health and Social Behavior* 31(2): 162–172, 1990.

McLeod, J., and Shanahan, M. "Poverty, Parenting, and Children's Mental Health." *American Sociological Review* 58(3): 351–366, 1993.

———. "Trajectories of Poverty and Children's Mental Health." *Journal of Health and Social Behavior* 37(3): 207–220, 1996.

McLoyd, V. "The Impact of Economic Hardship on Black Families and Childhood Psychological Distress, Parenting, and Socioemotional Development." *Child Development* 61(2): 311–346, 1990.

McNeil, B. "Poverty Causes Child Abuse." In Koster, K., and Swisher, K., eds., *Child Abuse: Opposing Viewpoints*, pp. 91–95. San Diego, CA: Greenhaven Press, 1994.

Mensch, B., and Kandel, D. "Underreporting of Substance Abuse in a National Longitudinal Youth Cohort." *Public Opinion Quarterly* 52: 100–124, 1988.

Meyer, S. "Trends in the Economic Well-Being and Life Chances of America's Children." In Duncan, G., and Brooks-Gunn, J., eds., *Consequences of Growing Up Poor*, chapter 4. New York: Russell Sage Foundation, 1997.

Milford, N. *Savage Beauty: The Life of Edna St. Vincent Millay.* New York: Random House, 2001.

Mills, K. *This Little Light of Mine: The Life of Fannie Lou Hamer.* Lexington: University Press of Kentucky, 2007.

Milner, E. R. *The Lives and Times of Bonnie and Clyde.* Carbondale: Southern Illinois University Press, 1996.

Mistry, R., et al. "Economic Well-Being and Children's Social Adjustment: The Role of Family Process in an Ethnically Diverse Low-Income Sample." *Child Development* 73(3): 935–951, 2002.

Monroe, M. *My Story.* With Ben Hecht. Lanham, MD: Taylor Trade, 2007.

Moren-Cross, J. "The Effects of Life Course Poverty on Depression." *Gerontologist* 44(1): 650–651, 2004.

Morgan, H. *Drugs in America: A Social History, 1800–1980.* Syracuse, NY: Syracuse University Press, 1981.

Mossakowski, K. "Is the Duration of Poverty and Unemployment a Risk Factor for Heavy Drinking?" *Social Science and Medicine* 67(6): 947–955, 2008.

Mr. T. *The Man with the Gold: The Autobiography of Mr. T.* New York: St. Martin's Press, 1984.

Mulia, N., Schmidt, L., Bond, J., Jacobs, L., and Korcha, R. "Stress, Social Support, and Problem Drinking among Women in Poverty." *Addiction* 103(8): 1283–1293, 2008.

Muntaner, C., Eaton, W., Diala, C., Kessler, R., and Sorlie, P. "Social Class, Assets, Organizational Control, and the Prevalence of Common Groups of Psychiatric Disorders." *Social Science and Medicine* 47(12): 2043–2053, 1998.

Musto, D. *The American Disease: The Origins of Narcotics Control.* New Haven, CT: Yale University Press, 1988.

Nathanson, C. *Dangerous Passage: The Social Control of Sexuality in Women's Adolescence.* Philadelphia: Temple University Press, 1991.

National Institute on Drug Abuse. *Drug Use, Drinking, and Smoking: National Survey Results from High School, College, and Young Adult Populations.* Rockville, MD: NIDA, 1993.

Nielsen, K. *Beyond the Miracle Worker.* Boston: Beacon, 2009.

Nott, R. *He Ran All the Way Home: The Life of John Garfield.* New York: Limelight Editions, 2004.

O'Meally, R. *Lady Day: The Many Faces of Billie Holiday.* New York: Arcade, 1991.

Orcutt, J., and Turner, J. "Shocking Numbers and Graphic Accounts: Quantified Images of Drug Problems in the Print Media." *Social Problems* 40: 190–206, 1993.

Parton, D. *My Life and Other Unfinished Business.* New York: HarperCollins, 1994.

Peck, L., and Segal, E. "The Latent and Sequential Costs of Being Poor: Exploration of a Potential Paradigm Shift." *Journal of Poverty* 10: 1–24, 2006.

Peele, S. *The Diseasing of America: Addiction Treatment Out of Control.* Lexington, MA: D. C. Heath, 1989.

Pelton, L. "Child Abuse and Neglect: The Myth of Classnessness." In Pelton, L., ed., *The Social Context of Child Abuse and Neglect*, pp. 23–28. New York: Human Sciences Press, 1981.

Perlman, S. *A Theory of the Labor Movement.* New York: Macmillan, 1928.

Pierce, J., Fiore, M., Novotny, E., and Davis, R. "Trends in Cigarette Smoking in the United States." *Journal of the American Medical Association* 261: 56–60.

Popporich, F. *Larry Bird: The Boy from French Lick.* West Bay Shore, NY: Blue Marlin Books, 2009.

Porter, D. *Steve McQueen: King of Cool.* Blood Moon Productions, 2009.

Pryor, R., with Ted Gold. *Pryor Convictions and Other Life Sentences.* New York: Pantheon, 1995.

Putnam, R. *Bowling Alone: The Collapse and Revival of the American Community.* New York: Simon and Schuster, 2000.

Rainerman, C., and Levine, H., eds. *Crack in America: Demon Drugs and Social Justice.* Berkeley: University of California Press, 1997.

Robinson, D. *Chaplin: His Life and Art.* New York: Da Capo Press, 1994.

Rogak, L. *Haunted Heart: The Life and Times of Stephen King.* New York: St. Martin's Griffin, 2008.

Room, R. "Stigma, Social Inequality, and Alcohol and Drug Use." *Drug and Alcohol Review* 24(2): 143–155, 2005.

Rosoff, J. "For Most Teens, Chastity Isn't a Choice." *Wall Street Journal*, July 13, 1994: 12.

Ross, S. *Hollywood Left and Right*. Oxford: Oxford University Press, 2011.

Rothman, D. *The Discovery of the Asylum: Social Order and Disorder in the New Republic*. Boston: Little, Brown, 1971.

Rowley, H. *Richard Wright: The Life and Times*. Chicago: University of Chicago Press, 2001.

Sanger, M. *The Autobiography of Margaret Sanger*. Mineola, NY: Dover, 2004 [1938].

Saraceno, B., and Barbui, C. "Poverty and Mental Illness." *Canadian Journal of Psychiatry/Revue Canadienne de Psychiatrie* 42(3): 285–290, 1997.

Schneider, P. *Bonnie and Clyde: The Lives behind the Legend*. New York: Henry Holt, 2009.

Schwartzenberg, B. "'Lots of Them Did That': Desertion, Bigamy, and Marital Fidelity in Late 19th Century America." *Journal of Social History* 4: 573–600, 2004.

Singer, M. "What Are You Afraid Of?" *New Yorker*, September 7, 1998: 56.

60 Minutes II. "The King of Rap." Interviewer Bob Simon. CBS, New York, 2002.

Sklar, R. *City Boys: Cagney, Bogart, and Garfield*. Princeton, NJ: Princeton University Press, 1992.

Smelser, M. *The Life That Ruth Built: A Biography*. Lincoln: University of Nebraska Press, 1975.

Smelser, N., Wilson, W. J., and Mitchell, F., eds. *America Becoming: Racial Trends and Their Consequences*. Commission on Behavioral and Social Sciences and Education, National Research Council. Washington, DC: National Academy Press, 2001.

Smith, J., Brooks-Gunn, J., and Klebanov, P. "Consequences of Living in Poverty for Young Children's Cognitive and Verbal Ability and Early School Achievement." In Duncan, G., and Brooks-Gunn, J., eds., *Consequences of Growing Up Poor*, chapter 7. New York: Russell Sage Foundation, 1997.

Snead, M. C., and Cockerham, W. "Health Lifestyles and Social Class in the Deep South." *Research in the Sociology of Health Care* 20: 107–122, 2002.

Solomon, D. *Jackson Pollock: A Biography*. New York: Cooper Square Press, 2001.

Sombart, W. *Why Is There No Socialism in the United States?* Translated by Patricia M. Hocking. White Plains, NY: International Arts and Sciences Press, 1976 [1906].

Spoto, D. *Marilyn Monroe: The Biography*. New York: Random House, 1995.

Stauffer, D., and Jayakody, R. "Prevalence of Mental Health Problems among Welfare Recipients: Implications for Welfare Reform." Paper, American Sociological Association, 1998.

Streissguth, M. *Johnny Cash: The Biography*. New York: Da Capo Press, 2006.

Taylor, R. L. *W. C. Fields: His Follies and Fortunes*. New York: St. Martin's Press, 1949.

Ten Broek, J. *Family Law and the Poor*. Westport, CT: Greenwood Press, 1971.

Terrill, M. *Steve McQueen: Portrait of an American Rebel*. London: Plexus, 1993.

Thompson, K. "Gender and Adolescent Drinking Problems: The Effects of Occupational Structure." *Social Problems* 36: 30–47, 1989.

Tiggs, L., Browne, I., and Green, G. "Social Isolation of the Urban Poor: Race, Class, and Neighborhood Effects of Social Resources." *Sociological Quarterly* 39(1): 53–77, 1998.

Tonry, M. *Malign Neglect: Race, Crime, and Punishment in America.* New York: Oxford University Press, 1995.

Topalian, E. *Margaret Sanger.* New York: Franklin Watts, 1984.

Toure. "The Book of Jay." *Rolling Stone,* December 15, 2005.

Tucker, C. "You Can't Spot an Abuser by His Table Manners." Syndicated column, June 23, 1994.

Turner, R. J., and Avison, W. R. "Status Variations in Stress Exposure: Implications of Research on Race, Socioeconomic Status, and Gender." *Journal of Health and Social Behavior* 44(4): 488–505, 2003.

Underwood, T., and Miller, C., eds. *Bare Bones: Conversations on Terror with Stephen King.* New York: Warner Books, 1989.

US Center for Disease Control. "Prevalence of Selected Risk Factors of Chronic Disease by Education Level in Racial/Ethnic Groups—United States 1991–1992." *Morbidity and Mortality Weekly Report* 43: 894–898, 1994.

Valdez, A., Kaplan, C., and Curtis, R. "Aggressive Crime, Alcohol, and Drug Use, and Concentrated Poverty in 24 US Urban Areas." *Journal of Drug and Alcohol Abuse* 33(4): 595–603, 2007.

Valliant, G. *The Natural History of Alcoholism.* Cambridge, MA: Harvard University Press, 1983.

Vance, J. *Charlie Chaplin: Genius of the Cinema.* New York: Harry N. Adams, 2003.

Vanneman, R., and Cannon, L. *The American Perception of Class.* Philadelphia: Temple University Press, 1987.

Votruba-Drzal, E. "Economic Disparities in Middle Childhood: Does Income Matter?" *Developmental Psychology* 42(6): 1154–1167, 2006.

Wagner, D. *Checkerboard Square: Culture and Resistance in a Homeless Community.* Boulder, CO: Westview Press, 1993.

———. *The New Temperance: The American Obsession with Sin and Vice.* Boulder, CO: Westview Press, 1997.

———. "The Universalization of Social Problems: Some Radical Explanations." *Critical Sociology* 23(1): 3–23, 1997.

———. *What's Love Got to Do with It? A Critical Look at American Charity.* New York: New Press, 2001.

———. *The Poorhouse: America's Forgotten Institution.* Lanham, MD: Rowman and Littlefield, 2005.

———. *Ordinary People: In and Out of Poverty in the Gilded Age.* Boulder, CO: Paradigm, 2008.

———. *The Miracle Worker and the Transcendentalist: Anne Sullivan, Franklin Sanborn, and the Education of Helen Keller.* Boulder, CO: Paradigm, 2012a.

———. *Confronting Homelessness: Poverty, Politics, and the Failure of Social Policy.* Boulder, CO: Lynne Rienner, 2012b.

Ward, G. *Unforgivable Blackness: The Rise and Fall of Jack Johnson.* New York: Vintage, 2004.

Watkins, M. *On the Real Side.* New York: Simon and Schuster, 1994.

Westen, R. *Oprah Winfrey: I Don't Believe in Failure*. Berkeley Heights, NJ: Enslow, 2005.

Wilkenson, R. *Class and Health*. London: Tavistock, 1986.

Williams, J. A. *The Most Native of Sons: A Biography of Richard Wright*. Garden City, NY: Doubleday, 1970.

Wilson, F. H. *Race, Class, and the Postindustrial City: William Julius Wilson and the Promise of Sociology*. Albany: State University of New York Press, 2009.

Wilson, W. J. *More Than Just Race: Being Black and Poor in the Inner City*. New York: Norton, 2004.

———. *The Truly Disadvantaged*. Chicago: University of Chicago Press, 1987.

———. *When Work Disappears: The World of the New Urban Poor*. New York: Knopf, 1996.

Wilson, W. J., and Taub, R. *There Goes the Neighborhood: Racial, Ethnic, and Class Tensions in Four Chicago Neighborhoods and Their Meaning for America*. New York: Knopf, 2006.

Wood, J., ed. *Malcolm X: In Our Own Image*. New York: St. Martin's Press, 1992.

Woodward, J. "Examination of the Effects of Race and Socioeconomic Status on Health Behaviors." PhD dissertation, Arizona State University, January 2001.

Wright, R. *Black Boy*. New York: Harper Perennial, 1989.

Yeung, J., et al. "How Money Matters for Young Children's Development: Parental Investment and Family Processes." *Child Development* 73(6): 1861–1879, 2002.

INDEX

Abandonment, of children, 13, 15–43, 163
Alcoholism/problem drinking, 6, 9, 22, 32, 43, 46, 49, 50, 52, 153, 158–159, 161, 175, 176–178
American Federation of the Blind, 127
American Laboratory Theatre, 33, 118, 137
American National Biography Online, 31, 36, 38, 61–66, 67, 103, 109, 135, 143
An American Tragedy (Dreiser), 20, 54, 121
Alger, H., 2
Anagnos, M., 95–96, 97, 118, 121, 126
Anti-authoritarianism, 13, 69, 93–115, 164–171
Argyle, M., 94, 172

Bangor, Maine, 164
Barrow, E., 101
Bastardy/illegitimacy, 20–21, 22, 31, 35, 38, 39, 42
Baxandall, R., 74
Beaver, J., 137
Bell, A. G., 79, 96
Benton, T. H., 50, 119

Berkeley, B., 103
The Big Knife (film), 104
Bird, L., 152–153, 168, 170
Black Boy (Wright), 29, 30, 59, 121
Black Muslim Party, 37
Bogart, H., 137, 138
Boissvain, E., 84
Bonds, B., 136
Brace, C. L., 125
Braddy, N., 18, 96, 97
Brando, M., 105, 137
Bread and Roses (film), 162
Bridges, H., 104
Bullock, S., 162

Café Society, 51
Cagney, J., 137
Call of the Wild (London), 49
Camp, H., 73, 74
Canby, M., 96
Carrie (book, film), 149, 157, 166
Carter, J., 52, 90, 120
Cash, J., 12, 14, 45, 48, 52, 90–91, 119–120, 122, 168
Censorship, 123, 128–130, 133
Cerf, B., 108

Index

Chaplin, C., 22–25, 42, 43, 54, 56–58, 59, 79, 86–88, 91, 103, 104, 114, 117, 119, 122, 123, 131–134, 142
Chavez, C., 138, 170
Chesler, E., 55, 56, 71, 99
Clarke, D., 35
Class consciousness, 69–92, 93, 105, 115, 131, 164–171; defined, 70
Cleaver, E., 138
Clift, M., 137
Cline, P., 91
Clinton, W., 145
Cloward, R., 94
Coburn, J., 112
Communist Party, 58, 71, 72, 74, 82, 85, 89, 104, 105, 119
Comstock, A., 125
Concentrated poverty, 5, 6, 8, 11, 174–175
Conrad, J., 24
Conservative view of poverty, 2
Coontz, S., 15
Cosby, B., 113
Cowen, T., 13
Coxey's Army, 82
Creamer, R., 26, 101
Crime, 6, 10–11, 94, 176–178
Croteau, D., 94
Cultural capital/social capital, 117
"Culture of poverty" debate, 2, 172

Day care, 8
Debs, E. V., 73, 80, 81
Dell, F., 84
De Niro, R., 137
Depression (psychiatric), 5–6, 21, 35, 44, 49, 54–60, 158, 161–162, 173
Depression of 1873, 16
Depression of 1893, 54
Diagnostic Statistical Manual (DSM), 9
Dies Committee, 104
DiMaggio, J., 142
Dodge, M., 99
Domestic violence, 6, 8, 10–11, 15, 43, 51, 178
Doubleday (publisher), 128
Downward mobility, 20, 21, 22

Dreiser, T., 12, 19–20, 22, 42, 54–55, 72, 79, 81–82, 119, 121, 123, 125, 127–129
Drug use, 5–6, 9, 42, 49, 51, 52, 53, 59, 114, 155–156, 158–159, 160, 161, 176–178
Du Bois, W. E. B., 85
Dyson, M., 75, 139, 140

Ellis, H., 99
Environmental causes of life differences, 7–8
Equi, M., 73–74

Fairbanks, D., 57
Fame, 13–14, 110, 116–142
Flynn, E. G., 71–74, 105, 118, 120, 124, 138
Forbes (magazine), 167
Force of Evil (film), 104
Foster, G., 133
Friedman, B. H., 32, 89
"Frost King" episode, 95–96

Gans, H., 133
Garfield, J., 32–34, 42, 93, 102–105, 119, 136–138
Garson, H., 167
Gehrig, L., 47, 48, 135
Gender and personality types, 44
Genetics, 7
Gentlemen Prefer Blondes (film), 142
George Lopez Show, 153, 162
Gifford, B., 28, 109
Gilman, A., 96, 97
Gilmore, A., 46, 106–107
Goldman, E., 55, 129
Goldwater, B., 139
Gould, J., 25, 84
Graham, S., 167
The Great Escape (film), 111
Greenberg, C., 50, 89, 121–122
Guevara, C., 140
Guggenheim, P., 50

Haley, A., 36, 49
Haley, J., 21, 22

Index

Hall, A., 161
Hamer, F. L., 71, 72, 73, 74, 76–78, 120, 138
Harper's Weekly, 130
Hays Code, 127
Hecht, B., 59
Hegemonic masculinity, 44
Hermann, D., 97
Hill, J., 138
Holiday, B., 34–35, 42, 43, 45, 48, 51–52, 55, 93, 122, 124, 134, 140–141
Hollywood studio system, 102–105, 137
"Home Run" Baker, 100
Hopper, H., 104
House Un-American Activities Committee (HUAC), 34, 103, 104–105, 138
Howe, J., 95, 126
Howe, S. G., 95, 125, 126
Huggins, M. 101
Hugo, V., 88
The Human Comedy (Saroyan), 109
Huss, J., 91

Industrial School, 26–27
"In kind" benefits, 3

Jay-Z, 145, 155–157, 162–164
Johnson, J., 44, 45–47, 48, 93, 105–107, 119, 122
John Barleycorn (London), 49
Johnson, L., 77
Jones, Mother, 72
Juvenile delinquency, 94
Juvenile homes, 15, 34, 40, 43

Kael, P., 114
Karno, F., 57, 119
Keller, H., 19, 73, 79, 81, 83, 86, 93, 95, 96, 97, 118, 121, 123, 125, 126–127
Kelley, K., 159–160, 168
Kelley, R., 75
Kershaw, A., 21, 49, 82, 83
King, C., 77, 148–149, 157–159
King, M. L., 75, 77, 122, 138

King, S., 148–149, 164–166
Krasner, L., 50, 89, 119
Kristofferson, K., 91

Labeling theory, 8–10
Landis, K., 102
Lash, J., 19, 95, 96, 97
Leaming, B., 38, 59
Lee, C., 78
Lee, L., 28, 109
Lee, S., 36
Leggett, J., 108
Levy, D., 59
Lingeman, R., 19, 20, 55, 81, 128
Loach, K., 162
Louis, J., 47
Life expectancy, 4–5, 7, 8, 15
Liberal-left view of poverty, 2
London, J., 21–22, 25, 31, 32, 35, 42, 45, 48, 49–50, 51, 72, 79, 82–83, 119, 121, 125
Lopez, G., 14, 153–155, 161–162, 168, 169–171
Loving, J., 54, 81, 127

McClusky, A., 40, 41, 113, 114
McGwire, M., 136, 144
McKee, G., 38
McQueen, S., 39–40, 42, 43, 45, 93, 110–113, 119, 122, 137
MGM, 109
Macy, J., 126
Magistrale, A., 164, 165
Malcolm X, 14, 35–37, 42, 43, 45, 52, 71, 72, 73, 74, 75–76, 105, 117–118, 122, 124, 138–140
Malcolm X (film), 36
Mann Act (1910), 46, 107
Marcy Housing Projects, 155
Maris, R., 136
Marmot, M., 8, 173
Marxism, 69, 70, 82, 89, 92
The Masses (newspaper), 84
Maugham, S., 57
Mediating and mitigating circumstances, 10–11
Merton, R., 94

Index

Middle class sample, 61–66
Milford, N., 83
Millay, E. S. V., 12, 25–26, 30, 42, 45, 72, 79, 83–85, 118, 119, 120, 121, 134, 136, 140
Miracle Worker (film, play), 127
Mississippi Freedom Party, 77
The Mist (S. King), 167
Mohammed, E., 105
Monroe, M., 37–39, 42, 43, 54, 59–60, 104, 105, 119, 121, 137, 140, 141–142
Moore, D., 144
Moreno, B., 153
Moses, B., 77
Mr. T., 149–150, 170

Nation of Islam, 75–76
Native Son (Wright), 85, 121
NAACP, 77, 78
Newman, P., 137
Newton, H., 138
Nott, R., 33, 103, 104, 105, 137

Obama, B., 168
Ohlin, L., 94
O'Meally, R., 34, 51
Oprah Winfrey Show, 152, 159, 167
Orphanages, 15, 23–24, 28–29, 30, 38, 43

Papillon (film), 112
Parton, D., 146–148, 168–169
Patri, A., 33
Pauperism, 6
Pax Americana, 11
People of the Abyss (London), 83
Perkins School for the Blind, 12, 18, 19, 80, 95, 96, 118, 126
Phil Donahue (television show), 159
Picasso, P., 89
Pickford, M., 133
Pleschette, S., 112
Polansky, A., 104
Pollock, J., 31–32, 35, 42, 45, 48, 50–51, 55, 88–90, 91, 93, 94, 119, 121–122

Poorhouse/workhouse, 15, 16–19, 20, 22–25, 43, 118, 126
Poor relief system, 17
Porter, D., 40, 111, 112
Poverty: absolute versus relative, 2, 3; definitions of, 2–4, 172–173; as a disability, 1–12; education and, 6; health and, 4–7; level/rate, USA, 2–3; life expectancy and, 4–5, 173–174; mental health and, 5–6, 9, 23, 31, 36, 37, 38, 43, 49, 174–175, 175–176; obesity and, 5; working class and, 4, 86
Prostitution, 29, 30, 34, 39, 40–41, 46, 51, 141
Pryor Convictions (book), 113
Pryor, R., 12, 40–42, 45, 48, 53–54, 93, 110, 113–114, 120
Public service announcements, 10
Pulitzer Prize, 25, 28, 108–109

Racial concentration of poverty, 11
Radical feminism, 98
Ramperson, A., 36
Random House, 108
Redbook (magazine), 167
Reitman, B., 129
Rhinestone (film), 169
Rivera, D., 88
Robinson, D., 132
Robinson, J., 47
Rodgers, J., 91
Roosevelt, T., 107
Ross, A., 133
Ross, S., 131, 133
Rupert, J., 101
Ruth, B., 26–27, 30, 43, 44, 47–48, 51, 71, 93, 94, 100–102, 107, 118, 120, 122, 134, 135–136, 144

Sanborn, F. B., 96, 97, 126
The Sand Pebbles (film), 112
Sanger, M., 12, 54, 55–56, 71, 72, 82, 93, 98–100, 118, 119, 120, 121, 122, 123, 127, 129–131
Saroyan, W., 28–29, 31, 42, 43, 45, 93, 107–110, 121

Index

Schulberg, B., 109
Screen Actors Guild, 103
Serrano, A., 155, 161
Shame of poverty, 13, 15–43, 147, 157
The Shining (King), 157
Simmons, R., 156
Sinatra, F., 112
Sklar, R., 103, 137
Sister Carrie (Dreiser), 20, 54, 81, 121, 128
Slee, J. N., 99
Smelser, M., 26, 48, 101, 135
Smith, A., 2
Sosa, S., 136, 144
Southern Christian Leadership Conference (SCLC), 77
The Story of My Life (Keller), 126
"Strange Fruit" (song) 51
Streissguth, M., 90–91
Stress and poverty, 8
Student Non-Violent Coordinating Committee (SNCC), 77, 78
Students for a Democratic Society (SDS), 164, 166
Social class, 3, 71
Socialist Party, 73, 83, 99, 120
Solomon, D., 32, 89
Spoto, D., 37, 38, 59, 141
Stallone, S., 169
Sullivan, A., 12, 16–19, 22, 42, 43, 72, 73, 79–81, 83, 85, 86, 93, 95–98, 118, 120–121, 123, 125, 126–127
Swank, H., 144, 145

Taylor Homes, 150
Teen pregnancy, 6, 9, 176

Terrill, M., 39, 110–111, 112
Time of Your Life (play), 108
Topalian, E., 99
Tragic America (Dreiser), 82
Tramp, as image, 22–23, 87–88, 114, 122, 131–132
Tresca, C., 73, 74
Twain, M., 79, 96

Unnatural Causes (film), 8, 173
United Artists Company, 103
United Negro Improvement Association (UNIA), 36
US Department of Agriculture, 2–3

Waiting for Lefty (play), 103
Ward, G., 105, 106
Warner Brothers, 103, 104, 137
Washington, B. T., 107
Watkins, M., 53, 113
Werther, D., 91
Westen, R., 167–168
White Fang (London), 49
Whitman, M., 167
Why You Crying? (Lopez), 153–154
Wilkins, R., 77
Williams, J. A., 30, 85, 86
Winfrey, O., 151–152, 159–161, 166–168, 169, 170
Wobblies (IWW), 71, 72, 73, 74, 88, 98, 130, 138
Works Progress Administration, 89
Wright, R., 29–31, 32, 43, 54, 58–59, 79, 83, 85–86, 117, 119, 121, 124

Xaverian Brothers, 27

ABOUT THE AUTHORS

David Wagner, Professor of Social Work and Sociology at the University of Maine, is the award-winning author of eight previous books, including *Confronting Homelessness: Poverty, Politics, and the Failure of Social Welfare.*

Jenna Nunziato is a recent graduate of the MSW program at University of Southern Maine.